Intimacy and Italian Migration

CRITICAL STUDIES IN ITALIAN AMERICA

series editors: *Nancy C. Carnevale and Laura E. Ruberto*

This series publishes works on the history and culture of Italian Americans by emerging as well as established scholars in fields such as anthropology, cultural studies, folklore, history, and media studies. While focusing on the United States, it includes comparative studies with other areas of the Italian diaspora. The books in this series will engage with broader questions of identity pertinent to the fields of ethnic studies, gender studies, and migration studies, among others.

Intimacy and Italian Migration

GENDER AND DOMESTIC LIVES IN A MOBILE WORLD

Edited by *Loretta Baldassar and Donna R. Gabaccia*

FORDHAM UNIVERSITY PRESS NEW YORK 2011

Library of Congress Cataloging-in-Publication Data

Intimacy and Italian migration : gender and domestic lives in a mobile world / edited by Loretta Baldassar and Donna R. Gabaccia.
p. cm.—(Critical studies in Italian America)
Includes bibliographical references and index.
ISBN 978-0-8232-3184-3 (cloth : alk. paper)—ISBN 978-0-8232-3185-0 (pbk. : alk. paper)—ISBN 978-0-8232-3186-7(ebook)
1. Italians—Foreign countries. 2. Immigrants—Family relationships—Italy. 3. Italy—Emigration and immigration—Social aspects. I. Baldassar, Loretta, 1965– II. Gabaccia, Donna R., 1949–
DG453.I68 2011
305.85′1—dc22

2010026348

Printed in the United States of America
13 12 11 5 4 3 2 1
First edition

Contents

Ethnographic Studies of Family, Community, and Nation

Acknowledgments

This volume represents a complex, international, and interdisciplinary project that has benefited from the support of many people and institutions. Loretta Baldassar recalls the meandering, cross-border, and at times deeply intimate development of this volume, beginning with Donna Gabaccia's visit to Perth for the Europeans Program, hosted by the Institute of Advanced Studies at the University of Western Australia in 2003 with the impressive support of Professor Terri-Ann White and her team there. Donna had in fact been invited to Perth two years earlier, but that visit was abruptly canceled because of the complete cessation of all air travel in the days following the September 11 attacks. Sharing this global tragedy and its immediate repercussions fostered a greater appreciation of the importance of mobility (especially for people living in isolated Perth) and seemed to generate a need to reinforce ties across distance, even among academics. As is often the case, planning that international visit resulted in an increase in e-mail conversations and a sharing of ideas that led Loretta and Donna to coordinate the Intimacies and Sexualities in a Mobile World Symposium within the Europeans Program, and to the participation of several important scholars, including Michael Herzfeld, Ghassan Hage, Linda Reeder, Giovanna Campani, Anne-Marie Fortier, Ien Ang, and Pnina Werbner. Loretta was sorry to have to miss the Pittsburgh conference, which was the follow-up to the Perth meeting, despite Donna's generous offer to accommodate her and her very new baby. Loretta feels particularly indebted to Donna for agreeing to work on this project in a way that was not governed by the usual time pressures, facilitating a more flexible and less stressful approach to its progress. She offers thanks, too, to all the participants for accommodating this pace. Many of them benefited from the unhurried evolution of the manuscript. The intellectual exchanges among participants never ceased despite the distances involved in the collaboration; intellectual exchange was increasingly augmented with more personal and private news, which served to make the shared work more and more rewarding. Special thanks also go to Anne-Marie Fortier and, in particular, Ralph Grillo, who participated in the virtual exchange of ideas that consolidated the volume.

Donna Gabaccia remembers with great fondness the excitement of visiting Perth in 2003, and she thanks Loretta Baldassar, Pam Sharpe, Terri-Ann White, and Richard Bosworth for all they did to make her summer sojourn there such a pleasant one. Many in the United States helped to nurture the project that eventually emerged from her first meetings with Loretta. She thanks, in particular, Kenyon Zimmer, her graduate student in Pittsburgh, and the University of Pittsburgh's Global Academic Partnership Program for financial assistance. Both helped to make possible the April 2005 gathering of historians, folklorists, sociologists, anthropologists, and Italianists that was titled Love of Country. Not all the papers presented at that conference found a place in the present volume, but all the scholars who participated contributed their enthusiasm for thinking about the meaning of intimacy, the private sphere, and personal relationships in the complex process of nation building in Italy and around the world. Donna thanks Franca Iacovetta, Sonia Cancian, and Liz Zanoni for their helpful readings of the introduction, Loretta for her warm heart and steady intelligence, and all our contributors for their considerable patience.

Intimacy and Italian Migration

Home, Family, and the Italian Nation in a Mobile World

THE DOMESTIC AND THE NATIONAL AMONG ITALY'S MIGRANTS

Loretta Baldassar and Donna R. Gabaccia

That nations are not natural phenomena but rather products of human imagination and (to varying degrees) choice has become a truism of modern intellectual life. Recent historical scholarship on international migration has made it equally obvious that the imagining of Italianness and of Italy occurred as much across as within the political boundaries that nation-states worked so hard to draw; impose; and, once formed, enforce. Nations cannot create such boundaries independent of an international system of nations that recognize them as significant. The movement of people, ideas, and goods across borders has often played a part in the emergence of nations and national identities. Nevertheless, nation-states have, more often than not, struggled to regulate these border-crossing movements, often viewing them as unnatural and as threatening to their sovereignty.

Much of the scholarly literature on Italy's modern migrants and on the consolidation of Italy through border-crossing movement has focused on wage earning, politics, proletarian mobilizations, and residential districts as key sites of Italian nation building.[1] Inevitably, perhaps, such studies have highlighted the nationalization of men and the activities of men in creating the nation. Men have, of course, figured centrally in nation building and in the imagining of nations, as well as in Italy's migrations. Still, it is quite striking that, across cultures, Italianness is often associated with or symbolized by femininity, passionate emotions, or elements of domestic life—the Italian mother, a peculiarly "Italian" intensity of family solidarities, the ardor of romantic love, or the pleasures of eating and of the table.[2] Precisely because affective ties, and life outside the workplace, remained somewhat shadowy in such works as *Italian Workers of the World,* and *Women, Gender, and Transnational Lives,* we felt that a third international collaboration—and one that was different from the collaborations that produced these two volumes—should specifically pick up these themes.

Thus, while we share with earlier works on Italians around the world a keen interest in the imagining of nations across national borders, our focus here is the intimate and domestic lives of individual men and women, their families, and the communities they loved, and within which they married, procreated, raised children, and dreamed of familial and communal transcendence even as they left Italy to work and live in faraway lands, sometimes to repatriate, and often to visit and revisit their original homes.[3] We focus on intimacy across borders because we believe it holds important and often misunderstood clues to the process of nation building and the acquisition of male and female identities in Italy and abroad. In particular, we believe that women's relationships to the nation, women's transformations of identities through migration, and women's participation in nation building are more likely to be captured by our approach than through studies of politics and work.

The intimate relationships developing among men, women, family, and community and nations point to themes that are central to the development of human life around the world in the twentieth and—we assert—twenty-first centuries. The consequences of intimate and emotional relationships between nations and citizens, historians remind us, can be devastating. The history of the twentieth century provides evidence of just how powerful was the emotional cocktail formed through national intimacies. The millions who died in international, regional, anti-colonial, and civil wars did so, presumably, because they had learned (or were forced) to "love" their countries so intensely that they gave themselves, their bodies, and their children's bodies to the nation. Nor does our own world suggest that such deadly emotions are things of the past: Around the globe, individuals continue to die for religious faiths, nations, and national ideologies that are intimately part of personal, familial, and communal identities.

Emotions, nations, and migrations attract attention in many disciplines. We begin, therefore, by pointing to the junctures we have found between concepts and theories developed in several scholarly fields. We concentrate, of course, on those intersections and connections that have most assisted us in compiling and ordering the rich variety of case studies on offer from our contributors.

Theory, History, and Method in the Study of Italy's Mobile Millions

Scholars have demonstrated that many different types of nations—including self-conscious nations of immigrants such as the United States; multicultural nations such as Canada and Australia; the radically republican and secular nation of France; the racially amalgamated nation of Brazil; exclusionary, mountainous, and often isolationist Switzerland; and even regionally diverse and ever-mobile Italy—came to be imagined amid the sweeping population movements of the nineteenth and twentieth centuries. International collaborations and collections of essays published in the past fifteen years, and associated with the project we once termed "Italians Everywhere," have explored how migrations out of Italy helped to make modern, multiethnic nation-states and complex national and ethnic identities in many lands.[4] These provided us with a model for our own project. They sketched a basic chronology—fourteen million departures from Italy between 1870 and 1914, four million more in the interwar years, and another eight million after 1945—and drew a map of the changing locations of *altre italie* ("other Italies") over time. They showed the differing ways that nations could be and were imagined in North and South America and in southern, northern, and western Europe. They also highlighted the distinctive identities that emerged among the children and grandchildren of migrants in Australia, Europe, and the Americas. In doing so, they successfully extricated the history of nation building from the study of single nations and encouraged cross-national comparisons and a deeper understanding of connections between nations and between specific home places based on class and national or regional identities. As a result, we can now better understand nation building and the international system of nations as global phenomena with histories of their own.

Our unbinding of the study of the national from its usual location in political and labor histories of Italy's mobile citizens, and our focus on intimacy and border crossing, is theoretically driven by our interest in modern nations and identities. At least since Benedict Anderson's early work, historians have insisted that nations are imagined communities.[5] But while Anderson traced the emergence of imagined communities from the public world of print capitalism, we (along with others) assert that nations, like all communities, rest also on some degree of intimacy among their members and participants. Communities, furthermore, are not simple products of voluntary association or of affiliations in a public sphere or civil society but often reflect and can also foster deeply felt emotional solidarities that more resemble those of domestic and familial life. Similarly, families are increasingly understood as sites of disagreement and contest, particularly along gendered and generational lines, as well as of bonds of emotion that, along with economic concerns, often provide the affective drivers for migration.[6] It is in the spaces of what A. L. Epstein called "intimate culture" that symbolic and affective national identity attachments are constituted. These subtler expressions of identity "revealed in the ongoing life of the home, in the company of friends, or at ethnic gatherings" indicate clearly how individual migrants, as emotional and intimate beings, reflect but also mediate within and among structures of family, community, and nation.[7]

Yet the affective dimension of social life has until recently often been overlooked and undervalued in history and the social sciences.[8] On this point, theorists in anthropology have proved particularly helpful in guiding our thinking. Anthropologists once emphasized the long war that early religious and secular dynastic states waged against local kin groups in their efforts to wrest from them control over marriage and thus over legitimate procreation (and also interpersonal violence) as sanctioned tools of governance.[9] More recently, they have called attention to the ways that nation-states depend upon the existence and changed meaning and symbolism of emotional, deeply embodied, and seemingly natural and private and familial everyday behaviors. Body language, gendered family relations, and modes of sexuality might ordinarily seem to define privacy, domesticity, and intimacy as arenas apart from the public world of states and politics. During nation building, however, they typically become markers of national belonging and racialized national difference.[10] Intentionally or not, the idiosyncratic, private, and deeply felt practices of individuals become cultural expressions of national solidarity—the Greek man, the Australian mate, the Italian mother, or the Latin lover. Nation building, some anthropologists, sociologists, and historians have suggested, requires nation-states not only to "go home" into households, private lives, and personal relationships but to "embrace" key elements of intimate and domestic life as distinguishing characteristics of the nation itself.[11] In this process, as several of our contributors suggest, the theoretically sharp line between public and private is muddied, and intermediate spaces that combine elements of private and public lives mingle.

Just how does this happen? And how does this happen when nation building occurs in the midst of vast population movements? We cannot answer these historical questions by attending exclusively to labor movements, the workplace, or the public arena of politics and state-controlled education as sites of nation building. Our intention is to delve deeper than the political rally or school text, into the hearts, minds, and imaginations of mobile people as they confront nation-states seeking to embrace them and have their love.

And so, with considerable excitement, we turn to feminist theorists of the private (or "domestic") sphere, seeking to connect the theoretical debates of the 1970s to the questions about the gendering of nations and national belonging raised in the 1980s and 1990s.[12] Although early theorists of the public-private divide certainly popularized the study of "separate spheres" for men and women across cultures, most also vigorously criticized the utility of treating the two spheres as disconnected. More recently, theoretical work has pointed to the naturalization of separate spheres as a key factor in creating gendered inequalities and in creating and perpetuating modern notions of distinctive racial, ethnic, and national groups that are reproduced biologically and culturally through family, kinship, and community.[13]

Like nations, private and public spheres have generally been understood as spaces or as territories, with women confined within the domestic sphere, and with men as travelers across the boundary separating the two. At least since geographer E. J. Ravenstein wrote his "laws of migration" in the 1880s, scholars have had difficulty imagining women as long-distance movers. Traditional models of stages of labor migration, in particular, invariably begin with the lone male setting off in search of fortune, while the final stage of successful settlement in the New World is characterized by the arrival of his wife and family.[14] Immigration policies often reflected, reinforced, and shaped these gendered ideas about migration processes.[15] Others have noted as well how concern with moral danger and collapse typically emerge and accompany female movement beyond the domestic, spatially fixed household or national territory.[16] Women have been essentialized as, by nature, anchored to home and hearth and the private sphere, enclosed within an equally territorial space, a nation. Only through the nurturing provided by relocated women were immigrant families imagined to integrate and put down roots in new lands and so develop new homes and communities with emotional attachments to receiving nations.

If, however, the domestic is neither unitary nor unilocal, then the family and the community too are not inevitably the small, private geographic domains from which emerge patriarchal nation-states imagined as fixed to a particular, if larger, sovereign territory.[17] Analyses of immigrant communities and voluntary associations are often assumed to be examples of activities in the public sphere, outside and separate from family and household—a point that many of our contributors eagerly dispute. A focus on intimacies across borders necessitates a more processual and less spatial understanding of mobility, identities, sociality, and nations. Essays in this collection focus on Italy and on several sites in Europe, in the Americas, and in Australia. An analysis of the intimacies that form across boundaries thus promises to shed light not only on nation building but on the resistance to national, racial, and gendered identities that can also emerge within intimate relations.

Throughout the volume, readers are exposed to the legacy and unresolved nature of recent ferment and debate surrounding the most appropriate analytical concepts for studying linkages among identities, mobility, and nation building. Debates over the usefulness of studying these relations as transnationalism, translocalism, or diasporas have been particularly intense. Those who study mobile Italians have used, defended, and criticized all these terms, as have some of our contributors.[18] To give one example of the terminological confusion, "trans-" (as it is commonly used in theoretical works on both transnationalism and translocalism) may mean "across," "between," or even "above" or "beyond."[19] "Transnational" and "diasporic" are sometimes used interchangeably and are regarded as closely related phenomena.[20] The purpose of our volume is not to resolve these complex theoretical issues or to privilege one approach over others. Rather, our comments here are intended to highlight the relevance of these concepts to an analysis of intimacies across borders.

Debates about diasporas tend to center around identity politics, and critics have pondered the role of the nation-state in diaspora formation.[21] Some scholars focus on the existence or absence of a "diasporic consciousness" that encompasses all the people of a given diaspora and their descendants.[22] Khalid Koser, for example, has argued that claiming diaspora status is a demand for recognition alongside and in the same terms as those to whom the term originally referred.[23] Others have been more hesitant to define diasporas so narrowly. More have built on the work and typologies of Robin Cohen in taking the Greek origins of the term "diaspora" to signify merely a scattering in multiple directions of people without fixed identities.[24] In contrast, discussions of transnationalism commonly focus on questions of mobility and connectedness. Pnina Werbner, for example, draws a distinction between transnationalism and diaspora studies by arguing that the former focus on movements including communication across borders, and the latter on the formation of "a permanent condition of ethnic and communal living."[25] Critics debate whether the focus on border crossings implied in transnationalism obfuscates or conflates the continued importance of the nation-state.[26]

Whatever their other differences, studies of the transnational and of diasporas most commonly focus on the supposedly public issues of labor, capital, and citizenship.[27] Only relatively recently have their more quotidian and domestic aspects been acknowledged through the notion of "transnationalism from below."[28] Scholars have posited the existence of a diasporic public sphere—suggesting the possible significance of a corresponding diasporic private or domestic sphere as well.[29] A focus on intimacies across borders, whether transnational or diasporic, unfastens the boundaries of the private sphere by locating it in a space larger than that of a single nation.

Rather than develop or impose on our contributors a single analytical frame, we sought work that engaged with the existing controversies while focusing empirically on intimate relationships among the mobile. This, we hope, will give readers the opportunity to learn from but also to problematize in new ways the many concepts our contributors have chosen to use in their analytical work. The national or Italian element of migrant identity has possessed widely differing meanings over different times and places. As essays in this collection suggest, the word "translocal" may at times best capture the social relationships of migrants, yet nations continue to matter in migrants' lives: Not only do they define the rules of movement; they also draw on emotions nurtured "transnationally" and often make extraordinary demands on personal identity formation through citizenship, schooling, and expectations of military service. Migrants' attachments to their homes in Italy can remain intense and can be shared "diasporically" through global networks, but such attachments are less often to the Italian nation than to a particular place in Italy and to the scattered former residents of that local place. This in turn suggests where, and in what ways, mobile persons have escaped or resisted the entwining of intimacy and nation suggesting that love of country is not the only, natural, or inevitable result of human mobility. Dual and multiple citizenship, hybrid identities, and cosmopolitanism are all potential outcomes.[30]

To highlight the key themes of the personal, the family, and the community in relation to nation building, we have chosen to organize this volume in three sections. The first uses biography to explore the Italianization, or national "marking," of particular expressions and practices of masculinity and femininity, in private and in public, among individuals who lived their lives within and beyond the national territories of Italy. In the second part, oral methodologies complement written texts in explorations of two of the veritable icons of Italian intimacy—the Italian mother and the Italian marriage—but are explored across several generations and in many national settings, not just in Italy itself. Finally, the third part combines ethnographic and oral historical methodologies to suggest how private, or domestic, and public arenas—especially in community associations and in families—develop across borders. Of course, this division is in many respects somewhat arbitrary: Most chapters touch on the interconnections of individual, family, community, and nation, and many of the authors employ a mix of methodologies.

The National in the Personal through Biography

One of the best places to explore the emergence of the national, and the ways in which nation-states seek to embrace the intersection of public and private practices and personae, is in the lives of individual men and women. Most national cultures—and certainly all the ones that migrants from Italy encountered in the course of their own migratory lives—accept that men will move, while imagining women as ensconced within the family or household and thus within a single nation. Any study of nation building across borders must, then, be a gendered one.

Nevertheless, it is no simple matter to examine how movement across borders complicates the nexus of the national and the local or the dichotomy of public and private, let alone how it disrupts or reinforces the creation of a sense of intimate connection between individual and nation-state—even in the lives of men, although perhaps more poignantly in the lives of women. This is particularly true because most mobile Italians before the mid-twentieth century were illiterate; they left few traces of any kind in the written record. Scholars inevitably write about the exceptional rather than the most representative migrants as a result. Still, by including biographical studies of both men and women in this volume, we open what we hope will be a long debate about how nation building across borders has been gendered. And occasionally, as author Carol Stabile shows, the exceptional working-class immigrant or child of immigrants does aspire to write about his or her life.

In the first part, four contributors respond to the challenge with studies of the explicitly nationalist exile Giuseppe Mazzini and his followers and friends Giorgina Craufurd and Aurelio Saffi, the equally well-known film star Rudolph Valentino, and two little-known Italian Americans—a labor activist, Katie DeRorre, and the working-class soldier Mike Stabile. Collectively, these chapters respond to Gabaccia's call "for more biographical analysis of the theory and practice of gender and sexuality in the ideas, politics, movements and personal lives" not only "of the nineteenth century Italian nationalists in exile" but also of Italian migrants in general.[31]

Historian Ros Pesman explores how Italy's early nationalists imagined a nation emerging from the cradle of a family life of intimacy and love between men and women. The public regeneration of the nation of Italy was envisaged as a private and deeply moral action to be taken by Italians in their private and domestic lives. Moral and spiritual decadence had been Italy's bane; family ties and proper gender relations at home would help to create a new nation. A concern with morality has of course been common to nation building in many places; in the case of Italy, secular nationalists faced the particularly challenging task of seizing from the Catholic Church its power to legitimate sexuality and procreation (through control of marriage) without provoking fears of moral chaos.[32]

Central to Pesman's story of intimacy and nation building is the life of Giuseppe Mazzini, the republican conspirator and founder of both Young Italy (an Italian nationalist group) and Young Europe (which was composed of nationalists committed to democratic governance). As a nationalist conspirator, Mazzini was forced to live most of his adult life in exile, and much of that time in England. Scholars have long recognized the importance of English supporters of Italian, and especially of Mazzinian and Garibaldian, nationalism in the making of Italy itself.[33] In her essay, Pesman examines this well-worn theme through a careful exploration of the intimate relations of friendship, love, and marriage within Mazzini's circle of English and Italian nationalist co-conspirators, revealing the difficulties of fixing individual identities firmly within one nation or the other.

Mazzini was attractive to English Protestants, many of them women, precisely because of the distinctive persona he developed as an individual in exile. His nationalism was as spiritually expressed as it was political in its intentions. Mazzini abjured sexual relations; his followers in England, in turn, seemed to perceive him as having taken his ideal of a new Italian nation as his only bride. At the same time he embodied for them a suffering Italian nation they clearly viewed as feminine, prostrate, and in need of their assistance. Pesman particularly emphasizes the appeal of this Mazzinian persona to English women, some of whom felt themselves to be wedded to Mazzini spiritually and emotionally, even as they described themselves—like brides of Christ—as "converts" to his cause. In the world of Mazzini and his followers, exile, love, self-sacrifice, friendship, and intimacy underwrote and enabled political action during several key moments in the history of Italian nation building (even though the unification of Italy in 1861 under the House of Savoy and the king of Sardinia increasingly positioned Mazzini and his secular and republican followers on the margins of state power).

By exploring the marriage of two of Mazzini's most devoted followers—Aurelio Saffi and the Italian-born and -raised but nevertheless English-speaking and British

Giorgina Craufurd—Pesman offers readers an Italian case study of an exceedingly common trope of republican nation building.[34] That trope defines families as the cradles of nations. Among republicans in North America and Europe, furthermore, the same trope defines women such as Craufurd as mothers of the nation. (That the same trope would later become even more powerfully associated with militarist fascist movements, including Mussolini's fascism in Italy, is not something the republican nationalists foresaw.)

Saffi and Craufurd defined their love less around maternity, however, than around mutual sacrifice and collective duty to a shared cause. Craufurd did not follow Saffi's leadership in politics; mutuality and communication between wife and husband—not maternity—was the focus of their companionate marriage. Despite increasingly stressful political disagreements that resulted from Saffi's election to office (at a time when Mazzini called upon his followers to abjure cooperation with the Italian monarchy—a position that Craufurd, but not Saffi, supported), the couple committed themselves to creating a new Italy at home and a new home in Italy. This would be one of their many contributions to nation building. Craufurd may have been a "republican mother," but with Saffi also clearly committed to "republican fatherhood," the rearing of children for Italy was not understood to be female work in this family.[35] On the contrary, Pesman paints a portrait of Craufurd and Saffi as a companionate couple determined to make of their marriage a "country of the heart," borrowing from Mazzini's beliefs in the connections among nation, spirituality, and intimacy.

It seems at first a long leap from the highly spiritualized love expressed by Saffi and Craufurd and from the passionate but asexual friendships of Mazzini and his English women supporters to the filmed kisses and overtly sexualized persona of Rudolph Valentino, the Italian migrant who helped to make the Latin lover a persistent stereotype in the cool theory of academe and the hot pleasures of popular culture. Film studies scholar Giorgio Bertellini asks readers to ponder why the great age of nationalism and international migration in the nineteenth century generated increasingly public and popular literary and theatrical exhibitions of intimacy as forms of entertainment. (Students of television and film in our own times now also write of the impact of globalization on desire, as ever-larger numbers of viewers in the poor global south learn to desire the Western wealth that they can see and that they imagine themselves enjoying.)[36] Mass circulation of images through print, theater, and film and through large-scale migration increasingly attached dramatic and public displays of intimacy to men and women—many of them singers and performers—from the Mediterranean. Together with the working-class migrants, individual performers such as Enrico Caruso and Luisa Tetrazzini and the actress Eleonora Duse (who died while on tour to Pittsburgh) dramatically challenged the idyllic visions of the Italy that earlier Americans and Europeans had encountered through tourism and the Grand Tour. Increasingly, the performative associations of Italy's culture were embodied by physical sensuality and romantic love.[37] Thus Valentino, according to Bertellini, was not just a Latin lover and a transatlantic star but a racialized man as well. Bertellini explores how viewers established meaningful and in some sense intimate relationships with legally white performers who nevertheless, much like Valentino, were imagined as "dark" or swarthy. It was these racialized and eroticized immigrant stars who most often made love and kissed in the liminal arenas of the silver screen and theater.

As in the case of Mazzini, however, Valentino's seductive masculinity generated continual critiques of his supposed femininity, and by the twentieth century, Americans were beginning to view this linkage as somehow perverse, and associated with gender and sexual abnormality. Bertellini reminds us of the survival of nineteenth-century notions of a feminine Italy that lived on in the highly racialized Italian south—the home of most of the migrants traveling to the United States in the years between 1880 and 1920. Like the migrants from Italy—whose migrations the United States decided to restrict in the 1920s—Valentino inherited his masculine seductiveness, with its purportedly feminine undercurrents, from the racially mixed populations of the Mediterranean.

Perhaps for this reason, Italian and Italian American audiences did not understand or criticize the on-screen physical intimacy or the public persona of the seductive Valentino in quite the same ways. Indeed, some Italian critics explicitly questioned the Italianness of the Latin lover's masculinity. But even they felt compelled to discuss Valentino as a racial type, albeit one that differed rather sharply from racialized masculinity of Italy's new duce, Benito Mussolini.[38] Ironically, Italians tended to represent the man whom Americans viewed in highly embodied ways as darkly physical and sexualized yet also effeminate and as possessing a sublimely spiritualized *italianità*, which shared considerable resemblances to the ways English women had imagined Mazzini. Both men enjoyed the adulation of women of the English-speaking world for exactly this combination of spirituality and soulful appeal.

The identity and sexuality of Mike Stabile, a working-class American soldier, provide a further contrast to the uplifted and spiritualized yet also Italianized masculine persona imagined by Mazzini's and Valentino's physically distanced yet emotionally connected women fans and supporters. Mike Stabile was a man and a soldier—and, most exceptionally, a diarist and avid letter writer—who rarely thought about the national elements of his identity—whether as American, Italian, or Italian American—but who found himself, as a soldier, asked to die for his country. (While Stabile was in fact wounded in Okinawa in 1945, he leaves us with little doubt that he was not fighting for his country: For Stabile the army was just another job, and a job where more powerful men bossed him around and kept him from earning money, much to his anger and dismay.) Despite Stabile's apparent indifference, if not hostility, to national identities, he formed relationships with other Italian-origin, largely second-generation "guys from New Jersey," whom he identified as being much like himself—that is, lower class and marginal as Americans. Much of Stabile's interaction with the "guys from New Jersey" revolved around a search for sex across gender and racial boundaries in wartime Hawaii. Author Carol Stabile—Mike's daughter—makes a solid case for his whiteness, albeit within a hierarchy that—again—includes a type of dark-white masculinity that carried resonances of Valentino's identity. This dark whiteness was both the key element of Stabile's identity and a major shaper of his sexual adventures in Hawaii.

Stabile was not Valentino, and he was certainly no Mazzini, yet some dimensions of his masculinity will seem familiar to those who read Pesman's and Bertellini's accounts. Mike feared being feminized by the U.S. Army. He especially resented KP—

kitchen work, which included serving and cleanup—which he viewed as women's work. Throughout the war, he suggested in his diary that he and other young men from New Jersey were being assigned more than their fair share of KP. Mike's fellow soldiers, furthermore, saw his interest in writing as giving him special skills that could help them in romancing women, either locally (which involved Mike speaking for them on the telephone) or back home (via letters that Mike penned on their behalf). Indirectly, at least, Mike enjoyed a reputation as a Latin lover.

Mike's (dark) whiteness and his Italianness both figured in his sexual activities in Hawaii; indeed, it is in relationship to sex that Mike seemed most often to think about race and nation. Mike was as fascinated with racial difference as one might expect of a man whose own sense of whiteness was fragile. Did his matter-of-fact descriptions of same-sex intimacy and his involvement with openly and not-so-openly queer local men—as matchmaker, as friend, as sexual partner, as "'Q' hunter"—call attention to his Mediterranean origins? Italianists and students of same-sex relationships in other Latin cultures such as that of Mexico remind us that such relationships were broadly tolerated among young men and that the label of "queer" and social stigma attached only to mature men who were penetrated by other men.[39] As Stabile points out, however, Mike was fully aware of and sometimes also expressed American hostility and revulsion toward the same queer men he embraced—emotionally and physically—as friends in Hawaii. In between, in both his racial and national markings, the working-class Mike was refreshingly unwilling to accept the nation's claims on him; he was, as Carol Stabile notes, less inclined to resist his racialization as white.

Mike Stabile often viewed women in ways stereotypically associated with Italy's Roman Catholic and Marianist culture—as either angelic mothers or potential whores.[40] But it was as an American that Mike layered these older tropes of femininity with racial assumptions. Italian American women in Hawaii, as in New Jersey, were sexually off limits to Stabile. (And we learn from author Stabile that he did not ultimately find a wife from within his New Jersey Italian American community, but one with deeper American roots.) By contrast, Mike Stabile seemed to assume that all Hawaiian women of Asian descent were sexually available, even when they were not working as prostitutes and even when he met them in decidedly familial contexts.

To understand how Italian migrant women negotiated the equally complex terrain of gender and sexuality during the same years, Caroline Waldron Merithew introduces readers to Katie DeRorre. DeRorre's life as a mining activist in Illinois took a completely different direction from Stabile's, especially in her resistance to racism, while revealing a resistance to nationalism that curiously mirrored his. Merithew tells DeRorre's story as one that merged the private and political, at least in part because of the transformations in gender identities and the struggles between the generations that migration fostered. DeRorre (known as Sister Kate) was atypical of female migrants in many ways, of course. Gender and power relations within her family were particularly unusual: She was active politically, while her husband stayed home with the children. She was seen by the men and some of the women in the movement not as equal to but as different from other activist women, and she was the only woman they called "Sister"—an acknowledgment, perhaps, of how decidedly outsiders associated her Italian roots with the warmth of family and kinship-based life, even though her family departed so sharply from Italian community norms.

Merithew defines DeRorre (who arrived in the United States as a child) as a 1.5-generation immigrant, and she highlights the competing identity choices typical of this group. DeRorre decided to have nothing to do with her mother once she married and left home, presumably to avoid the pressure exerted by her mother for her to fulfill her role expectations as married daughter and mother (a position examined at length in the chapters by Miller, De Tona, and Rieker in the second part). Yet DeRorre nevertheless continued to be part of a transnational Italian community and was a member of various Italian political associations. Unlike many of her co-nationals, however, Katie rejected both racial and gender discrimination.

Merithew argues that DeRorre's keen sense of social justice grew out of her personal experiences as the daughter of an abusive mother who gave privileges to her sons while denying the needs of her daughters. Other personal experiences, namely the death of one of her young children, led DeRorre to build her politics out of a conscious decision to combine domesticity and activism, creating what Merithew calls a "third sphere." Here we see the potential for change, transmutation, and resistance to nationalization offered by migration. According to Merithew, this intermediate space, or third sphere, was both physical and psychic and developed out of necessity in living rooms and household kitchens, as well as public parks and hobo camps, locales that became simultaneously public and intimate. This notion of a third sphere is reminiscent of the space that is defined by the liminal, characterized by *communitas,* a coming together of people who experience a sense of collective belonging in their transition to a new social status.[41] It was places like DeRorre's kitchen and living room in which women were transformed into activists, and that allowed disparate actors, including black women as well as individuals of various political and religious convictions, to join in a common cause.

That history has forgotten Katie DeRorre reflects a scholarly tendency to overlook the connections between domestic lives and political concerns. Yet when private troubles are shared by many in the community, they become public issues.[42] DeRorre's life demonstrates the intricate connections between the intimate and private hardships of Italian immigrant daughters, whose lives were tightly controlled by patriarchal values and made worse by poverty, and the broader marginalization and exploitation of immigrant labor, particularly in the heavy and dangerous work of the mines. That DeRorre bridged this divide through the transformation of the home into a kind of transnational yet also multiethnic third sphere—and was then promptly forgotten—underlines the importance of intimate relations in naturalizing the nation and making invisible the role of emotions in its creation. These themes become even more visible and poignant when the focus is marriage and motherhood.

"Italian" Motherhood and Marriage through Oral Narratives

What makes a mother "Italian" and why do so many nations around the world view a particular type of motherhood as a central trope of Italianness? Is the Italian mother imagined differently in Italy than in countries where Italian immigrants form only a small minority of the larger society? Given their role as bearers of culture and mothers of nations, a focus on migrant women's friendships and courtships, marrying and mothering, and childbearing and rearing necessitates an analysis of intimacies across borders. It is these quintessentially private matters of intimate culture that reveal most clearly how personal ideas and aspirations can both confirm and contest, challenge and channel, the more public cultural expressions of identity practices and national belonging. The testimonies of migrant women on motherhood, gender roles, and family life bring into sharp relief the role that border crossings often play in cultural transformation, particularly if viewed across the generations. What their narratives reveal is that the direction of change is not unilinear and never straightforward—and that mothers, whether in Italy or elsewhere, rarely understand themselves in exactly the same ways, or in the same national terms, as does the society around them. Another key finding is how migrant women struggle within and among themselves to both support and resist powerful stereotypes of Italian motherhood. On the one hand, these stereotypes can be limiting and restricting; on the other, they provide important boundary-forming devices for the creation of diasporic community.

At the broadest level, each of the chapters in the second part deals with the role of families in migration and with the role of women within them. Particularly striking is the way that women, their being and doing and their bodies and practices, come to represent "good" or "bad" culture (both national and ethnic) and how the processes of migration often accentuate and confound what nation-states and ethnic communities try to fix as appropriate beliefs and behaviors for women.[43] What is "right" and "proper" in the old national context is often outdated and inappropriate in the new. Discourses of honor and shame are often involved, and it is often women who impose these belief systems on each other. Of course, these tensions mirror the broader and more public debates about gender roles and identities that have powerful currency, particularly in the media and in major institutions of the Church and the state. Migrant women's struggles to deal with at least two sets of often conflicting gender and generational discourses in both home and host countries can create shared experiences for them but also produce diversity of—and thus contestation over—gendered practices. At the heart of these contestations we find battles between women. In Miller's chapter on Australia and De Tona's chapter on Ireland, these contestations center around migrant grandmothers, mothers, and daughters, while Pojmann's chapter on Italy focuses on relations between migrant women domestics and their Italian women employers. Rieker's chapter examines how individual women themselves have struggled to understand the enormous changes in marriage and motherhood that accompanied migration from Italy to Germany.

Oral testimony proved to be an excellent (and possibly the most appropriate) source of insider information on the especially intimate issue of making the "right" number of babies. Replete with frank, and often bawdy, discussions of contraceptive techniques, Miller's chapter examines three generations of Italian migrant women in Australia and compares their conceptions of selfhood and motherhood, altruism and individualism, by analyzing their thoughts and decisions on parenting and family size. Miller's informants overtly identified the broader political contexts of both their home and host societies as influences on their childbearing decisions. The experiences of economic, linguistic, and social marginalization in the host country all contributed to the development of a community identity and consciousness. Furthermore, the lack of opportunities and a limited safety net in Italy meant that the Italian migrant family in Australia had to do all it could to create its own security. In this context, the notion of a diasporic private sphere, with its political implications, seems perhaps more pertinent than the actual lived experiences of transnational intimate relationships.

A key theme in Miller's chapter is the changing relationship between motherhood and altruism, and thus the interconnections among notions of the self, family, and nation. The older generations share an understanding of motherhood that foregrounds selflessness and sacrifice, with the inherent expectation that children will reciprocate through strong bonds of emotion, respect, and closeness. In contrast, the younger generation takes a more individualistic approach to motherhood, wishing to balance self and others. The fact that contemporary psychologists define the older generations' altruism as a mental health issue brings home just how significant social change has been for these women over their lifetimes. Miller shows how a focus on personal lives provides insights into wider social arrangements, and how changing notions of Italian motherhood outside Italy highlight the impact of neoliberalism and the demise of the welfare state. In doing so, she queries how the transition from a more communal and family-oriented notion of self to a more individualistic one can be explained within the larger social context.

Being a mother in Italy at the turn of the twentieth century often meant working long hours in the fields as well as having many children who themselves began to work at an early age. In contrast, being a working-class mother in postwar Italy and Australia meant waged work outside the home, necessitating a stricter limit on family size, particularly in Australia, where the support of extended family was absent. In both places, the middle-class ideal of the selfless, altruistic mother devoted to domesticity (see Pojmann's chapter) exerted a strong influence, defining womanhood as motherhood. Miller notes elsewhere that the dramatic drop in fertility in Italy has been linked to the power of patriarchal family life there, noting that women resist by not having children, thus avoiding altogether the roles of wife and mother. Despite the clear evidence that Italian Australian migrants of all three generations have been concerned with limiting their family size, the fact that members of the third generation, in particular, have more children than their counterparts in Italy is perhaps an indication of the potential for increased autonomy that migration often provides Italian women, at least in the Australian context.

Just how these changes in gender roles affect women's own sense of Italianness and national identity remains an open and unresolved question. It is clear, for instance, that younger mothers are very aware of the generational contract implied by the altruism of their own mothers and define this as an Italian trait that they respect and aim to uphold by, for example, caring for their mothers as they age. Even as they increase their levels of education and commitments to professional work, younger women are developing relationships with their mothers that Miller defines as involving "new forms of emotional economy." Younger mothers challenge the notion that personal happiness and mental health rest on the "compulsory altruism" of their mother's generation. This not only affects their actions as mothers, many choosing to juggle children and careers, but also makes them uneasy about being recipients of their mother's selflessness. Tensions between the generations often result as adult daughters contest the generosity and self-denial of their mothers and try to encourage their mothers to look after themselves. At the same time, the younger women rely on their mothers' generosity and selflessness in caring for their own children so that they are free to pursue their careers.

There is some evidence in Miller's chapter to suggest that the newer practices of the younger mothers are attributed by the older generation to the impact of Australian society. The first-generation migrants thus face the realization that their migration, often justified as providing more opportunities for their children, has resulted in rejection of what they might define as traditional ways of mothering. However, the maintenance of a strong sense of respect for elders among the younger women, reflected in a commitment to close contact and care for the aged, tends to be defined by all generations as particularly Italian and is implicitly contrasted with the attitudes and behaviors of Australian families, whom they see as being less close. Here, as in other chapters, the conflation of nation with particular family practices is particularly striking.

A similar set of tensions around notions of mothering based in commitments to family and to self-sacrifice versus ideas about individualism and self-actualization are at the heart of Carla De Tona's chapter on Italian migrant experiences of motherhood in Ireland. However, the distinctions here do not appear to neatly follow generational lines. More than Miller, De Tona examines how motherhood is played out transnationally. Italy is much closer to Ireland than is Australia, and 80 percent of Italians in Ireland come from a single province in Italy (Frosinone, located between Naples and Rome) and work in the same industry (fish-and-chip shops). The result is a very high level of transnational activity between the two places. De Tona focuses on how women as mothers interact (in both imagined and practical ways) across distances and national borders. Notions of a transnational family and a transnational domestic sphere capture the lived experiences of these families, whose members retain their sense of collectivity and kinship, along with their attendant obligations and the resulting tensions, in spite of being spread across space and time.[44]

De Tona argues that although migration has the potential to be emancipatory, it can simultaneously constrain women in ways that force mothers and daughters into conflict. Among the Irish women of the three-generation Frosinone migration chain, which began in the late 1800s, conflicting values and practices of motherhood are played out among grandmothers, mothers, and daughters in Ireland. For recently arrived professional women who departed Italy in the 1960s, the same conflicts play out transnationally between Ireland and Italy. Daughters in both Miller's and De Tona's studies have acquired more social and sexual freedom and, as a result, wish to move away from the limiting gender models of their mothers and grandmothers. These same mothers and grandmothers encourage their daughters to move away from gender constraints but, in so doing, must push them away from themselves, as well as from the projects for which they have been asked to sacrifice their lives. The result is a set of tensions and negotiations of power that are brought into sharp relief by migration. Among migrants, women are often charged with the important role of defining ethnic community and national identity, which creates contradictions of diasporic motherhood that have no easy resolution and that involve a series of often painful processes of readjustment to new myths of motherhood.

De Tona finds that narratives on motherhood have been central to the women's self-ascription and self-positioning, and that motherhood, particularly among the older generations, was conflated not only with independent female selfhood but also with the essence of what it means to these women to be Italian. She highlights the power that migrant mothers have to define Italian culture and identity in host settings through both behavior and storytelling as well as through their control over their daughters' actions. De Tona argues that because migrants tend to invest in preserving cultural traditions as a hallmark of their identity, the tensions of the generation gap can be more severe in migrant settings than in the homeland. What might be viewed as the emancipation of the younger generation in Italy is imbued with concerns about the loss of ethnic and national identity in diaspora.

This is not to suggest that Italy and transnational kin play no role in the lives of the older migrants. Women bemoan the fact that migration disrupted their female kin and quasi-kin networks, rendering their lives as mothers more difficult. Whenever possible, and when needed, they call on such networks in Italy to provide support and they offer reciprocity in return. Recent professional migrants, for whom Ireland can represent an escape from possessive mothers and the space to develop more individualized notions of identity, do not experience the same losses. De Tona argues that despite competing generational tensions, mothers and daughters from all groups and generations invest in the notion of Italian motherhood as a key feature of migrant community identity and belonging in Ireland. Following Gans's notion of symbolic ethnicity, we might call this symbolic (Italian) motherhood. It does not impede Irish Italian migrant women from embracing more emancipated gender roles and relations and developing new ideals and practices, while continuing to define themselves as Italian, through their dedication to close family relations, frequent contact with family, and a commitment to mother-daughter bonds, all of which they define as quintessentially Italian.[45]

Rieker finds many of the same tensions in identity as she focuses on the marriages of Italian migrant women in Germany. She describes such women as reinterpreting their restrictive upbringings and marriage choices in light of newfound beliefs about female autonomy (which most do embrace) more often than through struggles with their daughters. Rieker's focus on changing ideas and practices surrounding courtship, love, and marriage provides insights into the often silent and hidden pain of intimacy, while also placing the transformation of practices among migrants in long-term historical context. The oral testimonies of the men and women she interviewed convey the overwhelming power of the gendered restrictions on social relations that characterized their youth in southern Italy in the 1950s. Rieker also provides a clear picture of the limited opportunities for social interaction and the harsh penalties for transgressions, particularly for women. She notes how women were obliged to marry to guarantee their economic support, given the absence of any viable alternatives.

Women struggled to make sense of such significant changes in social values and practices, particularly as they looked back at their limited educational and employment opportunities. Some lamented their lost youth and forbidden freedom. In Rieker's analysis of border-crossing marriages, the question of the emancipatory effect of migration for women remains germane. Because it opened opportunities for wage earning, for women as well as for men, migration also provided opportunities for marriage for those too poor to contemplate it in Italy. In addition, the relative isolation from extended families often resulted in a need for greater solidarity between husband and wife, and an increase in autonomy for the wife. But these newfound freedoms often also prompted a questioning and rejection of old ways. To now find meaning and companionship in their arranged marriages, in a social setting where notions of romantic love dominate, proved difficult for many women. By examining migrants' lives within the context of a long history of contestation over romantic love, Rieker suggests that the adoption of notions of romantic love may require a spatial frame of reference that is larger than that of the local village, with its face-to-face interactions among kinship groups. Whether or not the intensive self-reflection that romantic love encourages inevitably leads to a questioning of marriage itself remains an open question. According to her account, second-generation German Italians appear to uphold marriage as an important dimension of their Italian identity. However, unlike their parents, they embrace the notion of romantic love and the ideal of individuals making marital choices based on romance as the necessary foundation of a community of two partners for their lifetime.

Whereas the other chapters in this volume focus on migrants who left Italy, Wendy Pojmann tackles the issue of mothering in contemporary Italy, where a growing number of immigrants now also live. Like Miller, Pojmann considers the changing relationship between public discourses about Italian motherhood and changing private lives. She compares popular notions of Italian motherhood, including *mammismo* (mothers doting so much on children, especially sons, that they prefer to remain at home rather than marry), alluring motherhood (representations of pregnant movie stars that suggest mothers can be sexy), and motherhood in crisis (represented by immigrant mothers who are portrayed by the media as living in tragic circumstances). She then ponders how conflicting ideas about motherhood and feminist ideas affect the relationship of Italians to the increasing number of immigrant women who work for them in their homes.

Pojmann focuses on the legacies of middle-class motherhood as it developed in postwar Italy. In order to sustain middle-class lifestyles and ideals of motherhood, Italian women needed to become wage earners and employers of domestic help (since only with help could they preserve high standards of household cleanliness and fulfill the moral obligation to care for small children and the elderly at home). This has been the price, Pojmann shows, of neoliberal goals of individual and personal fulfillment. Its hidden costs have been borne by immigrant women workers in Italian homes, and they have been greatest for those who have to leave their own small children and elderly parents in distant homelands. By tracing the historical development of Italy's notions of motherhood in relationship to contemporary immigration, Pojmann raises the question of whether it is necessary to consider a diasporic private sphere that encompasses all women. This notion provides an interesting perspective on the concept of global care chains, introduced by Yeates.[46] Does this "import[ation of] maternal love" contribute to the creation of a diasporic private sphere among women?

Pojmann's analysis reveals how Italy's weak welfare state has been shaped by, and in turn constructs, Italian understandings of motherhood. She highlights the implicit contradictions in Italian women's practice of employing immigrant women as domestics in order to free themselves from domestic drudgery. By their actions, they condemn immigrant women not only to the boring, menial tasks of domesticity but also to bad pay and limited security. Furthermore, the employment of other women in the home serves to reinforce the patriarchal and gendered nature of domestic work while doing little to advance a more equitable division of labor in the home. And this private sphere is not particularly intimate. Italian middle-class housewives attempt to preserve the intimacy of their own families by employing immigrant domestics (rather than using Italy's limited institutional care facilities), but they do so without learning much about their immigrant employees. They commonly accept the media's negative stereotyping of the very women they employ and disregard the fact that these women are often mothers too. The invisibility of immigrant woman as mothers and caregivers exacerbates the relative invisibility of the domestic sphere of Italian families in which they work.

According to Pojmann, Italian feminists helped secure some of the most generous maternity leave entitlements in OECD countries, but immigrant women workers are not eligible for them. Scholars are increasingly recognizing the role of Italian women (and women in other Western industrial countries) in the feminization of migration and global care chains. But Pojmann notes that Italian women rarely recognize either their place in these global care chains or the loneliness of the immigrant women working in their family spaces (although groups such as Punto di Partenza[47] do call attention to these issues). Here Pojmann demonstrates how migration challenges notions of families as microcosms of nations comprising citizens.[48] A similar set of challenges to nationhood is often posed by migrant communities.

Ethnographic Studies of Family, Community, and Nation

The chapters in the third part point to the existence of a distinctively female public sphere and to intimate public spaces that resemble in some ways DeRorre's kitchen, the meeting locales of the *autocoscienza* associations in Italy, and perhaps even the movie theaters where people enjoy following the intimate if fantastical lives of screen sirens in relatively public locales. Migration has helped to create many intermediate spaces between the public and the private. All the chapters in this section examine how Italian migrant women, and Italian migrant communities in general, have navigated an often hostile public domain by domesticating it through rituals that are an extension of the private—for example, through wedding ceremonies, feast days, and family reunions. Each case study attests to the role of community and extended family networks as the link between macro (state) and micro (family/individual) levels and processes. They also reveal community to be the locus of social capital, which is so important to migrants and their families, who often do not have access to state support and services.[49] Extended family and community networks are well-known sources of support for immigrants in the new host country. Less well known is their role in transnational settings. These chapters reveal how intimate culture can be employed in public settings to reinforce ethnic and national identities.

Carol McKibben's chapter offers a classic example of a private and domestically based community: the enclave settlement of Monterey Sicilian fishing communities. Unlike most other groups, fisher people tend to form tightly knit and endogamous, self-sufficient communities that are dominated by women, particularly as the lives of the men are characterized by frequent movements away from home to follow the fish. Sicilian fisher people have incorporated homeland communities into their closed but transnational networks of kin for over three generations. Indeed, what is striking about the community of Sicilians that McKibben describes is its high and sustained level of transnational interaction. There is constant travel for visits between Monterey and Sicily, and migration, for intermarriage as well as for other purposes, between the local communities in the two places. Monterey Sicilians represent perhaps one of the most active transnational communities of Italian origin today.

An outcome of this high degree of transnational intimacy is that the boundaries between the first, second, and subsequent generations are not clearly defined and the sense of national and ethnic identities is fluid. Furthermore, as migrations to California from Southeast Asia, Latin America, and the Caribbean increased, Monterey Sicilians "began to enjoy a sense of themselves as welcome European immigrants," based on their whiteness. In such a context—Monterey Sicilians were well respected and clearly contributed to local development—the acquisition of American citizenship nevertheless became "a detail often overlooked." Even when Italy and the United States were at war, Sicilians on both sides of the Atlantic cared mainly about their ability to stay in touch, to send much-sought-after goods to each other, and to maintain their relationships of reciprocity and their trust. The often hotly contested issue of dual citizenship had little to do with overt political issues of national allegiance and infinitely more to do with facilitating transnational caregiving practices, the intimate relations across borders that sustain family and community ties.[50] Still, the gendered consequences of this mode of transnational community building were noticeable in Monterey. McKibben argues that the political indifference of the female-based and -controlled community stymied the efforts of some of the local men to organize themselves politically, with the result that men had no political visibility at all. Only during the Second World War did politics become an issue for Monterey Italians, and even then its salience proved short lived. Given the still high rate of immigration from Sicily today, interest in acquisition of American citizenship and in local political activism has again declined.

McKibben provides a portrait of a very well-defined transnational, or perhaps translocal, community identity. Monterey Sicilians appear to be at home both in their Sicilian hometowns and in Monterey. The extent of their travel between the two suggests that many spend equal amounts of time in each. This cross-border existence in some respects mirrors the way people's lives plays out fluidly across private and domestic spheres too. McKibben explains that home is "both a public and private space," creating "a transnational identity that fuses an occupational identity (as fisher people) developed in public with private rituals of family and Sicilian ethnicity." With the menfolk away fishing for extended time periods, the women organized all aspects of daily life, often communally, from dinner menus to holiday camping trips, fostering a strong sense of community. In doing so, the boundaries of individual families were blurred, as McKibben makes clear: "It was these gatherings that built the Sicilian fishing community. It was, and is, in these casual meetings that women decided everything from what to make for dinner to whose children ought to marry."

McKibben explores how the Sicilian Monterey community coped with the demise of its primary industry—sardine fishing—by reviving the local tourist industry. Despite this significant change in economic structure, the community managed to retain its Sicilian and (more broadly) Italian identities. Employing widespread practices from their fishing days, the women reinvented key community festivals as public tourist events and, in so doing, developed a public marker of both ethnic and national identities. But women's access to the public domain was not complete. While they could chart a course from within their communities to the outside world through their organization of rituals, they still had little involvement in the politics or governance of American society.

Like the Monterey Sicilians, the Swiss Italians described in anthropologist Susanne Wessendorf's chapter enjoy a high degree of transnational exchange and activity, aided by the relative proximity between Italy and Switzerland. However, unlike the Monterey Sicilians, Swiss Italians have been constantly preoccupied with citizenship rights since World War II. The harsh limitations of Switzerland's guest worker scheme (which denied guest workers permanent residency and afforded them limited welfare services or access to health and education) meant that Italian migrants were initially overwhelmingly single males. Settlement and family life were curtailed, and children were left behind with relatives in Italy. In this context, Italian ethnic identity was carefully monitored and policed, so migrants were able to develop little sense of belonging to Swiss society, at least for the first generation. Connections to Italy remained strong, as everyone anticipated eventual repatriation and settlement there. Wessendorf shows how, in this comparatively hostile environment, the ideal of the united Italian family became a key symbol through which Swiss Italian migrants defined their identity as Italians.

Each year Italians in Switzerland engage in the performance of what Wessendorf calls a "united family" through visits home to Italy. The public displays of affection at the train station on departure and arrival, as well as during the long journeys to and from Switzerland, served to reinforce a sense of tightly knit community, providing a psychic buffer from the perceived hostilities and isolation of Swiss society. Yet at the same time, migrants are defined as *Svizzeroti* by their compatriots in Italy, a half-joking, somewhat condescending term that refers to the more emancipated, urban nature of Swiss Italian identities, attitudes, and behaviors and so marks them as different from Italians in Italy. For Italians in Switzerland, these regular contacts and the fostering of lively transnational relationships have not prevented the development of differing experiences among migrants and non-migrants. Forty to fifty years of emigration and spending more than half of their lives in a foreign place makes it difficult for migrants to reintegrate socially and culturally into a village in Italy that they have not experienced in everyday life for several decades.

In such active transnational communities, connections might better be defined as translocal, highlighting how the primary connections are between local communities. Unlike, for example, Katie DeRorre's transnational connections with Italy through political associations, these migrants almost exclusively associate with family and friends in their home villages in Italy. Of course, this does not eliminate national influences, since local-to-local linkages continue to operate within two national contexts (which Salih refers to as "plurinational").[51] Wessendorf employs the term "translocal" because it emphasizes the local connections even though these occur across national borders. Wessendorf acknowledges the continued role of the nation-state in shaping these translocal connections by coining the phrase "state-imposed translocalism" to refer to the way the regulations controlling residency and family reunion contributed to Italian migrants' continued connections to their homelands by ensuring that their connections to Switzerland remained provisional and insecure.

Wessendorf reveals how the influence of state-imposed translocalism has endured through the legacies of guest worker policies, which are still clearly evident today. Even once these restrictions were lifted, and migrants were granted permanent residency, their dreams of return persisted. But the myth of return proved difficult to achieve. A number of structural conditions—including limited job opportunities in Italy and a better health care system in Switzerland—impeded return. But, arguably, most important of all is the sense of cultural estrangement experienced by many during their time in Italy, as well as a reluctance to leave adult children now more permanently settled in Switzerland. This is particularly true when the migrants themselves had to endure lengthy separations from their children in the early years of migration.

Making a point that might be applicable to former guest workers and sojourners in other national settings, Wessendorf describes how separations contributed to a "myth of the family" and to a dream of "being united" *(essere uniti)* as key symbols of identification for Italians. In Switzerland, the migrants contrast their tightly knit families to Swiss families, which they see as more individualistic and colder (see the chapters by Miller and Baldassar for similar findings in Australia). Here is an example of a trope of intimacy becoming nationalized because it was adopted as a transnational identity. Wessendorf suggests that the idealization of family solidarity reflects continued resistance to efforts by centralized states and the Church to control family affairs, such as marriage and procreation.

The enduring role of family ideologies of solidarity as emblematic of Italian nationhood in migrant settings is further explored in Baldassar's chapter. Through an analysis of a century of visits and communication between Italy and Australia, this chapter explores the particular entwining of national and familial emotions of love and caring. The popular and much cherished image of the close *famiglia italiana* highlights not only the attachment of children and parents but also how a collective national sense of belonging is intrinsically related to family culture. The myths and contradictions of close Italian families arguably have a deeper resonance and greater resilience in migrants' lives because of the ways stereotypes of Italy—and the roles of families and women in enacting them—figure in the genesis of ethno-national and diasporic identities.

Drawing on a sample of Italian migrants living in Australia and their aging parents living in Italy, Baldassar contemplates how the obligations of transnational family caregiving are manifest in the related emotions of longing for homeland and nostalgia, or homesickness. She argues that notions about the importance of family closeness and co-presence ("being together") that characterize Italian conceptions of health and well-being are linked to ideas about connections to place and nation. These obligations to be with kin and to be in the homeland motivate individuals to create a sense of spatial co-presence, which can be achieved through physical, virtual, and imagined visits, as well as visits by proxy, in both migrant and transnational settings.

Baldassar concludes that the function of visits home in the Italian diasporic imaginary is not simply to assert family identity and solidarity as a marker of ethnic and national identity but also to foster connections to place, both local and national, sustaining a collective sense of Italianness. Longings for family and for homeland become entwined and in that way facilitate the conflation of family and national characteristics, building on the trope of the family as the cradle of the nation. By teasing out the relationship between family and nation in the processes of migration, this chapter offers a framework for understanding the work needed to maintain contemporary transnational relations and affective ties to both kin and country.

Through its focus on the very intimate processes of family caregiving and how these practices are linked to longing for and belonging to particular places, this chapter is particularly effective as the volume's concluding chapter. Not only does Baldassar refer to almost all the other studies presented in this book, but she also highlights key arguments made by other contributors, with a particular emphasis on the role of affective ties, imagination, and desire in the development of national myths and identities in transnational migrant lives.

Conclusion

In 1898, the Sicilian anthropologist and scientific racist Alfredo Niceforo referred to southern Italians as *un popolo-donna*—a feminine or womanly people—who were emotional, lovers of beauty, committed to their families, and as a result moral in private but immoral in their behavior outside their private and domestic worlds.[52] Ideas such as Niceforo's traveled the world in the nineteenth century, shaping the reception abroad of migrants from all of Italy, not just those from the south, particularly in English-speaking Canada, Australia, and the United States and in Germany and Switzerland.[53]

Although they cover more than a century of history and a global geography that includes Europe, North America, and Australia, the essays collected in this volume reveal the persistence of imaginings of Italy as a nation that is marked largely by distinctive domestic, private, and intimate relations among men, women, and children. That marking emerged in Italy but was re-elaborated and solidified abroad. Both outsiders and Italy's migrants contributed to the perpetuation of the notion of Italianness as a national culture defined more by its intimacies than by its public expressions of nationalism. *Intimacy and Italian Migration* suggests that the persistence of such associations with Italianness is not just discursive but the product of constant negotiations between mobile people struggling to understand their changing worlds, selves, and private lives and nations driven either to embrace or to exclude them. Still, the absence from this volume of studies of migrants in other Latin nations such as France, Brazil, and Argentina leaves open the possibility that the dynamics of nation building illustrated here are not typical of every corner of Italy's many diasporas.

The feminized masculinity of Italianness seen in the lives of men such as Mazzini, Valentino, and Mike Stabile may have existed largely in the eyes of non-Italians. But admiration of the emotionalism and open sexuality of eroticized Mediterranean men and women was also rooted in efforts of the Catholic Church and the Italian state to impose their own kinds of order on the lives of Italy's rural poor. The struggles over womanhood and motherhood between migrant mothers and daughters and migrant husbands and wives, as well as the constant creation of intimate intermediate spaces, where private needs drove behavior in public and vice versa, demonstrate how much migrants themselves imagined Italianness, and their own ethnic, national, and individual identities, as rooted ultimately in private relationships and in the domestic sphere of family and community. And in their relationships with the immigrant women from Asia and Africa and eastern Europe who now work to guarantee that standards of Italian domesticity are maintained at home, middle-class women in Italy continue to draw national boundaries by excluding such women from the intimacy normally associated with the domestic sphere.

The relationship of family and nation-state emerges in these studies as a complex and contentious one. Mobility itself contributes to this fraught relationship. While nationalists hoped a morally revived Italy would emerge from marriages such as the one formed by Saffi and Craufurd, and migrants made of their gendered family relations symbols of the Italian nation abroad, individual men and women also transformed their family and sexual relations in order to survive and to resist the demands of nations on them. In fact, the nationalization of their families and their personal lives as Italian, fostered through transnational and translocal connections, was often an explicit way for migrants to resist cultural pressures in host societies. Mike Stabile, together with his friends from New Jersey, scoffed at wartime patriotism by transforming military service into just another job where a good scam could be run, but private pleasures were sought off the base in transgressive sexual relations. Monterey's Sicilians more often than not regarded nation-states and the demands of citizenship as irrelevant or as significant only when war threatened. Both, however, also felt the power of nation-states to make demands, and to interrupt private goals, during wartime. Similarly, those who traveled between Switzerland or Germany and Sicily made of their transnational families and marriages both a bulwark against the restrictions of the Swiss and German states, with their exclusive understandings of belonging, and a way of escaping the economic and social limitations of small-town Italian life. In the essays collected here, then, the strength of an Italianness rooted in private solidarities actually defines the limits of the Italian nation as a focus for identity and identification. In Italy, and among the descendants of Italian migrants living abroad, a connection to Italy is often, still, expressed through identifications with particular friends and family and particular local home places and deeply felt obligations to stay connected with them, as well as with the pleasures of kinship, domestic life, and cuisine, while the nation and the nation-state remain objects of suspicion when not of outright scorn and contempt.

The National in the Personal through Biography

The Marriage of Giorgina Craufurd and Aurelio Saffi

MAZZINIAN NATIONALISM AND THE ITALIAN HOME

Ros Pesman

Italy in the nineteenth century was a nation imagined and made as much abroad as at home by Italian exiles and by foreigners, and particularly British men and women, who provided material and legitimating support. The most articulate and prolific Italian nationalist, Giuseppe Mazzini, lived almost all his life from the age of thirty-two as an exile in London. There he conspired and proselytized for the realization of his vision of a united and independent, democratic, and republican Italy in which all classes, and women as the equals of men, would participate. The republican nation was to be created and sustained by popular commitment and action and would be based on the moral regeneration of the nation, on duty, and on self-sacrifice. Once realized, Mazzini's nation would move on to fulfill its historic mission in the march of progress and lead humanity beyond the staging post of the nation to some higher and wider form of association—a term Mazzini often used for voluntary cooperation and activism. Mazzini's dream was but one imagining of the nation. The new Italian state, while united and independent after 1861, was a conservative and authoritarian constitutional monarchy, far removed from Mazzini's idea of the nation.

In exploring the intersections of mobility, patriotism, and intimacy, Donna Gabaccia has recently called for more biographical analysis of gender and sexuality in the ideas, politics, movements, and personal lives of the nineteenth-century Italian patriots in exile.[1] This chapter takes up that call in an exploration of the relationship and marriage of two of Mazzini's most devoted disciples: Aurelio Saffi (1819–1890), a refugee in Britain from 1851 to 1860, and Giorgina Craufurd (1827–1911), an upper-class British woman who was born and brought up in Florence. For Saffi and Craufurd, intimacy and politics were inextricably intertwined; they saw their relationship and marriage as the union of equal partners working toward the realization of Mazzini's republican nation of virtuous citizens. Theirs was also a union that crossed national borders. Giorgina Craufurd was one of a group of remarkable British women with whom Mazzini developed extraordinarily close ties.

Mazzini's political teaching did not amount to a coherent system. His ideas, expressed in a very large corpus of writings in a variety of genres, were derived from Romanticism, his understanding of Saint-Simon and Fourier, and his strong religious sensibilities. Religion was to be the foundation of his new nation, and while his was not a religion of hierarchy and institution but a civic religion, he wrote in the Christian rhetoric of faith, redemption, mission, salvation, and martyrs.[2]

Mazzini also wrote and spoke about the national importance of the private and the personal, of the family, association, friendship, and love. His republican nation was sustained by the bonds of fellowship and love: "It is the sentiment of love, the sense of fellowship which binds together all the sons of that territory."[3] According to Roland Sarti, Mazzini used the language of love to call on his generation to extend the bonds of love and friendship beyond the family to the political realm: "Let us love one another for all living beings are born to love."[4] Through love, the individual reached out first to the family and then to the *patria* (homeland) and finally to humanity. In speaking and writing of love, Mazzini included and shifted among the public and private, sacred and profane, Eros and agape; the love of mothers; the love between sisters and brothers and between a man and a woman; and the love of the savior who sacrifices himself for humanity, his people, and the sacred cause.

The family was central to Mazzini's view of nation building. It was "the country of the heart," the primary form of association and the cradle of the nation, the place where children were educated to fulfill their role as the future citizens of the virtuous republic.[5] Within the family, the wife and mother, "the angel of the family," was the provider of solace and comfort, and because of her superior virtues, she assumed a preeminent role in the education of children.

Mazzini's views on women as the angels of the family, as different from men, and as possessed of distinct and superior moral virtues meshed well with Catholic teachings in Italy, with Evangelical and Nonconformist teaching in Britain, and with Europe's prevailing bourgeois ethic. Nevertheless, Mazzini held, alongside John Stuart Mill, the most advanced ideas on female citizenship in mid-nineteenth-century Europe, and his followers were prominent among the leaders of early feminism in both Britain and Italy.[6] While he was consistent with his time and place in emphasizing the moral superiority of women and their prime role as mothers and wives, Mazzini went beyond both in advocating the complete equality of men and women and hence women's right to education, to the vote, and to membership in the legislature of the state.[7] Mazzini argued that any current inferiority of women (like that of the working classes) was the result of oppression. The very last words of his best-known work, *The Duties of Man,* addressed to the Italian working class, called for the emancipation of women, which "should always be coupled by you with the emancipation of the working-man. It will give your work the consecration of a universal truth."[8]

In Mazzini's view, women had to work for their own emancipation: "Nobody conquers unless deserving."[9] Emancipation was not a question of right but one of duty. As he told one of his English feminist followers, their cause was "a religious one," and it should not be narrowed down to a right: "Let Duty be your ground."[10] The emancipation of women, the working classes, and other subject peoples was not an end in itself but a necessary step on the upward path of humanity. The education, equality, and political participation of women were necessary for the regeneration of Italy: at the core of Mazzini's teaching was a view of gender relations based on equality and respect.

Aurelio Saffi wrote that Mazzini lived his doctrines.[11] If religion, the family, the bonds of affection, and the equality of women and their role in the making of the nation were central to Mazzini's creed, it can be argued that they were equally important to his life, and particularly to his life in exile.

British support for the Risorgimento (the Italian nationalist movement) is now well-explored terrain. Maura O'Connor's recent *The Romance of Italy and the English Political Imagination* has added a gender perspective to the role of Italy in shaping the cultural imaginations of the nineteenth-century English middle classes.[12] Compared to Garibaldi, Mazzini was adored by a rather restricted circle, for the most part a group of men and women who shared a Nonconformist religious background (mainly Unitarian) and radical political views (including advocacy of the emancipation of women), and who were closely connected by ties of marriage, friendship, and social life.[13] Distinguishing the network was the overlapping of the personal and political, the conspicuous presence of women, and the total devotion of Mazzini's followers.

Mazzini's supporters responded to him as a person and to his teaching. As an exile from Italy, a revolutionary patriot, and a conspirator, he came clothed in Romance. In account after account of their meetings with Mazzini, both men and women emphasized his personal magnetism and the impact of a carefully crafted presence: beautiful, brooding, intense, always dressed in black (as if in mourning for his country), and endowed with charm, integrity, and an empathetic sensibility. In his teaching, it was his religious and moral messages; his vision of a resurrected, regenerated, and virtuous Italy; and his appeal to Duty that made his mission so compelling. Emilie Ashurst Venturi, in her short biography of Mazzini, wrote that she would show that his "whole existence was a living religion," and after the death of her second husband, Carlo Venturi, she told his sister that she continued to live "because living is a duty (*dovere*)."[14] In the eyes of his English supporters, the Italian patriot carried the moral credibility of total dedication and self-sacrifice and the aura of martyrdom.[15] For his cause, he had been forced to leave the family and country of his birth and had renounced sexual love and marriage and taken Italy as his betrothed. More than that, he was a Christlike holy figure, Jessie White Mario's "Cristo del Secolo," Sara Nathan's "essere divino," and Emilie Ashurst Venturi's sacrificial savior, whom Italians had "crucified."[16]

In Mazzini's relations with his followers—particularly, although not exclusively, with women—political commitment was closely linked to friendship, intimacy, and love.[17] He established very close ties with the women of this British network, and his extensive correspondence with them is full of expressions of love and intimacy. His letters to women point to his extraordinary capacity for a gendered sociability; he wrote to his women friends in terms of their concerns and needs, showing great interest in the events and vicissitudes of their lives. At the same time, Mazzini took women seriously and wrote to them about political events in Italy and his own plans and disappointments and expected them to work assiduously for his cause. He argued that women were attracted to him because he sympathized with them and supported their emancipation, which indeed he did. Certainly the ranks of his most devoted disciples included feminist women, who in turn influenced his own thinking, which became more radical in his later years.

Fueling Mazzini's intimate friendships with his women followers were the loneliness and needs of an exile. His family in Italy had been central in his life and the bonds with his mother were extraordinarily deep and close. What he sought and found in Britain were surrogate family ties and loving relationships with women, with his "sorelle amorose." He described the Ashurst family, the center of his support network, as his family, and the wider grouping as the "clan." The four Ashurst sisters were his "loving sisters," and they indeed fulfilled all the roles of ideal sisters while working for his cause. He in turn became a source of comfort and solace to them, their "loving brother."

Although upholding the family as the cradle of the nation, Mazzini never married and, indeed, seems to have abjured sexual relationships after he arrived in Britain.[18] But there were a number of marriages among his Italian followers and British women, marriages that lasted.[19] Among them were those of Aurelio Saffi and Giorgina Craufurd, Alberto Mario and Jessie White, Carlo Venturi and Emilie Ashurst, and Pellegrino Rosselli and Janet Nathan. The British women met their husbands while working for the Italian cause. All were Mazzinian disciples when they met their husbands, and Mazzini was to be a central figure in all the marriages.

Aurelio Saffi arrived in London as a thirty-two-year-old political refugee in 1851. He initially lived with Mazzini, who introduced him into the British network. Born in Forlì in the Papal States in 1819, Saffi grew up in a family of the lesser nobility with reform and patriotic traditions, his maternal grandfather a Jacobin, and his father involved in the 1831 uprisings.[20] It was also a family of strong patriotic women, and like Mazzini, Saffi had the support of a loving mother in Italy.[21] He studied law at the University of Ferrara, where his strong interest in literature exposed him to Romanticism. After working for a time in Rome, Saffi returned to Forlì in 1844 and participated in opposition politics, emerging as a local leader. In January 1849, after the overthrow of Papal rule, he was elected as a deputy to the parliament of the Roman Republic, and two months later, he became, alongside Mazzini, a member of the Second Triumvirate.

Saffi was captivated by Mazzini, by his virtue and dedication to his mission, by the perfect simplicity of his life, and by his charm and ease of manner.[22] He had almost daily contact with Mazzini during the triumvirate and then in exile in Switzerland. Sharing lodgings in Lausanne, he noted that "our spirits embraced with increasing intimacy, like sisters."[23] For Aurelio Saffi, Mazzinianism was above all a religion, and he became the most convinced and faithful convert, the "ultimo vescovo."[24] He shared in Mazzini's radical democratic political vision and in the conviction that moral and religious regeneration were necessary for the creation and the maintenance of a republican nation that drew no distinction between private and public morality. For Saffi too, the family, as the first site of education, was the central institution of the nation, and increasingly as he grew older, he devoted his life to acting on his belief that education was the means to regeneration.

Saffi espoused the equality of women and men and women's suffrage.[25] But following Mazzini, he also emphasized the different tasks assigned to women and men on the path of human progress and, as much as Mazzini did, gave women responsibility for the creation of virtuous citizens.[26] Like Mazzini, Saffi, who enjoyed enormous moral authority with all patriots, was seen to live out his beliefs in his public life and in his personal relations, but also in the additional roles of exemplary husband and father.[27]

Among the followers of Mazzini to whom Aurelio Saffi was introduced when he arrived in London was the family of Sir John Craufurd, a Scottish gentleman, and his wife, the aristocratically connected Sophia Churchill, and their daughter Giorgina and Aurelio Saffi fell in love. Giorgina Craufurd had been born in Florence, where she lived until the family moved back to Britain in 1849. The family was of liberal persuasion and sympathized with aspirations for the unification and independence of Italy and while living in Florence entertained opposition figures in their home in Piazza della Carmine as well as aiding patriots after the 1831 uprisings.[28] Sir John Craufurd met Mazzini in London in 1838, the Italian patriot describing him as "un ottimo vecchio" and as one of the best Englishmen he had met.[29]

In later recalling her "conversion," Giorgina Craufurd wrote within the rhetoric of Romanticism. A significant event in her story of her transformation into Mazzinian disciple was the secret visit to her home in 1840, when she was thirteen, of a mysterious veiled women who spoke of arrests, persecutions, and exile. The woman was Giuditta Sidoli, active patriot, widow of a patriot, mother, and intimate friend of Mazzini: "I, inexperienced young girl, felt myself in her presence a woman and at the same time an ardent conspirator."[30]

The salutation would have fed into Giorgina Craufurd's ambivalent sense of national identity. Many of Mazzini's British followers had Italian connections, but Giorgina Craufurd had been born and brought up in Italy: Italian was her first language. Only at age twenty-two did she set foot in Britain, first living in the family home in Scotland and then in London. A poem in her personal papers, apparently written by Giorgina soon after she arrived in Scotland, stereotypically contrasted south and north and recorded her longing for her real home—Italy—and Aurelio Saffi informed his sister in a letter announcing his engagement that his betrothed considered the country where she was born her *patria*.[31] Her marriage to Saffi and their subsequent settling in Italy allowed Giorgina Craufurd to become truly Italian. Indeed, on her death, she was lauded as "italianissima fra le donne italiane."[32]

On their return to London, the Craufurd family became part of Mazzini's British network, and Sophia and her daughters Giorgina and Kate collected funds for Italy, translated essays and articles for the press, and helped newly arrived exiles. After meeting Mazzini, "nostro Grande Santo Amico e Maestro," Giorgina Saffi's life became one of discipleship, of total devotion to the man, and of firm and intransigent commitment to his regenerated Italy.[33] She wrote four years after meeting him: "Oh, I will never be able to express what I feel near him. It is a holy and profound emotion, almost a ray of better life. I forget my egoism, my doubts, my fears, and I dare to say that I feel a better person, nearer to God."[34]

For Giorgina Craufurd, Mazzini was above all a religious thinker, the "teacher of the 'new religion' of Humanity," and like other women, she cast him in a Christlike role: "He was the highest and most perfect man who had lived on earth since Christ."[35] What Giorgina Craufurd embraced most in Mazzini's teaching, and what became the constant refrain in her correspondence and public writing, was self-sacrifice and duty: Mazzini's was "the great Religion of Duty, which was the essence of life."[36] As she grew older, her understanding of duty became increasingly joyless and deadly; in 1878 she published a letter in the first Italian feminist journal, *La Donna*, with the title "Life Is

Duty," a duty to be accepted and lived to the end, and she questioned the origins of the idea that life was given to us for happiness.[37]

Giorgina Craufurd's personal relationship with "nostro Grande Santo Amico e Maestro" was never quite what she desired. Mazzini paid a price for the adoration he aroused in women. Accompanying their constant offers of hospitality, gifts, and services were demands for recognition and appreciation. While his construction of himself as the self-sacrificing, pure martyr may have rendered marriage and sexual relationships beyond reach, it could not restrain possessiveness and jealousy among the women of his inner circle, as well as competition to occupy the role of most appreciated and favored acolyte, to translate his works, to tend to him in times of trouble, to sit at his deathbed.[38] According to Mazzini, Jessie White disliked Giorgina Saffi, whom she referred to as "quella donna," and relations between the two women after they both settled in Italy were barely cordial.[39] There was also tension between Giorgina Saffi and Emilie Ashurst Venturi. Saffi was particularly bitter when Ashurst was admitted by General Medici to the fortress in Gaeta, where Mazzini was held prisoner in 1870, while she, who had also journeyed to be of service, was left at the gate.[40] Giorgio Asproni wrote in his diary at the time of Mazzini's death that Giorgina Saffi and Sara Nathan were carrying on like the Virgin Mary and Mary Magdalene at the foot of the cross and that they did not want any other women near the body or to accompany it to the station at Pisa for transport to Genoa.[41]

While the letters of Giorgina Craufurd and Aurelio Saffi leave no doubt as to their long and lasting affection, love, and devotion, her older sister Kate thought that their differences in personality and character would hinder the development of any lasting relationship. She doubted whether the amiable scholar filled with "noble principles and sentiments" and "lovingness of character" was "the strong and severe man" who would eventually win over Giorgina, a strong-minded young woman, an "anima ribella" who had displayed from childhood "a mania for independence." Kate believed that much of Saffi's appeal was the "romance" of the Italian patriot exile.[42] But more compelling than this, for Giorgina Craufurd, was the fact that Saffi was Mazzini's closest and most devoted friend and ally.

The relationship of Giorgina Craufurd and Aurelio Saffi—founded on an indivisible private passion and mutual commitment to Mazzini and his vision—is documented in the intimate and frank letters that they exchanged during periods of separation. It is a correspondence that needs to be handled with some care. When she was organizing their papers in preparation for her death, Giorgina Saffi copied out much of the correspondence, including that of their courtship—"an intimate story sacred to us"—and then asked that the originals be placed in her coffin and buried with her.[43] She also instructed her sons that the copies were for their eyes only and that they were never to allow others to see them. (The letters are now open to the public in the Biblioteca Comunale dell'Archiginnasio in Bologna.) The archive itself is Giorgina's creation, subject to her ordering and censorship. She also played an active role in the selection and preparation of the fourteen volumes of Aurelio's writings for publication after his death.

A year after they met, Saffi wrote to Giorgina Craufurd that she gave him courage and virtue and that their joint love for Italy and its future were the first ties in their friendship: "The image of the *patria* and of you are indissolubly joined in my heart."[44] Four years later, just before their marriage, he told her that their life together would be a continuing and diligent labor for the regeneration of Italy.[45] In turn, Giorgina wrote to Aurelio in 1862 that their union was not the earthly and egoistical passion that most people understood love to be but a guiding light pointing the way to a better existence, where souls more than passions would understand each other in a sublime embrace of faith and holy love.[46]

The path to marriage for Aurelio Saffi and Giorgina Craufurd was far from smooth: Her father would not approve of her union with a penniless exile, even after Aurelio obtained a position teaching Italian in Oxford. In 1854, Aurelio wrote to Mazzini, telling him of the ending of his relationship with Giorgina: She, stronger than he, had decided that to fulfill their duty, his to his *patria*, hers to her family, they must "sacrifice" their love.[47] As it happened, the sacrifice was only temporary, and after a period of separation, Craufurd and Saffi met again in 1856. Her father finally gave his consent, and they were married the following year, with Oxford as their home base until 1860.

The marriage was not easy, and the early years were especially difficult as the Saffi family moved between Britain and Italy and within Italy—Florence, Naples, Turin, Genoa, Forlì. Their peripatetic life brought long periods of separation, which Giorgina, in particular, found difficult to accept. She suffered—volubly—when she did not receive letters from Aurelio and suspected his fidelity to her.[48] According to Giorgina, by 1865 there were rumors of divorce circulating.[49] From 1859 at least, increasing differences over political issues had become obvious—differences not on ends, as Aurelio continually pointed out, but on immediate tactics. The tensions sprang from Giorgina's desire that Aurelio pursue a more active and revolutionary path in bringing about the Mazzinian popular revolution—although what she understood by "popular revolution" is not clear. Their disagreements derived in part from, and were accentuated by, their different temperaments and intelligences. Aurelio was reflective, a man of reason and tolerance whose beliefs were intellectually grounded and underpinned by a classical and literary education. Giorgina was the inflexible and intransigent true believer, little able to cope with difference of opinion. Indeed, her adherence to Mazzinianism appears less flexible than that of the Master in the area of tactics in the 1850s and 1860s.

While Aurelio Saffi continually affirmed his unswerving commitment to the realization of the regenerated united republic, he also believed after 1860 that the republicans should try to work within what he saw as the interim phase of the Savoy monarchy so that the democratic forces remained part of the nation. Thus he accepted his election to the first Italian parliament, as he did his appointment to the commission of inquiry into brigandage in the former Kingdom of Naples. For Giorgina, such cooperation was betrayal of Mazzini. Her letters to her husband through the first half of the 1860s declare her love, but they are also full of expressions of disillusionment, disappointment, and despair at what she saw as the splintering of the personal and political discipleship that was the very foundation of her marriage. In letter after letter, Giorgina pleaded, begged, and harassed her husband to return to her intransigent position, arguing that only isolation from the nation, compromise, and corruption could result from cooperation. He should resign, devote all his energies to writing and working for the Mazzinian revolution, and place himself at the head of the *popolo*; popular action was the only means of creating the regenerated nation. Was he afraid of appearing revolutionary? she asked.[50] Her words, as Giorgina constantly wrote, sprang from a heart that was full of anxious affection for him, from a soul in which he had the principal seat and that wanted to feel complete harmony of convictions and aspirations.[51] She would give half her existence to see him take up a more energetic and effective role that was more in harmony with his faith and principles.[52]

Aurelio Saffi had no illusions about the new Italy or the contrast between the Mazzinians' aspirations and the course of events. As he explained to his wife over and over again, often with exasperation, he was living in Italy as it was and could see that the present, "a time of transitory chaos," was not the time for popular revolution; the people were not yet ready.[53] Parliamentary participation was yet another way to prepare the country to fulfill its destiny; increasing the representation of those who represented popular interests and aspirations was a step forward on the path to Italian democracy.[54] As to his joining the commission in Naples, "how could I refuse to go and face brigandage?"[55] Aurelio was firm in his convictions; while he explained his thinking to his wife in long and loving detail, he also told her that in continually arguing with him, she was wasting her words.[56]

By the time that he accepted the appointment to the commission, Aurelio Saffi had become increasingly skeptical about the possibilities of progress through parliament, and he resigned in January 1864.[57] But the political differences between husband and wife did not disappear. Indeed, Aurelio appears to have become more alienated from his wife as she continued to rebuke him not only in her own name but also in that of Mazzini. She conveyed to him Mazzini's disappointment that he was not doing more, disappointment that Mazzini himself also expressed in Saffi, accusing him of preferring contemplation, inertia, and lack of initiative.[58] For Giorgina Saffi, Mazzini's words took precedence over those of her husband.

Later in her life, Giorgina Craufurd Saffi represented herself as a humble, weak, and retiring woman, a "poor weak woman with no authority," and as she grew older, her letters do suggest a woman of great anxiety and insecurity, of high puritanical expectations for both herself and others.[59] But the other side was the strong-willed woman observed by her sister. This woman criticized and challenged her husband's political positions. Giorgio Asproni, who was often in the company of the Saffis in Naples and Turin in the early 1860s, wrote in his diary that Aurelio Saffi did not have "any initiative or force," but his wife, who rebuked him for his weakness, was something very different.[60]

The marriage of Aurelio and Giorgina Saffi seems to have reached a crisis in 1865, which was resolved when they decided to end their long separations by settling in his *paese* of San Varano, just outside Forlì, a move that would give their sons stability and a sense of belonging. The political disagreements between them did not cease, but both were increasingly committed to living out the ideal of the Mazzinian family, to selfless patriotism, and to responsible citizenship. In time their partnership became an exemplum eulogized in republican circles. In a book of messages published in 1911, after Giorgina's death, to mark the fifty-fifth anniversary of the Saffi marriage, the Genoese Mazzinian Felice Dagnino wrote that to commemorate the marriage of Aurelio and

Giorgina Saffi was to give homage to the ideal of the Family, understood as a work of high civic education for the shining glory of the *patria*.[61]

In the face of what he saw as the continuing degradation of Italy, the solace of the family, of the private and domestic, was a constant theme in Aurelio's letters to Giorgina: All his hopes and aspirations were concentrated in the family, which was like a sanctuary, a place of renewal for action in the wider world.[62] The letters of Giorgina and Aurelio bear witness to the delight that both took in their family life when their sons were young, and Aurelio played an active and loving part in their upbringing.[63] As both she and her sons grew older, Giorgina increasingly saw parenthood and education for a regenerated Italy as a heavy responsibility. She wrote to Aurelio in 1865 of her fears as a mother, imagining all the temptations that her dear and still young sons would encounter: "Oh please God grant us enough strength and virtue to educate them so that they would find themselves doubly equipped to confront with courage and faith the long battle of life."[64] Her anxiety increased after one of her brothers was arrested for debt and fraud and two of her four sons became a source of problems and concern.[65] She came to feel that she had failed in her primary duty of providing their moral education.

Mazzini still remained at the center of Giorgina and Aurelio Saffi's family life after his death as they celebrated not only private anniversaries but also important dates in the history of Mazzini and Mazzinianism. Writing to Felice Dagnino in Genoa in June 1875, Giorgina Saffi referred to the anniversary of Mazzini's birth, or rather to the day that "the great and holy soul" came down on earth, "a sacred *festa* for our sons."[66] The pain of loss was still too close for Giorgina and Aurelio to engage in celebration. The Saffis also played a considerable part in maintaining Mazzini's memory for posterity. Aurelio took on the task of editing the later volumes of his works, providing lengthy introductions to each volume. Giorgina assiduously collected Mazzini's letters. Those to his mother were "a sacred deposit" that would be handed over to a future national archive in Rome, but only "when Rome and Italy [were] worthy of raising such a temple to his Memory," and she sought to control their publication. It was as if only she and Aurelio could be trusted to preserve the purity of Mazzini's teaching.[67] After Aurelio's death, Giorgina organized an edition of the Master's letters to Aurelio, herself, and her family.[68]

If the family was a sanctuary for Aurelio Saffi, it was one from which he moved into the world, to his teaching at the University of Bologna, his writing and journalism, and his participation in the communal government in Forlì and republican politics in the Romagna. Consistent with his belief that the days of insurrection were over and that the education of the *popolo* was now the means of realizing the democratic and virtuous republic, he was particularly involved in workers' associations (*società operaie* and mutual aid societies). It was among these proliferating societies in the 1860s and 1870s that Mazzini's influence remained strongest.[69] For Aurelio and Giorgina Saffi, these associations were significant in promoting not only economic and material progress but also education and moral regeneration and hence the development of all the virtues of Italian patriotism.[70] Both Aurelio and Giorgina Saffi saw the working class as the best element in the country: For Aurelio, members of the working class were "the less corrupt, the less dominated by egotistical interests," and for Giorgina, it was among the "sons and daughters of the *popolo*" that the most noble examples of "self-sacrifice, courage, constancy, devotion to the *patria,* and fraternal charity" were to be found.[71]

Giorgina Saffi was particularly active in promoting these associations among woman workers in Forlì. While she believed with total conviction that the primary and most important role of women was in the home as mothers, her devotion to Mazzini took her into the public sphere. He had taught her that it was the duty of everyone to work to "*realizare l'anima della donna* in Italia," because without the moral, intelligent, and efficacious participation of women, every step of man on the road to the realization of "il Bene" would be futile.[72] Giorgina Saffi had worked for Mazzini's cause in England, and when she and Aurelio went to Naples in the wake of Garibaldi, she took up Mazzini's request to form a women's association, the Comitato Femminile per la Sottoscrizione Nazionale per Roma e Venezia, and in these first years in Italy was assiduous in trying to raise funds for the Mazzinian press and for the acquisition of Venice and Rome. Mazzini wrote to her in 1861 commending her for all that she had done.[73] Her recent Italian biographer, Liviana Gazzetta, has argued that in the early 1860s, Mazzini implicitly entrusted Giorgina Saffi with the role of coordinating women's activities in the Party of Action.[74] When the women in the Società di Mutuo Soccorso di Forlì established their own autonomous association, the Associazione Operaia Femminile di Mutuo Soccorso di Forlì, Giorgina Saffi accepted her election as director in 1863.[75] Her mother, who was also very interested in the formation of associations, wrote at the time to an acquaintance that Giorgina seemed to be gaining influence among the people, "helping them to understand and thereby winning them over to the good cause, especially the women."[76] Giorgina Saffi again took control of the association in 1873 after it had begun to languish.

In her public statements and journalism, Giorgina Saffi spoke in her capacity as a mother; her emphasis in her work with the women was on their role as mothers, and her vocabulary was that of the Mazzinian family. Woman's first duties were to plant in the heart of their men the love of family, of the *patria,* and of humanity; to comfort them in the struggles of life and, at times, return them to the right path; and to educate their children.[77] Women themselves had to be educated to raise citizens for the virtuous republic and to teach their children love of country and social duty.[78]

The world of both Aurelio and Giorgina Saffi was constructed totally within the moral vision of Mazzini: For Giorgina, "without morality there is no liberty."[79] After 1870, they were both deeply committed to the campaign against licensed prostitution, a campaign linked to Josephine Butler's British and Continental Federation for the Abolition of the State Regulation of Vice, in which Mazzinians were prominent in both Italy and Britain.[80] The activities of Aurelio and Giorgina Saffi were directed toward mobilizing workers' associations. The campaign became the focus of her public activities, including her contributions to *La Donna,* and she directed her crusade particularly toward mothers and the young.[81] In her writing, Giorgina Saffi was uncompromising and extreme; she attacked the double standard for women and men and male licentiousness and demanded chastity from the nation. For her, the worst tyranny was that of the senses.[82] Aurelio Saffi took an even more prominent role in the campaign, presiding over and delivering the inaugural address at the Congress of the Federation in

Genoa in September 1880.[83] He argued that the source of prostitution lay in materialism and sensuality; in prevailing systems of education in Europe, particularly in Catholic countries; in men's arrogant claims to superiority; in the subjection of women as perpetual minors; and in the authority of the priest.[84] Prostitution degraded society, particularly women and the working classes. The solution lay not in regulation but in the ending of prostitution: This great struggle for the moral redemption of society could only be won through changed consciences and hearts.

As they grew older and the realization of the Mazzinian nation was pushed further into the future, Aurelio and Giorgina Saffi (particularly Giorgina, who lived well into the era of liberal Italy) expressed growing despair over the state of the nation. The decade after the return of the Saffi family to Forlì saw both the consolidation of the conservative and authoritarian constitutional monarchy and the surge of both international anarchism and Marxism at the expense of Mazzini's vision (which rejected class struggle and advocated the cooperation of all classes). The influence of the Saffi model marriage as a private commitment to family and children and a patriotic and civic commitment of equal partners to the realization of a democratic and regenerated Italy was limited to the dwindling republican circles. Their aspirations to remake the Italian people in their own image and to create a just and equal society had failed.

Donna Gabaccia has recently suggested that a significant minority of the political exiles of the Risorgimento lived personal lives that departed sharply from the ideals of Christian sexuality set forth by the Council of Trent.[85] This is hardly surprising, since the exiles, particularly after 1848–1849, were for the most part unattached and unmarried young men who had rebelled against prevailing political and social systems. The Catholic Church and the enemies of the republican democrats were quick to label the Mazzinians immoral, irreligious, and enemies of the family. But the marriages in the Mazzinian circles of foreign women and Italian patriots were based on mutual affection and patriotic commitment. "God, *patria,* family" was a conservative and Catholic slogan as well as a Mazzinian one, but the Mazzinian view of intimacy and family was radical because at least some of his devoted followers lived out their ideal, accepting the equality of women and rejecting the double standard of sexual morality.[86]

The Atlantic Valentino

THE "INIMITABLE LOVER" AS RACIALIZED AND GENDERED ITALIAN

Giorgio Bertellini

In the late nineteenth century, the passionate exhibition of emotional and physical intimacy enjoyed an extremely receptive audience on stage, in the pages of novels, in paintings, and in prints. Unrestrained hugs, caresses and kisses, and other displays of affection figured spectacularly in late nineteenth-century artworks, theater productions, and even films. *The Kiss* was the title and theme of an 1886 Rodin sculpture and an 1892 Edward Munch painting. Repeated kisses were the great attraction of the 1895–1896 American stage adaptation of *Carmen* and the Edison film *The John C. Rice–May Irwin Kiss* (1896), which inspired mocking handmade frame enlargements in newspapers and spawned imitations and remakes.[1] Writing openly about passion and intimate relationships brought fame to literary authors—Hugo, Flaubert, Proust, Lawrence, and James—and their uninhibited characters. Romanticism—that bedrock of so many nationalist movements of the nineteenth century—made melodrama and what Peter Brooks has called the "melodramatic imagination" the privileged literary and theatrical form for the expression of passion and intimacy.[2] In the nineteenth century, the expansion of theatergoing and reading as pastimes transformed melodrama into a commodity for public and private consumption.

In Victorian America, public displays of affection dovetailed with ideas of national and racial difference. The 1895–1896 production of *Carmen* starring Olga Nethersole exuded southern European sensuality and a sense of the forbidden. Because Nethersole was known to be of Mediterranean ancestry, viewers were tolerant of (without condoning) her passionate kisses with multiple partners. At the same time, *The John C. Rice–May Irwin Kiss* was introduced as a more "wholesome" American response.[3] This contingent craze for public displays of affection over several months in 1896 pointed toward the emergence of a celebrity culture. The circulation of printed media and the novelty of illustrated newspapers and films offered the masses voyeuristic access to famous individuals' private lives (whether real or fictionalized) and in turn turned such private experiences as physical intimacy into a public performative genre. At the same time, improved transportation across the Atlantic and modes of communication offered Europe's major performers, usually opera and theater stars, more frequent contact with their adoring American fans. A few of these performers were Italian—Enrico Caruso, Luisa Tetrazzini, and Eleonora Duse.

The same infrastructure that increased American knowledge of Italian stars also enabled the mass migration of millions of Italians to the United States, often to identical destinations, although with quite different prospects of reception. Transatlantic Italian stardom and Italian migrations were by no means separate phenomena; they affected each other and helped to define the contours of the Italian nation in American eyes. The heavy baggage of the racial and sexual stereotyping of immigrants often informed the popularization of the alleged passion and fervor of famous Italians. Reports on the "warm-blooded" Neapolitan tenor Caruso, for instance, insisted on his heightened sensuality, bodily exuberance, and inbred brutality. "Caruso was not Don José for an instant," the reviewer for the *New York Journal* wrote about his performance in Gounod's *Carmen*. "He sang divinely. But he was a Calabrian brigand all the time."[4] By the 1920s, the national and transnational significance of passion found in the phenomenon of film stardom an emblematic illustration. Film stars' expressions of affection became overtly linked to ideologies of gender and racial difference. No star better illustrates this linkage than the *divo* Rodolfo Valentino, the clearly racialized male lover of the silver screen.

Valentino helped to crystallize what we may term an "Atlantic Italianness," a transnational notion of Italy. Traversing the Atlantic Ocean in both directions since the time of the Grand Tour and intensified, if also challenged, by recent mass migrations (and seasonal mass returns), master narratives about Italy and Italians could be either complimentary or derogative. Invariably, however, they featured passion as a national trait. Although the intimacy that audiences in Italy and America felt they shared with Valentino's on- and offscreen personae was not identical, the star operated as a vessel of sexual appeal and desire that the modern commercialization of gender and racial typecasting generally accepted as national fantasy. The phenomenon of Valentino reveals a persistent tension between the discursive exigencies of stardom engaged in emphasizing the unique and inimitable features of a popular icon and the discursive needs of racial typage engaged in showing the visually characteristic "Italian" dimensions of that icon. Valentino walked a fine line between Hollywood icon and immigrant/Latin lover.

In early twentieth-century America, perceptions of Italy and Italians filtered through long-standing literary and visual stereotypes that had, since the eighteenth century, granted Italian political and artistic history an idealized position of universal prominence.[5] Americans' idealized notions of Italian culture, however, could not easily survive the arrival of millions of highly racialized Italian peasants, who were viewed with hostility, resentment, and condescension. Richard H. Brodhead has described the conflict for Americans posed by the coexistence of a "touristic-aesthetic Italy," embodied in artworks and exotic landscapes, and the "alien-intruder Italy," characterized by othered and dangerous immigrants.[6] In Italy, absorption of the literary and visual stereotypes produced by the Grand Tour led to parallel geo-cultural and racial dichotomies. What ensued was a similar juxtaposition of a supreme and ideal Italy and a defective and reproachable one, with the latter mainly identified with the south's alleged political, cultural, and anthropological inadequacies. During the fascist regime, as that dimension was minimized, the image of an ideal Italy again gained prominence.[7] Because Valentino became popular just as fascism came to power in 1921 and 1922, it is helpful at times to compare him to that other intercontinental and equally beloved icon with whom Valentino had constantly to compete—Benito Mussolini.[8] The two celebrities repeatedly crossed each other's paths, in terms of both their biographical and discursive identities, pushing and pulling the gendered meanings of Italianness between them.[9]

America's Valentino: Beyond the Racial Type

Valentino's success in America is a familiar Horatio Alger story. Born Rodolfo Pietro Filiberto Guglielmi in Apulia in 1895 to a fairly prosperous family, Valentino did not face the hard work and misery of the average southerner.[10] After a brief period in Paris, in 1913 he left for New York, where he first landed jobs as a gardener, then a dancer, and eventually moved to Hollywood to appear as an extra and a secondary character (often a dancer) in more than a dozen unremarkable melodramas of forbidden romance and social betterment.[11] At this point the vast majority of cinematic portrayals of Italians on the American screen relied on master narratives of exotic picturesqueness and, more often, associations with the Mafia.[12] After 1915, popular but now long-forgotten feature films starring George Beban, an American performer of Irish and Dalmatian background who specialized in Italian impersonations, inaugurated a genre of sentimental racial melodramas that, through stories of racial discrimination, destitution, and tragic deaths, cast Italian men and women as more sympathetic protagonists. Fostering a new poetic relationship between American cinema and racial difference, Beban's tear-jerking tenement dramas humanized Italian immigrants but also portrayed them as childlike and excessively emotional.[13] If Beban's increasingly psychologized characters discontinued the representation of Italians as "natural" criminals and outlaws—a radical change that the Italian American press quickly recognized—his screen personae never intended to or could establish intimacy or identification with the audience. Thus, Valentino's overt mobilization of erotic desire, on- and offscreen, was unprecedented for foreign, racialized characters (i.e., a Spaniard, Argentine, Russian, and Italian) played by a foreign, racialized actor.[14] How did this happen?

Beginning in the 1910s, the migration of thousands of African Americans from the rural South as well as northern urban centers and the arrival of other peoples of African descent from the Caribbean supported the emergence of the New Negro Movement at a time also shaped by race riots, labor strife, and frequent protests. This engendered, in Matthew Guterl's words, "a national mass culture obsessed with the 'Negro' as the foremost social threat." The former nativist emphasis on the racial heterogeneity of Europeans was complemented by a dawning polarization of black versus white, or "biracialism," best epitomized by the success of *The Birth of a Nation* in 1915.[15] Thus if color identified insurmountable divisions, race did so less. On-screen, racial difference was used to cast white European immigrants in a less antagonistic and more sympathetic and even sentimental light. This transformation occurred as the notion of racial identity itself was undergoing radical change. Social scientists and reformers had begun to place less of an emphasis on immutable racial inheritance and to consider the social, economic, and cultural environments in which people of different races lived. This emphasis on the critical role of the environment in both enhancing and delaying adaptation and assimilation soon acquired scientific recognition through the work of sociologists, criminologists, and cultural anthropologists (e.g., Franz Boas and, later, Robert E.

Park). Without utterly relinquishing the power of racial difference and typecasting, these new ideas allowed for more sympathetic literary, photographic, and cinematic narratives that addressed immigrants' capacity to adapt to their new environment through what Boas called the "plasticity of human nature."[16]

By the mid-1910s, with the development of feature-length films, American cinema displayed a solid interest in characters' psychological rendering. This occurred as the nation's thriving consumer culture significantly intensified the commercialization of familiar racial differences to evoke the spectacular, to arouse emotion, and for the sake of entertainment.[17] Valentino embodied the culmination of the Hollywood star system's growing sympathy for racialized (white) characters, who now even engaged in romantic pursuits with white women without eliciting fears of miscegenation and whose love stories were offered for public consumption. In the 1920s, newspapers, magazines, write-in campaigns, popularity contests, movie premieres, and photography captured the stars' lives *beyond* their filmed performances. Well-run film studios sought control over the entire process of film production and consumption through the pervasive intertextual discourses that developed around such products.[18] Whether real or fictitious, the private life and romantic involvements of the olive-skinned Italian actor became a crucial component of his public persona.[19] As the *New York Times* reported after Valentino's death, "a new mental attitude in vast multitudes of people" had emerged. For the first time, the article continued, fans had "come to regard a favorite screen actor as one whom they have known *intimately*."[20]

As the new Hollywood "machine" turned Valentino into a familiar persona, whom audiences felt intimate with, it also constructed a distinctive, special, and incomparable figure, endowed with unmatched taste and sexual appeal. More an artist than just an actor, more an idol than a mere film personality, Valentino found a number of superlative qualities attributed to him.[21] "The work of Valentino had reached a stage of perfection," noted in 1926 an enthusiast writer, the exotically self-named Ben-Allah Newman. "It caused the American dictionary, at least, to add a new meaning to the word 'Sheik.' . . . 'Sheik' has come to mean a Valentino-like man."[22] (See Figures 1 and 2.) As thousands of fans described him as the "greatest lover" and as the embodiment of passion and romance, the Western film actor and director William S. Hart spoke of him as "the finest of God's handiwork."[23]

Yet the copious praise for Valentino often singled out his racialized foreignness. At work here was a tension between the exceptional features attributed to him as a star and the typical and familiar characteristics linked to his Italian racial type. First, Valentino was depicted with polemical reference to indigent immigrants (or destitute southern Italians). Speaking of the ability "of the lowly to arise from where their kith have lingered for generations, maybe," Newman wrote that "the life of Valentino will furnish inspiration to many of *his countrymen* to do bigger things with their own lives."[24] Once the association with Italian immigrants was weakened (without ever being completely severed), the *divo* was also described with reference to Italy's cultural, artistic, and historical contributions.[25] His allegedly unique talent in seducing women ("the greatest lover in the cinema world")[26] came to be understood as quintessentially "Latin" or "Italian," thus without an American rival. Or, more eloquently, Valentino was hailed as the *ideal* model for the Latin type or Latin lover. Newman thus concluded: "He was

Figure 1. Stardom and the supreme display of intimacy: Valentino in The Sheik *(1921), with Agnes Ayres (Courtesy of the Museum of Modern Art/Film Stills Archive)*

never rated as a lover as a Don Juan might have been proud to be rated. He was of an order greater than all the conquests of a Casanova could have made him. He was the 'TYPE.' He was the embodiment of the word, the visualization of the thing itself on the screen."[27]

More than a decade later, Beulah Livingstone linked similar idealizations and abstractions: "What made him a unique figure and significant beyond all his contemporaries was that he represented a *symbol more than an individual*—a symbol of Romance in its most glamorous aspects. . . . Rudy personified the *ideal* lover—dark and dashing, handsome and headstrong, passionate and dangerous."[28]

Rather than being simply *a* Casanova, or *a* Don Juan, Valentino was described as *the* defining type, *the* prime measure of the Latin lover. As such he was connected to a known, familiar, even shared typology while standing, alone, at the *origin* and foundation of that very typage, or typecasting operation.

The predication of his uniqueness and stardom *upon* a Latin-lover typage was at the basis of an inevitable sexualization, which was unhesitatingly used to both exalt and disparage his persona. His sexual appeal as a star made him the "greatest seducer,"

Figure 2. Valentino and Vilma Banky in The Son of the Sheik *(1926), Italian publicity postcard (Giorgio Bertellini Collection)*

but his fetishization and objectification for mass voyeuristic desire also brought about allegations of femininity and perversity.[29] The sensationalist press insisted on his uniquely decadent lifestyle and his penchant for flamboyant furs and custom-made suits but also hinted at his sexual ambiguity, "evident" from his alleged fondness for slave bracelets and his effeminate dancing style.[30] This departure from any familiar norm of American masculinity (and even from earlier examples of Latin lovers) led to slander and contradictory charges of predatory lasciviousness and androgyny, which ran parallel to accusations of decadent unproductiveness and—possibly the most damning indictment of all in America—financial dependency on women.[31]

Unlike the praise bestowed on him, these allegations belonged to the conceptual currency of the "low" Italianness of southern peasants and migrants. At least since the second half of the nineteenth century, decadence and femininity had been linked to formulations of Italian "lower" racial types by Italian and American racial theorists and social Darwinists, fiction writers, cartoonists, and playwrights. The influential social determinism of the criminologist Cesare Lombroso and the anthropologist Alfredo Niceforo equated Southerners with other "lower" categories, including women, children, criminals, and urban crowds on the basis of an alleged inherent inability to exercise self-restraint, whether physical or emotional.[32] Once described as *popolo-donna,* or a "female people," southerners were now seen as embodying a converging set of negative attributions, including emotional susceptibility, moral weakness, intellectual inadequacy, and an untamable inclination toward selfish pleasure.[33]

The simple equation of Valentino and an Italian racial type was not what made him a *divo*; on the contrary, his on- and offscreen persona was described as *exceeding* the Latin-lover typage. Hence, more than visual appearance or superficial actions spoke of his still racialized yet extraordinary status. What was the ideological and rhetorical arrangement that allowed for this overdetermination of racial typage? This was possible, I argue, because of the persistence of popular notions of *inherited racial character,* even as scientists increasingly emphasized the influence of the environment on the formation of an individual's character. Indexing a neoplatonic distinction between body and soul, the concept of racial character expanded upon that of personal moral character, which was itself a recurring trope in the profoundly religious culture of nineteenth-century America. Since the second half of the nineteenth century, the notion of inherited racial character had informed, without fully coinciding with, visual racial type in enabling the recognition of racial differences *beyond* visible physical traits.[34] As a rubric of racial classification, the notion of racial character appeared in many urban "ethnographic" discourses, and in America's highbrow and popular cultural depictions of immigrant life.[35] By the early twentieth century, anthropology and other social sciences had learned from the literary habitus of characterization to draw *coherent* "racial types." Similarly, even as the environment was gaining greater explicatory power, "scientific" notions about an individual's racial character had become features of literary and theatrical characterizations that aided practices of dramaturgic coherence and verisimilitude. American cinema learned a great deal from the nonvisually coded racial characterizations sketched by racial scientists, moral reformers, political commentators, novelists, and vaudeville performers. The film medium could profitably emphasize and narrativize the *intangibles* of racial belonging as dramaturgic revelations. This could apply to almost all of a film's characters but was particularly true at a time when stars' behind-the-scenes biographies had become a major intertextual reference for both their film characterizations and their reception by the public.

By complicating the mere visual recognition of the racial typage, the inherited racial character became part of an equally cogent but more flexible and thus more accommodating identification of racial identity. Longer narratives made it easier to bestow psychological depth on racialized characters beyond the discriminating cogency of visual appearances, while offering the profundity of an ideal and shared human dimension. The exceptional singularity of Valentino's positions as a star further idealized his racial stance as different not only from American models of virility but also from past icons of sensualized Latin lovers. The protean dramaturgic plasticity and semiotic excess of his star image distanced his racial character from any strict biological and physical determinism, in favor of the more performative and elusive notion of personality. This opened safe new possibilities for audiences' relationships with him. A writer like Newman variously and repeatedly called this ethereal core "personality" and "charm": "There can be only one explanation of his enslaving the attention of the races of the Earth and that is the power of the personality he wielded. Charm at its greatest heights has ever been an indefinable something. It is known to exist, and though intangible, is definite in that it is actually there without being seen, it IS without being known or recognized."[36]

Referring to that "inexpressible" quality that Valentino possessed, Newman also noted that the Italian *divo* "was born as a distinct somebody with a definite IT about him," using the capital-lettered pronoun made famous a year later by the eponymous film starring Clara Bow.[37] Still, Valentino's IT personality could never aspire to a pure universal quality; racial associations originating in the Latin lover typage were also always intrinsic to it. Since love, as "indefinable emotion" and "the most powerful of human factors," defined and *possessed* him—as only Latin subjects could be possessed—Valentino suffered from what Newman called a "love complex [that] was the outstanding point in his subconscious emotions."[38]

In brief, the tension between stardom and typage produced in Valentino a significant semiotic novelty that capitalized on past crystallizations—the heavily sexualized Latin lover—but also expanded its semiosis in the direction of an Olympic transcendence. The communicative effects of such a move were unprecedented. In 1920s nativist and consumerist America, Valentino and Anglo-American women could safely be cast together in appealing narratives of seduction, lovemaking, and romance, although not without controversy and resistance.

Artistic Idealism in Fascist Italy

What kind of *divo* and what sort of Italian was Valentino in Italy's gender and racial culture? This question addresses the discursive space of modern and transnational Italianness within an Italian culture that, for decades, and with renewed urgency in the early 1920s, confronted questions of racial/national self-appreciation. Italy's Valentino can be examined through the lens of two interlocked phenomena. The first is a discourse on national and international media stardom that emerged in Italy from the late 1910s to the late 1920s, when Italian cinema was experiencing its worst crisis just as Hollywood was establishing its commercial dominance in the peninsula. The second is fascists' development of nationalist narratives, including their iconic embodiment in Mussolini's transnational figure, at a time of heavy traffic of migrants, goods, and aesthetic forms across the Atlantic.[39]

In the years following World War I, the Italian film industry lost commercial ground both in Italy and abroad, even as American films increasingly dominated domestic film exhibitions. The crisis of Italian cinema provoked intense debates about once profitable but soon unaffordable Italian female stars. The diminished popularity of the patrician *dive* Lyda Borelli, Francesca Bertini, and Italia Almirante Manzini was not just a box office concern. Comparing their histrionic excesses with the popular sobriety of the performers of 1920s American and French films, critics denounced the Italian female stars' unwarranted physical convulsions and repetitive tableaux, which served mainly as a means of showcasing their own inimitable and unreachable bodily presence.[40] The lack of realistic character interpretations and thus of narrative flexibility distinguished their solipsistic screen performances from the more naturalistic interpretations of American players.[41]

In the mid-1930s, critic Giacomo Debenedetti claimed that American performers were more attractive because the American star system had grasped cinema's difference from theater, where stars remained "inaccessible, far away, and supreme." By contrast, film icons were brought into "close, sensual contact with the audience." If "La Bella Otero was accessible to only an exquisite *côterie* of wealthy people and *viveurs*," he continued, "Joan Crawford belonged to everybody, including the blue-collar worker." Contemporary audiences, he concluded, demanded that cinema represent "that immediacy of relationships . . . that is typical of our times."[42] Only in the 1930s did explicit discussions of actors' social origins, particularly through the mediation of Soviet film theories and practices, open up the possibility of casting the faces and bodies of Italy's plebeians, thus offering a cinematic form of social realism. Furthermore, in the second half the 1920s, the notion of type was subject to another major ideological pressure exerted by fascism—that of *racial* identification. Valentino's acting style and persona, on- and offscreen, were both critiqued and admired in these debates, before and after his death.

Viewed through the Italian lens of gender, the performative quality of Valentino's stardom was rather old fashioned. His resembled an older model of masculinity—that of poet, writer, and Latin lover and modern aviator Gabriele D'Annunzio. Like *il vate* (as D'Annunzio was known), Valentino could be both charming and seductive, exquisite and sophisticated, almost feminine in his cosmopolitan tastes, but at risk of sexual excess and perversion.[43] Still, Valentino enjoyed considerably more popular visual exposure than either D'Annunzio or other decadent male lovers of the cinema of the *dive* ever did.[44]

Valentino's fame in Italy began after the 1923 release of *The Four Horsemen of the Apocalypse* (*I quattro cavalieri dell'Apocalisse*, 1921), two years after its American debut.[45] (See Figure 3.) In many respects, Valentino seemed a novel figure: His success was linked to a growing interest in Hollywood's powerful star system at a time when Italian film and popular periodicals increasingly focused on American stars.[46] They publicized Hollywood's modern and highly attractive and glamorous models of masculinity and femininity and romantic relationships and their individualistic (as well as libertine) lifestyles. The news that a southern Italian had made it in America's "dream factory" seemed to be compensation for the negative associations attached to Italian immigrants over the decades. Valentino's popular and exceptional sexual appeal as a Latin lover in Anglo-Saxon America also demanded official rationalization. The sexualization of his physical features, the passion that he appeared to exude, and the sense of sensual intimacy that he fostered with audiences resonated among Italians concerned with their national racial identity and with American modernity.

Italian understandings of Valentino's fame in the United States and in Italy were powerfully shaped by their ambivalent responses to Hollywood itself. Italian critics praised the American dream factory for its capacity to communicate to large social, cultural, and international constituencies. Yet they also harshly criticized its excessively commercial orientation. Their judgment relied on the familiar juxtaposition of cinema as an industrial enterprise—which Hollywood embodied to the fullest (and also to its detriment)—and the old and wishful, but rhetorically still powerful, notion of films as high art. Discussions of Valentino and his name, body, and acting style, as well as

Figure 3. Gracious masculinity: Valentino as superb tango dancer in The Four Horsemen of the Apocalypse *(*I quattro cavalieri dell'Apocalisse, *1921) (Courtesy of the Museum of Modern Art/Film Stills Archive)*

the characterizations and the settings of his films, constantly oscillated between two poles—Art and Commerce, which were then invested with national (and racial) connotations.[47] Aware of the dangers of physical racializations, Italian critics warned Italian audiences to look *beyond* the visual camouflage of Valentino's many exotic costumes and amorous postures and instead focus on his timeless artistry which, since it could be neither racialized nor commodified, was to be understood as distinctively "Italian."

On-screen, Valentino appeared to be an admirably modern presence, moving within fashionably decorated settings that the Italian audience adored. At the same time, however, his success challenged common ideas about Italianness. The more successful he became, the more intense the desire, and the more difficult it became to fully appropriate him as a full-fledged national hero. One reason for this tension was his name. Recognition of his (Italian) "artistry" went hand in hand with increasing complaints about how film credits "Americanized" his first name. In the pages of the fascist periodical *L'Impero,* critic Aurelio Spada protested the sensational Hollywood-style publicity campaign for *The Conquering Power* (*La commedia umana,* 1921), released in Italy in late 1923, and then sarcastically wondered whether Rudolph was Valentino's real name. He ultimately condemned the film as a vulgar adaptation of Balzac's serious literary classic.[48] A conflicted and fetishistic attachment to Valentino's national identity emerged at the time of the release of *The Sheik* (*Lo sceicco,* 1921), distributed in Italy in 1924 and, more than any other film, responsible for Valentino's notoriety in Italy. In Florence, reviewer Pier Giovanni Merciai of *La Rivista Cinematografica* juxtaposed the artistry of his interpretation to the story's lack of originality and appeal. While parenthetically and somewhat sarcastically referring to Valentino as an "Italian . . . Americanized!" Merciai praised his artistic talent by insisting on the delicacy and efficacy of his "characterization" (*personificazione*), and his ability, like that of a gifted sculptor, to reproduce even the most subtle emotional traits of his subject.[49] Similarly, a few months later, the reviewer for *L'Epoca* described the immigrant Valentino as a victorious emissary of "the artistic school of our country" to distant America.[50]

When Italian reviewers referred to Valentino's "racial type," they could not ignore the long tradition of racist allegations against the Latin race based on "scientific" descriptions of skulls, complexion, and eye color. The Anglo-Saxon, but more so the German, scientific discourse on Latins' anthropological inferiority, decadence, and feeblemindedness was quite well known in Italy, both before and after the rise of fascism.[51] Valentino's physical appearance appeared to confirm those racist characterizations and had to be disputed. Debates in Italy became particularly intense, creative, and eloquent after Valentino's death, which apparently resolved a dispute between the Italian *divo* and Mussolini regarding the desire of the former to acquire American citizenship for financial convenience.[52]

Not only did Valentino's sudden and unexpected death squelch accusations of betrayal and opportunism,[53] but it also eased his de-sexualization and re-categorization as the *ideal* Latin lover and Italian type. Beginning in the late summer of 1926, a number of his previously unreleased films began to circulate, from *A Sainted Devil* (*Notte nuziale,* 1924) and *Cobra* (1925) to *The Eagle* (*Aquila nera,* 1925). Italians' admiration was articulated in disembodied racial terms.[54] Valentino now became a representative of Italy's noble and artistic culture, as opposed to America's material vulgarity. The mere physicality of his appearance—a vessel of a dangerous passion in America—became in Italy an index of less tangible but no less powerful national traits, including character and spiritual beauty. About a month after his death, the reviewer for *Lo Schermo* connected Valentino's inner character with the widely admired artistic history of the Italian nation: "Rodolfo Valentino has indeed transfused his strong passionate Italian soul into the character, and he has incarnated his actions with the aristocratic bearing of our race. . . . And we wait to know, from those who have disparaged him, what they have done for Italy and for Art, since they feel entitled to condemn the one person who has represented with infinite and successful fervor Italian art and race all over the world."[55]

One year later, in an homage to his stardom in *Cinematografo,* a reviewer again made reference to Valentino's "spiritual beauty"—an intangible of great convenience that conveyed a most neoplatonic synthesis: "Yes, because [Valentino] was beautiful. Because in him there was that divine harmony that only our royal race possesses. . . . He was the proof of our superiority. Superior to everybody in thought, in art, and in body. Superior for that divine fusion that unifies body and soul, matter and spirit."[56]

Intimacy and Transcendence

Within the American star system, Valentino was considered exceptional because his on- and offscreen persona surpassed (without ever relinquishing) the characteristics of the Italian (immigrant's) racial type while embracing the sexualized but glamorous persona of the Latin lover. More publicly than anyone, Valentino demonstrated how the increasingly psychologized concept of racial character transcended mere physicality. This, in turn, granted the film roles he interpreted an aura of shared humanity. Once the public was able to see beyond his threatening or discomforting racial otherness, his body could become a vessel for higher forms of emotional intimacy coupled with safer projections of romantic and sensual enticement. In the increasingly racialized industry of desire fostered by Hollywood, the lover Valentino could convey the sense of both an emotional and romantic connection with audiences while transmuting his Italianness into a universal (white) characteristic of humanity larger than the sum of the roles he played as an Arab sheik, a Spanish torero, and an Argentine tango pirate.

In Italy, and particularly after his death, Valentino was deemed to be exceptional not just because he surpassed the Italian type but because he was the true embodiment of an *ideal* Italian type. In the 1920s, Italy's race-conscious culture conveniently played down Valentino's sensual physicality in favor of his more ethereal qualities, including his talent as an actor and an almost spiritual or divine aura. His physical appearance was described as exceeding ordinary Italian traits. Yet, most cogently, the depth of character, personal charm, and soulful appeal attributed to him ensured the safeguarding of an ideal notion of Italianness despite the fact that in his films he played an Arab, Argentine, Russian, and Spaniard.

On both sides of the Atlantic Ocean, then, the attribution of passion carried reifying dangers, whether racially or nationally defined. Help came from the semantic area of human interiority and spirituality, which was an implicit source of Valentino's Olympic star status. The term *divo,* as fans of opera know, is from the Latin *divus,* "divine." Since the late nineteenth century, the term had been used to refer to the new opera, stage, and, later, film stars, signifying their larger-than-life presence and their distance from mortal fans. "Mankind, which in Homer's time was an object of contemplation for the Olympian gods," wrote Walter Benjamin in 1936, "now is one for itself." The German critic read the demotion of physical materiality as the result of the fascist (and futurist) embrace of modern technology, including war.[57] Yet the fascist motto he quotes on the same page, *Fiat ars, pereat mundus* ("Let art be created though the world shall perish"), points to a broader urge for transcendence that Hollywood and fascist regimes addressed by both exalting and denigrating the vision of a tango-dancing body.

"George the Queer Danced the Hula"

MIKE STABILE, AMERICAN SOLDIER IN HAWAII

Carol A. Stabile

On 1 April 1941, eight months before Pearl Harbor was attacked, Mike Stabile, a twenty-two-year-old working-class Italian American man, was drafted into the U.S. Army. Mike was assigned to a gun battalion for the duration of the war; he performed a wide range of duties for his battalion, ranging from repairing motor vehicles to modifying equipment to building a washing machine. Mike's life differed from those of hundreds of thousands of other young men who served in the military during World War II in only one respect: From the day he was inducted until the day after he was discharged in 1945, Mike maintained a diary chronicling his life in the army, making entries on a daily basis.[1] After being wounded in Okinawa in April 1945, Mike smuggled the diary past the watchful eyes of military censors and back into the United States. The diary remained in a safe, along with Mike's wartime poetry and correspondence, until the late 1980s, when Mike's wife and youngest son transcribed the diary from yellowed scraps of paper and rusty spiral-bound notebooks.

Written by a working-class man living through a period of economic and political upheaval, the diary narrates both everyday experiences and historic events from a standpoint seldom represented in literature about World War II. Most representations of this generation of men, later dubbed the "greatest generation" by Tom Brokaw (a phrase that was immediately adopted by boosters of cold war masculinity), are recollections written after the fact extolling their courage, patriotism, love of family, and sense of personal responsibility. There are few representations of working-class men's transition from a Depression-era structure of feeling—one critical of authority, skeptical of the promises made by industry, and frequently cynical when it came to capitalism—to the structure of feeling now associated with that generation. Mike's perspective was little like that of Ben Bradlee, who was commissioned as an ensign in the U.S. Navy on the very day he graduated from Harvard with a major in Greek.[2] Rather, this is, as Carolyn Steedman put it when describing her working-class parents, about a life "lived out on the borderlands," one for which "the central interpretive devices of the culture don't quite work."[3]

Mike's diary recounts the everyday experiences of a working-class man removed from the community he understood and loved in New Jersey, who was trying to make sense of who he was within the diverse culture he encountered in the Pacific. For those studying the intersections of gender, race, class, sexual orientation, and national identity, nearly sixty-five years later, Mike's diary is a unique and unsettling document that reveals the disconnect *between* powerful androcentric ideologies about masculinity, heteronormativity, and patriotism, on one hand, and lived experience, on the other.

The Making of Italian Americans

One of thirteen children born to Maria and Salvatore Stabile, who immigrated to the United States from Naples at the end of the nineteenth century, Mike was born in Nutley, New Jersey, in May 1918 and died in February 1993. His mother died when Mike was sixteen; Mike memorialized this loss in his poetry and letters home. As the youngest male child, and the only boy remaining at home in a household of six women, he was very much indulged by his father and sisters. Mike dropped out of high school the year his mother died, worked at his father's trucking company until it went bankrupt during the Depression, and later did a series of odd jobs until he was drafted in 1941 (see Figure 1).

Mike began writing poems and letters while working as a truck driver on cross-country runs between New Jersey and Michigan in the late 1930s, but few of these writings were saved. Mike's first entry in his diary was on 1 April 1941 (the irony of which was not lost on him), the day he was inducted; the final entry in the diary is on 29 June 1945, the day he was discharged (see Figure 2). There is no evidence that he continued to write after this. Evidently, the routinized existence of a soldier provided a structure he would never have again, especially after he married and began fathering children. During his four years in the army, his output was prodigious. In addition to the diary, which totals almost four hundred pages of single-spaced typewritten pages, he wrote dozens of poems, some of which were published in army publications and newspapers. He also spent hours writing hundreds of letters home. He was much in demand for his services as a ghostwriter who penned generic love letters to girlfriends and wives for other soldiers, like the following, addressed to "Dearest Darling Irene": "Like an arrow, the thought of your letter sped swiftly to my heart. Never dreamed that pen and paper could make up so nice a package of Sunshine. It's really wonderful to know that from this life filled with the horrors of war, there is still something worth living for. You are that someone, and from you I get the energy and courage that keeps me going on" (24 April 1944). Although Mike clearly addressed a wider audience in his poetry and his letters (which were often passed around among the members of his large family), the audience for the diary remains unclear. His older sister Florence gave him the first book he used for recording daily activities, but the remainder was written in spiral notebooks or on whatever scraps of paper he could find. The contents of the diary suggest that it was not necessarily intended for his sister's eyes.

There is no single mode of address in the diary. Some sections simply record and reflect on the events of Mike's day, as in this entry from 1943:

> We limbered our #2 gun and moved it to #3 gun position. The U.S.E.D. men are fixing our mounts for the new type 155. The tractor tore up a section of the water line and I,

Figure 1. Mike during the Depression

> with some help, fixed it. At 11:45 A.M. we had to limber our gun up again and send it into Ft. Kam where the Ordinance is to install hooks for unloading the gun from a ship. Worked until 12:15 and then had chow. This noon Howe and I took off and relaxed until 4 P.M. In the chow line I met "Yank," one of the boys from our outfit of peace time days. I haven't gone A.W.O.L. for quite some time. This being a good boy in no way satisfies the nervous system. (29 Sept. 1943)

Other entries point to his consciousness of the significance of the historic events he was narrating. On 7 December 1941, Mike wrote, "Today has been my first in warfare. I don't feel scared. I feel mad as hell. The same goes for many other soldiers." Four years later, during the invasion of Okinawa, Mike more specifically recounted his own experiences of combat:

> Darkness came and I felt tired and miserable. My nerves were on edge and the counter battery duel between the Howitzers and the enemy did naught to lessen my feelings. I laid on my cot and tried to sleep, but sleep would not come. The rolling thunder of big

Figure 2. PFC Stabile

> guns beat my nerves unmercifully. At 20 minutes past ten Stig and I went on guard. It was very dark out and one couldn't see very much, not very far. The guards on #2 gun thought they heard something and the nervous pricks were afraid to investigate it. Sometimes flares would lite up the sky and only at these times could I see the surrounding sea. (1 May 1945)

Mike was also driven to write because of a sense that he was living in historic times, and that his observations of the historic world events in which he was participating were worth recording and his perspective on events, for the first time in his life, somehow valuable. In his battalion, Mike was known as a writer—he sometimes read aloud from his diary or entertained his friends with his poetry, and his services as a writer of love letters and other missives home were in demand. He understood that he alone among his cohort was recording events from the perspective of the lowest-ranked soldier. Later, Mike took care to preserve the diary and was openly proud of it, considering it to be one of the most significant achievements of his life.

"Those Mamas with Grass Skirts": Ethnicity and Color in Hawaii

Nearly three months into his stint in the army, in June 1941, Mike volunteered for assignment to Hawaii. Mike, like many working-class audience members, would have been familiar with the mythic version of Hawaii then current in Hollywood cinema and popular culture. Films like *Honolulu* (1930), *Waikiki Wedding* (1937), and *Hawaiian Nights* (1939), as well as the popular radio program *Hawaii Calls*, which began broadcasting in 1935, conveyed an image of Hawaii as a tropical paradise, where white women danced the hula in grass skirts and leis.[4] The first mention of Hawaii in Mike's diary directly reflected this understanding of the islands. On 21 June 1941, Mike wrote, "I volunteered to go to Hawaii. A call for volunteers was out to go there. I sure would like to see those Mamas with grass skirts. Boy, oh boy!" For servicemen like Mike, Hawaii offered the opportunity to travel to a place billed as an exotic paradise, one that appeared to be far from the conflict in Europe.

In the 1940s, Hawaii was, as Beth Bailey and David Farber put it, "the last strange place" in terms of its "mixture of racial and ethnic groups [which made it] unlike anywhere else in the United States." Whiteness did not have the same valence in Hawaii as it did on the mainland, and despite the enormous influx of largely white military personnel and civilian workers that poured into Hawaii after the Japanese attack on Pearl Harbor, Hawaii remained a place where "white men were suddenly made to feel that *they* were the ones who were different."[5] For Mike, color and sexual identity were mainstays of his identity as an American. Both were unsettled by his experiences in Hawaii.

Mike obviously considered himself white, so white, in fact, that the issue of his own ethnicity never directly surfaced. At home, his mother had spoken very little English, and his father spoke heavily accented English. His older siblings spoke some Italian, but as one of the youngest members of the family, Mike never learned. Mike's kinship and friendship networks in New Jersey had been made up almost exclusively of other Italian Americans, not surprising, given the influx of Italian immigrants after 1920. (Even today, Nutley's population is nearly half Italian American.)

Mike never directly mentions being Italian in his diary, although in one entry he described a "jeep [soldier] by the name of Tony who is a wop" (4 Jan. 1942).[6] Nevertheless, he surrounded himself with other working-class Italian men (Ernie Sampino, John Cafone, "Pussy Foot" Cantazzaro, Al Ciazzo, Joe Bizzaro, Ralphy Dimarsico). On one occasion, he mentioned meeting at a party in Waipahu another soldier who "had the Jersey talk right with him. His name—Joe Nurado" (24 Dec. 1942). In certain ways, Mike understood New Jersey, "Jersey talk," and Nutley to be synonymous with an Italian American background.

Of course, traces of Mike's ethnicity run throughout his writing. Mike romanticized his "little Mother" as an "angel" (by all accounts, Maria Stabile was a sizable and temperamental woman) in a manner consistent with Roman Catholic understandings of motherhood and maternal sacrifice, and many of his poems center around the relationship between mothers and sons. In an untitled, undated wartime poem, one of the few places where he talks about combat, Mike invoked what many of us would recognize as a specifically Italian rendering of motherhood:

The crashing sound of metal
As it struck on human bone
A blue clad figure hurtled
And landed lying prone.

A twisted mass of flesh and bone
And blood spurting from his chest
I kneeled to ease his suffering.
I tried to do my best.

His pain-wracked body trembled.
From moaning lips, there came this cry,
"Oh! Mom Mio, How this hurts me.
Ma, I don't want to die."

His sense of masculine entitlement was also consistent with the patriarchal privileging of male children within a large Italian American family. As the youngest boy, Mike was pampered by his older sisters, who often sacrificed their own desires in order to provide Mike with treats and toys during the lean years of the Depression. This treatment continued during the war, when Mike was the frequent recipient of packages of salami, mortadella, and olives from his sisters. But he refers to consuming this Italian comfort food only in passing: "We ate salami sandwiches and olives to soothe the system" (4 June 1944). Since his closest companions were other Italian Americans, there would have been little cause for comment on the ethnic origins of the food.[7]

The diary does contain hints of pressures to assimilate while in the army. Two years into his stay in Hawaii, Mike offhandedly began one diary entry by declaring he had "Decided that I'd report to the hospital to be circumcised" (30 Aug. 1943). Several days later, he mentioned that he "was too embarrassed to tell" a female lover why he was in the hospital (3 Sept. 1943) and he later confessed that he could not tell female friends about the circumcision "because I didn't know how. It isn't everyday that a fellow gets circumcised" (9 Sept. 1943). Although he acknowledged the significance of this procedure—"It isn't everyday that a fellow gets circumcised"—he reported it with no further commentary.[8]

Joe P., Mike's closest friend in the army, believed that Italian Americans were assigned the least popular duties in their unit, especially cooking and KP.[9] Allan Bérubé has written that "The stereotypically feminine domestic and service duties were the jobs into which classification officers sometimes channeled black GIs who seemed to be gay or effeminate."[10] Mike's diary makes no open reference to how his identity as an Italian American affected the division of labor in the military, but in a poem complaining about his chronic assignment to KP, Mike implicitly acknowledges the hierarchical ordering that determined soldiers' assignment to undesirable, feminized tasks. In a poem titled "Dear Sergeant," Mike wrote:

If I get a Jap for you,
Better yet—I'll make it two.
Will you be nice to me
And never give Stabile K.P.?

In a longer version of this poem, Mike makes it clear that only the racialized enemy would be lower on the military food chain than he.

Usually, Mike's complaints about feminized jobs refer to the gendered nature of this labor, emphasizing that in the hierarchical universe of the military, he and his friends did not feel they were treated like men: "It is a great relief to be off K.P. and I do feel like a man instead of a woman" (10 Aug. 1941). On another occasion, he observed, "My bed had to be made up. Bet my sisters would get a big laugh from watching me make a bed" (25 Nov. 1944). In a more sympathetic vein, Mike wrote, "I again tried my hand at washing clothes. When the scrubbing was done and my back was aching, I was convinced that a woman's job is a hard one. My sympathy goes out to them" (10 July 1944).

While Mike was only subtly conscious of ethnicity, his sense of class was pronounced. Indeed, Mike primarily understood the Italian "boys from New Jersey" with whom he socialized through the lens of class. For Mike, in a rigidly hierarchical army, being a "jeep" and getting assigned to KP were markers of class identity more significant than being Polish (like his buddy Jasek) or French (like his friend Michaud). Mike was keenly aware of his working-class status in the army and resentful of the control exercised by his superior officers. Resisting what they perceived as arbitrary exercises of control, Mike and friends were chronically AWOL, feigned illness to escape particularly onerous duties, and sometimes openly defied orders. These young men were also entrepreneurs who accumulated forms of capital that made their superiors dependent on them for supplies and services that could be difficult to obtain. For example, Mike and his best friend, Joe P., owned the only motor vehicle in their camp. This allowed them to visit town frequently but also forced other soldiers, including their officers, to hitch rides with them. Mike and Joe further owned a seemingly limitless supply of blank passes (given to them by a grateful officer) that allowed them to pass most challenges on their frequent AWOL excursions. As cook for the unit, Joe was also in charge of purchasing food and drink from local suppliers, which meant that his contacts among local people were extensive and often profitable. In short order, Mike and Joe became their battalion's contacts for a whole range of commodities and services, not all of them technically legal.

Mike's class background also structured a more positive encounter with the army. For the first time for many of these men, they had access to regular dental care and health care. Mike's diary contains numerous references to his use of available services to address chronic health problems. He was a frequent visitor to the dentist and was hospitalized several times for long-standing problems with abscesses, fistulas, hemorrhoids, and digestive problems. Army life also offered benefits like three square meals a day, housing, and entertainment in the form of books, magazines, films, and the occasional USO show.

Where class formed the basis for solidarity, color marked the borders of American identity. Hawaii proved a disorienting place in this regard for Mike and other white soldiers. Thomas Guglielmo argues that the most effective way to understand "Italians' secure whiteness *and* their highly problematical racial status" is to distinguish between race and color rather than race and ethnicity.[11] Mike would have agreed. For Mike, accustomed to the racial dynamics of metropolitan New York, color signified the divide between whites and blacks. In Hawaii, the army itself was at first entirely white: African American soldiers did not appear in Honolulu until 1942.[12] But Hawaiian society itself was, as Bailey and Farber observe, a multiethnic one that did not have the same deep-seated racial conventions or the same history of race and racism. Segregation was neither as fixed nor as widespread as it was on the mainland. Black wartime workers and soldiers reported discovering "a more welcoming environment than the one they had left behind" and spoke appreciatively of "Hawaii's wartime racial fluidity."[13]

This very fluidity caused a backlash among white soldiers. As reflected in Mike's diary, conflicts among soldiers were many after the arrival of black troops in 1942. On 11 June 1943, he disapprovingly remarked that the Malakole Post Exchange "was crowded with Negro doggies." The following day, Mike and a group of Italian American men left a bar because it had become a popular gathering place for African American soldiers: "As usual, niggers were there" (12 June 1943). On 13 June, a Sunday, a group of drunken white soldiers went to Ewa (a town near the army camp) to eat and Mike reported:

> A few Negroes were there and because of a few curse words a fight resulted. Harry Coester was in the restaurant getting the sandwiches while Molnar, Joe and I waited in the truck. The nigger made a wisecrack and Harry called him a black bastard. Joe ran in the joint with an ax and I had all to do to quiet him down. A top kick was there and he helped, also. Took off in a hurry and the M.P.s were after us. Lost them and then went to Camp. As usual, we were A.W.O.L. and at this rate we'll get nabbed one of these days. (13 June 1943)

Encounters between racist soldiers like Mike and his companions could turn violent quickly. The diary does not record any similar conflicts with the Chinese, Japanese, Filipino, and Hawaiian peoples who shared public spaces with U.S. soldiers—perhaps because Mike and Joe relied on them in their successful attempts to benefit from the lively black market economy on the island. In addition, and owing to stereotypes about Asian masculinity, men from these backgrounds did not pose the same threat to white masculinity that African American men did. Color, understood primarily as "blackness," defined the white masculinity that Harry, Joe, and the "top kick" sought to defend in the bar brawl at Ewa.

Mike's racist androcentrism meant that any challenge on the part of those perceived as black (largely African Americans) would precipitate a violent response from those invested in policing the color line, especially when black soldiers did not understand their literal and metaphoric places. As long as blacks remained in the positions prescribed to them, as long as they behaved in the appropriate subservient manner, relations could remain cordial. During one of his many stays in the hospital, Mike remarked, "I get a kick out of batting the breeze with Jenkins, the Negro. Just to look at him makes me laugh" (7 Sept. 1943), a statement that illustrates how the presence of blacks was tolerated, as long as they fit into racist stereotypes, in this case as comedic objects of white ridicule.[14]

Still, Hawaii clearly confused the binary logic of Mike's existing racial categories. For the first time in his life, Mike experienced everyday contact with Chinese, Japanese, Hawaiian, and Filipino people. People of Asian descent were clearly not "white" like

Mike and his brethren in arms, and racist sentiment against the Japanese military and soldiers appears throughout the diary.[15] Racial distinctions between white soldiers and people of Asian descent appear throughout the diary, but without the consistency with which Mike described African Americans. Moreover, Mike pursued a whole range of relationships with Chinese, Japanese, Hawaiian, and Filipino women and men that he would never have pursued with African Americans. Describing a meeting with a woman he curiously described as a "haole," a Hawaiian word used to refer to white people, Mike reprovingly wrote, "Her sister, Elizabeth, was there and she is married to a Gook" (12 June 1943); elsewhere he recorded how he caught a ride to Waipahu, where he found his friends drinking with "another 'gook'" (13 June 1943). During the course of the Ranger training that preceded his battalion's departure for combat in Saipan, Mike wrote, "As we'd make these daily trips we'd pass a gook's house and wave to the girls as they sat on the porch" (24 Jan. 1944). In this entry, the "gook's house" is distinct from "the girls" sitting on the porch, which underscores Mike's contradictory usage of this term.[16]

In Mike's eyes, African Americans were clearly at the bottom of a racial hierarchy. Although the diary contains a number of references to "gooks" (mainly in relation to the Japanese, who are also referred to as "little yellow men"), Mike established social and working relationships with Asian men. Mike was constantly performing a variety of services for Mr. Lee (a Chinese man who owned one of the many small stores that sprang up to serve U.S. troops), and Japanese merchants provided Mike and his friend Joe P. with liquor and other items. Mike and his friends frequently visited Joe Pie, a gay Hawaiian man, as well as "George the Q." and his father (Hawaiians who lived on Barbers Point). Later, on the island of Leyte, Mike commented that the Filipinos "are wonderful and I can't stop giving them things. To the men I give shorts and undershirts—the children—candy and centavos and for the women—I have canned foods and get them bread" (21 Dec. 1944). Provided he could occupy the intertwined roles of benefactor and liberator, Mike's relationships with the Asian people he encountered were, from his perspective, gratifying and warm. The oppressive implications of a colonizing mind-set that demanded gratitude and obedience from those who were dominated were most evident in his dealings with women.

"Native Gals" and "Notch House Broads"

Estimates of the ratio of males to females in wartime Hawaii range from one hundred to one to one thousand to one. Mike put the figure at "263 men to one broad" (30 May 1943). The resulting competition over women meant that many soldiers' most intimate contact with Asian populations was with women whose sexual availability marked their liminal status between white and black. Mike considered the daughters of Asian women and men, unlike the daughters of white women and men, a sexual resource, outside the bounds of respectability or marriage. Whereas Mike never mentioned having sex with black women (and very few black women lived in Hawaii before the postwar period) and perceived white women (especially Italian American girls) who enjoyed the protection of their fathers as off limits, Asian women were another matter altogether—sexually available in the short run, but not marriageable.

To Mike's thinking, Asian women were not black, but they were not white either. Shortly after his arrival in Hawaii, he wrote: "The native gals talk filthy, but a soldier or any service man stands little chance of making them. I couldn't get one to stand for while I snapped her picture. They look like niggers, but they are different" (18 Aug. 1941). Later, Mike noted a similar slippage in writing about Rosie, a Filipino woman with whom he had been involved while stationed on Leyte: "Hans Jeggins asked to see the pictures I got yesterday. They were taken on Leyte with Rosie, Anna, Rosario, Dee-Dee and Patsy, and of course, Rosie's youngster, Victorio. They came out none too good and I'm half ashamed to send them to Rosie, for she looks quite black in them" (19 April 1945).

One of his increasingly frequent complaints about life on the "Rock," as he came to refer to Oahu, further elaborates on such racial distinctions: "Women are scarce and crummy—there are a few nice ones, but not enough to go around. Many soldiers marry these women of mixed races. They are not to blame in a way. They want companionship and even a 'Gook' gives that to them—to an extent. However, seldom is it that one of these fellows takes their wife back to their home in the States. They, more or less, are ashamed of their marriage" (13 April 1943). Asian women's racial status allowed for sexual contact with the "few nice ones" (presumably those willing to have sex with U.S. soldiers), but this status also prohibited official, socially sanctioned relationships. This prohibition was official policy for the U.S. military as well, an institution that made marriage nearly impossible for interracial couples.

Although not white enough to marry, Asian women were acceptable sexual partners for white soldiers, providing that they understood and accepted their place in the raced and colored hierarchy of U.S. social relations, specifically recognizing that that they were entitled to neither emotional nor financial benefits. A case in point involved Mike's friend Joe P., an Italian American from Hazelton, Pennsylvania, who had a long-term relationship with Nancy, a Japanese woman whose father owned and operated a local hotel. "Nancy came out to meet us. She's pregnant and her baby is due in a couple weeks. Joe then will be a pappy. He has refused to marry her, so she is going to let the kid be adopted. She's a swell little Jap and is in no way trying to make trouble for Joe" (5 March 1944). Nancy was not trying "to make trouble for Joe": She was "a swell little Jap" who (according to Mike) accepted the army's policy of placing the products of what were considered unfortunate interracial relationships with adoptive parents.

Joe P. insisted when I interviewed him that Mike had also fathered a child in Hawaii, with the daughter of a Chinese grocery store owner with whom they did business. (See Figure 3.) Although Mike made references to this man's two daughters (one of whom Joe was dating) throughout his account of his life in Hawaii, he mentioned neither a sexual relationship with this woman nor a pregnancy, although he did make note of an argument they had in the spring of 1944. He mentioned his fondness for her but clearly marked the boundaries of the relationship in racial terms: "She is Chinese and for this reason I can't afford to be serious. Yet, there's something I like about her and it's got me going" (27 July 1943).

According to Cynthia Enloe, U.S. forces have long demanded sexual services from local populations. Women were expected to provide sexual services for soldiers and, in

Figure 3. Mike and infant daughter

so doing, bear the risk of disease, social ostracism, and unintended pregnancies. Cognizant of the problems that U.S. soldiers' sense of entitlement to sexual services could cause, particularly in terms of relations between the U.S. military and local, regional, and national governments, the military frequently established rules governing social and sexual contact with local populations.[17] In the Philippines, for example, Mike remarked, "The Army won't let us speak to the [local] women" (7 Dec. 1944), and the women's families often devised elaborate systems of chaperonage in order to prevent sexual contact.

In Honolulu, the vice district sat at the intersection of race and gender: Hotel Street, according to Bailey and Farber, "was in a corner of Honolulu's Chinatown."[18] Mike's diary chronicles numerous visits to brothels, or "notch joints," like the New Senator (his favorite), the Midway Hotel, and the Rex. These visits reflected the military's understanding of sex as recreation and a form of release: "After leaving the hospital, I went to the Midway Hotel, a notch joint. Vicky was there and no sooner I came—I went. Soldiers and sailors sure crowd these joints" (12 Jan. 1942); "We then went to the New Senator Hotel. Tobey was there and she was O.K. After 10 minutes of heaven, we left" (15 Feb. 1942); "Again I visited the New Senator Hotel. This time 'Bobby' gave me a half and half job—she was swell too" (27 Feb. 1942); "The Central was the best bet there and 'Dixie' took care of me" (2 May 1942); "Went up to the Camp Rooms and shot the scaben to Sonja" (5 July 1942); "The first stop in town was the Service Hotel. Sally was there and I had a swell time with her" (19 July 1942). Brothels, staffed by approximately 250 registered prostitutes, were open between 9 A.M. and 2 A.M., and men paid three dollars for three minutes. Hundreds of men waited in lines each day, and time limits were strictly enforced—prostitutes frequently set alarm clocks, and men were through when the alarm went off, regardless of whether they had reached orgasm. According to Bailey and Farber's estimates, nearly a quarter of a million men per month paid for sexual services during the war years.

Queers in Arms

For Mike and his fellow soldiers, military life offered other forms of sexual activity, too. As Eve Kosofsky Sedgwick, John D'Emilio and Estelle Freedman, and Allan Bérubé have documented, homosociality, particularly in the highly masculinized, gender-segregated confines of the army, engendered contradictions within the heteronormative confines of the institution.[19] As Bérubé succinctly put it, "The extreme demands of basic training disrupted the sexual patterns that each male recruit had developed as a civilian and forced him to reorganize them around his military experience. Segregation from wife and other women, total lack of privacy, and little free time immersed the trainee in an all-male military culture that was theoretically heterosexual but rife with homosexual tensions."[20] The male-to-female ratio in Hawaii, and the fact that only officers and more privileged military personnel had access to WACs and other white female wartime workers, meant that army GIs worked, lived, and played in an almost totally male environment. For some, as Bérubé also points out, this level of gender segregation and the "intensity of such an all-male world could force trainees to come to terms with their sexual desires toward men."[21] Certainly for Mike, the army proved to be a very queer place.

As both Bérubé and George Chauncey emphasize, World War II marked a transitional moment in the history of sexuality in the United States; sexual practices previously considered criminal were increasingly monitored and treated by psychiatrists and understood through the prism of psychiatric disorders and disease.[22] Gay men and lesbians serving in the armed forces during World War II had to be extremely cautious, since they risked dishonorable discharge and institutionalization should their sexual orientation be discovered. Nevertheless, a distinctive gay subculture emerged within the military, and Mike soon found it.

Mike's curiosity about the military's gay subculture emerges as early as 6 October 1941. With the island experiencing a blackout, Mike noted that men from his Barbers Point camp would "go to the beach at nite fall and chew the fat for awhile. Some of the boys visit George, the queer." "George, the queer," was Mike's shorthand for gay men, although in this instance it probably referred to a specific gay man. For Mike, gay men (native Hawaiians as well as military personnel like himself) became a distinguishing feature of the exotic landscape of Hawaii.

Perhaps Mike's sense of being marginalized within the military made him more inclined to identify with other outsiders and rebels. Maybe Mike was attracted to certain gay men. Whatever his motivations for participating in the gay subculture that he encountered, his interest in it was clear, and references to gay men and same-sex sexual practices run throughout the diary. In January 1942, he observed, "Today held for me quite a few surprises. I ran across five queers. Bill, George Smith, John and a male nurse and a kid named Ed. I am positively sure of George and the male nurse being queer. Of the others, I have a good suspicion" (5 Jan. 1942). The very next day, Mike met "George, the queer," on his way to the shower: "He was waiting for me at the ward door. He says he was in the mood, but I chased the lousy queer bastard away" (6 Jan. 1942). A few days afterward, Mike claimed that "George 'Q' made a play for me and I threatened to knock him on his ass. He hasn't been around any more" (10 Jan. 1942).

But Mike's situational homophobia and his resultant defensive posturing about heterosexuality did not line up with his sexual practices. During this same time period, when Mike was in the hospital, he met Smokey, "a swell kid . . . [who has] got a good connection in town" (5 Jan. 1942), meaning that Smokey had black market connections that Mike could use to his advantage. Mike recounted how he and Smokey shared not only sandwiches and coffee with a gay male nurse but sex as well: "Smokey copped a mope and I shot the sherbert to this Herbert" (8 Jan. 1942). Later, Mike complained, "Excitement is just a word here in Hawaii. Nothing has turned up since the memorable December 7th. My only sport is 'Q' hunting" (9 Jan. 1942).

While references to "'Q' hunting" may imply a level of homophobic aggression, Mike's curiosity about gay life in the military was more complicated. In addition to more casual brushes with gay military personnel, Mike sought out and became involved in the gay culture that already existed on the island. The connection between gay military cultures and local gay cultures was a crucial one for queer military personnel. During World War II, according to Bérubé, "When gay civilians threw wartime parties to entertain the new GIs in town, they drew on a long tradition in gay life. In the 1920s and 1930s, the private gay circles that existed in every city were often multigenerational, stable, and organized around a single man, woman, or couple who opened their house for get-togethers."[23]

Oahu was no exception. On 17 January 1942, Mike met a civilian gay man who figured prominently in the diary for the remainder of his stay in Hawaii. This "George," he wrote, "is another Mr. 'Q.' . . . He has a nice home and it's right on the beach. George himself is a good egg" (17 Jan. 1942). This particular "George" (whose actual name Mike records only once, on 2 May 1943) was a notorious and "flamboyant" con man and "bachelor," the son of a well-known Hawaiian folk singer. George claimed to be a Hawaiian prince (a direct descendant of native Hawaiian royalty).[24]

Both George and Mike considered themselves outlaws of sorts: George by virtue of his race and sexual orientation, Mike because of his class identity and problems with authority. Mike and his best friend, Joe P., proved useful to George through their ability to procure hard-to-find commodities, Mike's mechanical aptitude (he mentions performing handyman chores for George and his father on a number of occasions), and their willingness to experiment sexually. From 17 January 1942 on, Mike and Joe spent a good deal of time at George's home on Barbers Point, along with a bevy of other young soldiers. A photograph from the period shows George at the head of a table, surrounded by shirtless young men with drinks in their hands.

Mike described one of their first visits in the following terms: "I went to George's house and he didn't have any [plugs for Joe's car]. Fixed his frigidaire and he gave me 12 bars of candy. He's a swell egg. Joe's going to work him over for half a thousand" (18 Jan. 1942). Although Mike and Joe believed themselves to be consummate "bullshit artists," it took them some time to realize they had met their match in George. The two young Italian American men believed that they were "working" George "over" for his inheritance, unaware that George was running a scam of his own. George told Mike and Joe that he had "inherited $5,000,000" and was a Hawaiian prince descended from royalty. He promised that "He, Joe, myself and Rose, who lives with George and is a 'Q,' are going to tour the world when the war is over. George wants us to make the trip with him. He also intends to buy Joe a new Buick car" (20 Jan. 1942). Over the next few weeks, Joe, Mike, Rose, and George, as well as other soldiers, were frequent visitors to George's house on Barbers Point, where they dined and frequently had sex (Joe mainly with George, Mike with Rose).

Mike initially seemed convinced that George's promises of wealth were legitimate, recounting with all the verve of an ingenue: "Joe and I are as close to being millionaires as anyone can be. George says we never have to work any more for the rest of our lives. He wanted to buy us out of the Army, but this war don't allow it. If I live through this war, Joe and I are going to live like kings" (22 Jan. 1942).

Mike's enthusiasm for living like "kings" supported by a "queen" underscores his singular lack of discomfort when it came to his relationship with George and Rose and the manner in which class position (or living "like kings") mattered more in his musings about the future than being heterosexual. Mike's fantasies of touring the world with George, Rose, and Joe were hardly the vision of postwar heterosexual monogamy that soldiers were said to desire. Throughout the spring of 1942, Mike continued to express his belief that George was going to make these working-class Italian boys rich:

"Thinking of Joe, George and myself and that tour around the world, I head for my tent and sleep with a happy heart" (11 March 1942). Even after June 1942, when it became clear to both Joe and Mike that George was unlikely to deliver on these promises, they remained on friendly terms with him, continuing to exchange sex for money and other items: "For $26.00 bucks Joe threw the cylinder to George" (11 Jan. 1943). "Joe threw the Sceeben to George and boy was he (George) happy" (20 June 1943). A number of Mike's warmest memories of his time in Hawaii came after it became clear that George would not be sharing his millions with them:

> George and his Dad were cleaning house when we arrived. The twenty pound turkey was a cooking and while we waited for chow, Joe and I pitched in to help the old Man and George clean up the house. We finished one room and then quit. Sat down to a fine dinner, Turkey, dressing, vegetables, nuts, fruits, cakes, coffee, beer, cokes, sodas and lots of other things, including candy were before us to eat. George's father said a prayer in his native Hawaiian tongue and then we dug into the nutrition. The meal was tasty and satisfied my appetite to real perfection. Later, after the meal, George and the old gent sang some beautiful Hawaiian songs as we lounged about in the living room. . . . Today was truly the best day of my Army life. Only my discharge will equal it. Unless a furlough is given me. My thanks to George and his Dad. They are two fine people and knowing them sure is a pleasure. (25 Dec. 1943)

Ever prosaic, Mike understood his time with George and his father to be precious, equal only to a discharge or furlough. When this "George the Queer danced the hula," it was cause for reflection.

Mike's accounts of his interactions with George are warm, even after he realized that there was no financial gain in such a relationship. Mike and Joe seemed to identify with George's outsider status and to admire him because of it. Mike expressed considerable respect for what he was wont to refer to as "bullshit artists," particularly those who were accomplished and successful in this area. Working-class men of Mike's generation often made do during the Depression through various forms of hustling. Understanding themselves to have been "hustled" by an economic system manipulated by elites, they saw no shame in being "bullshit artists" but rather admired those who made a success of it. Importantly, Mike's relationship with George appeared unaffected by Mike's recognition that he had been hustled, with none of the homophobic backlash that we now expect to follow from such situations.

Mike's attitudes toward his queer comrades in arms complicate George Chauncey's research on turn-of-the-century New York City Italian communities' "tolerance of male homosexual relations."[25] According to Chauncey, for Italian immigrants, sex with a "fairy" or "queer" did not destabilize heterosexual identity, as long as putatively straight men "took the 'manly part.'"[26] Steven Cohan similarly points out that during the war, "Homosexuality was localized as a specific category of deviation (the 'sissy') while, at the same time, diffused throughout the same-sex culture of the military as one of the primary mechanisms by which men defined their relations to each other, bonded through their bodies, and, under the circumstances of sexual deprivation and if the desire was there, even found physical relief, without severely challenging their sense of normality."[27] While in some cases, Mike did refer to playing the stereotypical masculine role in same-sex sex, this detail seemed unimportant in his relationship with George. The diary mentions Mike having sex with Rose (George's lover) and Joe having sex with George, but it is uncharacteristically circumspect about George himself. George did represent himself as a Hawaiian "queen" of sorts, but Mike never refers to George in the derogatory manner reserved for women and effeminate men. George's exoticism as a man of color descended from Hawaiian royalty also affected Mike's attitude toward George. While George may have been queer, his ties to elite culture differentiated him from other people of color, as well as other gay men. Still, Mike's relationship with George was something more than the stereotypically casual sexual encounters typically attributed to bisexual men. While Mike's relationship with George may exemplify what Bérubé describes as "situational bisexuality," its affective dimension exceeds that description.[28]

Mike's diary contains additional references to the prevalence of same-sex sexual practices and relationships. Mike wrote about "ribbing" Michaud "about his Queer (my old one) Rose," an acknowledgment of Mike's previous relationship with Rose and Michaud's ongoing involvement with him. While in the hospital following his circumcision, Mike mentioned another patient named Simmerman who "is about 40 years old and appears to be quite queer" (8 Sept. 1943). The next day, Mike's suspicions were confirmed: "In short order, I found my suspicions about him being Queer to be true" (9 Sept. 1943). When Simmerman propositioned him, instead of taking umbrage, Mike fixed him up with a gay ambulance driver he knew, several weeks later casually mentioning another visit to "my friend Cpl. Simmerman whom I met in the hospital" (3 Oct. 1943). In another instance of playing queer matchmaker, Mike tried to set up Joe Pie with his friend Michaud (11 Feb. 1943). And in contrast to other writers who mention their military bisexuality, Mike never described these relationships as the result of the scarcity of heterosexual partners or as occurring out of sexual desperation. On the contrary, Mike continued to have sex with multiple women during the months he was involved with George and Rose.

The hyper-masculine culture of the military certainly supported the common belief that men's needs for sexual release were natural and a defining feature of masculinity, and that sex was necessary recreation for soldiers. "A 50–50 job" (fellatio followed by intercourse), according to Mike, served to boost his "morale to a record high" (18 Jan. 1943). This same logic was sometimes used to explain same-sex sexual activity among servicemen who, being men, could not be expected to remain celibate for any period of time. Years later, when asked about the many same-sex sexual encounters in her husband's diary, Mike's wife told me, "It was the war. You know men." During an interview in January 2005, Joe P. echoed this logic. When asked about one particular same-sex relationship, Joe P. simply smiled and said, "Boys will be boys."

In the end, however contradictory Mike's attitudes toward gay men were, they were never as consistently negative as his feelings about women. Mike regularly described other men's bodies in appreciative terms: He spoke of "Elmer, good looking, to the point where he seems pretty" (9 March 1943), and "Jasek," who "undressed and he had some monstrosity" (31 July 1942). These descriptions never expressed the same levels of revulsion and condescension directed toward women, who were routinely referred to as "broads," "pigs," "pooches," and "doggies." Mike's references to same-sex

sex sound as though they came directly from the hard-boiled fiction he liked to read: "I shot the bunion to Rose the onion" (23 Jan. 1942), "I know he wanted to eat it in the worst way" (13 June 1942), "I fed a pound to the hound . . . traveled the dirt road route and then knocked off for some sleep" (29 July 1942). But his similarly roundabout single reference to oral sex with a woman reflected an intrinsic revulsion toward the female body: "Met a young Hawaiian kid there [in Malakole] and he was telling a bunch of us how he almost ate it once. The stink was too strong and even if his friends like it, it was no good for him. His older friends snowed him that it tasted good and so he tried it, but couldn't stand the fishy smell" (26 June 1943). Women "stink" and have a "fishy smell," and the fact that this "young Hawaiian kid" nearly engaged in cunnilingus was significant enough to earn him the derisive nickname of "almost ate a snatch" (11 Aug. 1943).

Allan Bérubé believes that in the army, "some servicemen convinced themselves that casual sex with men was not queer if it was just between buddies."[29] As novelist Harold Robbins put it, "I was on a submarine, and if you're on a submarine for 22 days, you want sex. We were either jacking each other off or sucking each other off. Everybody knew that everybody else was doing it. . . . So we did it, it was fun, and it was over. I don't know whether any of them were really homosexual."[30] Since Mike's diary does not contain any justification for, or defense of, his same-sex sexual encounters, it is difficult to say whether Mike shared these sentiments. Certainly, the long-term relationship with George could not be understood in this fashion. It seems more reasonable to assume that Mike did not think that having sex with other men made a man queer. Behaving like a woman did. Men who were openly feminine, such as Private Dodd, who called himself Winifred and was eventually sent home, elicited open criticism from Mike: "Pvt. Dodd is bucking for a section eight. Not all of his actions are faked and the doctor in charge of him wants to know what the score is. Pvt. Dodd has told the doctor that Hazelwood and I are the two that ride him the most about him being queer. His ways seem to be on the feminine side and because of this he takes a lot of kidding. At the present time he is under observation at the hospital" (9 May 1943). Mike and his friends harassed Private Dodd not because he was queer—other gay soldiers, as we have seen, were treated with respect—but because his ways were "on the feminine side." Here again, same-sex sexual practices were not in and of themselves cause for concern or derision as long as the men engaging in them behaved like proper men and not like women. Mike's explicit references to same-sex sexual activities in a diary that was later given to his six children suggests that he was neither embarrassed nor ashamed but saw these activities as a part of his experiences in the military.[31] After all, Mike was only acting like a man.

If Mike did father a daughter in Hawaii and remained silent about it, this raises further questions about his relationships with men. Was having a biracial child with the Chinese grocer's daughter more shameful than his relationships with men? While boys may be boys and as such are granted space for sexual experimentation because of their "natural" sexual needs, fathering biracial children was another matter altogether. As John D'Emilio and Estelle Freedman observe in their history of sexuality in America, those who transgressed the sexual rules used to police racial boundaries "challenged not only a set of cultural values but also the basis of an emerging system of racial control"—a system of racial control that Mike was very much invested in defending, especially during the years following the war.[32]

Relations of Production

By way of conclusion, I should briefly explain my access to these unpublished source materials. I am one of the six children Mike had after the war ended (he married my mother in 1947), and I received a copy of the diary in the early 1990s, a few years before Mike died. My own relationship was with a much later incarnation of Mike: No longer the New Dealer of the 1930s and 1940s, like many of his class background and ethnicity, Mike had been transformed into a supporter of Joe McCarthy by the cold war and by the series of disappointments that working-class men confronted in their postwar pursuit of the American Dream.

As a scholar-daughter (an identity that is itself a fairly recent one), I have tried to be self-reflexive in considering my relationship to this material and to its author. My personal relationship with Mike was conflicted, to say the least. He could be incredibly authoritarian and patriarchal, but at the same time, he admired what he saw as my intelligence and spirit. In fairness to Mike, I am sure that it was extremely difficult to parent a child just as disobedient and resistant to authority as he had been, especially a female who read voraciously and had intellectual aspirations that never made sense to him.

Mike's generation of working-class Italian American men certainly did not invent the racialized androcentrism that they encountered in the United States and in the military, but many of them took to it like ducks to the water, using it to craft their own identities within the dominant social order. But in most cases, men like Mike who became petit-bourgeois spokesmen for cold war politics and masculinity did not benefit from this social order in the ways that more educated elites did, elites who knew enough not to overtly reveal their implicit support for racist, sexist, and homophobic ideologies. Like other working-class men of his generation, the postwar boom helped Mike achieve middle-class status, but it was a tenuous class position and he had to work every day for the remainder of his life to maintain it.

Mike's diary offers glimpses into Mike's own confusion about race and sexual orientation, his identification with the gender outlaws he encountered, and the ways in which his worst instincts were encouraged and rewarded by the institutions that governed his life and over which Mike and other working-class men had little control. His writings provide a complex portrait of a man who, for several years after the war ended, continued to send packages to the Filipino children he had befriended on Leyte. In one fund-raising letter circa 1945, he told Miss Troy, a teacher at his old grade school in Nutley, that "War makes no allowance for age and though the grown ups may die to pay the price of freedom, I think it is the children who suffer most." Mike could be an extraordinarily generous man who loved children, food, and good stories. At the same time, Mike was quick to invoke his race and gender privilege, particularly with people of color, gay men, and women in general. From an early age, it was clear to me that in Mike's world of racialized androcentrism, people of color (particularly African Americans), women, and—in a more contradictory manner—queer people occupied the wrong side of a binary that privileged white masculinity.

Mike always wanted his diary to be published. Long before the diary was transcribed, Mike would bring it up in conversation, ascribing to it the status of an historic artifact. Like many men who survived the war, he never talked about his military experiences; when pressed, he would say that someday people would read his diary and know what war was really like. For him, the diary spoke truths about World War II that were not represented elsewhere. His only request to my brother and mother as they began the tedious task of transcribing the diary was that they omit one section that described the death of a fellow soldier who had been killed by "friendly" fire. The family of this soldier, he explained, had been told that the Japanese killed him, and Mike did not want to resurrect old sorrows. Mike had no other reservations about going public with the document, although the diary remains a source of contention among his children. For the conservatives among his children, the diary shows that Mike was a largely godless young man who had sex before marriage with both women and men; it also abundantly demonstrates his lack of what is considered patriotism, as well as his disdain for authority. For his more liberal offspring, the diary offers numerous examples of Mike's sexist and racist behaviors. For his feminist daughter, the diary illuminates the contradictory nature of ideologies of gender, as well as the ways in which ordinary people both embody and contradict these in their everyday lives.

Domesticating the Diaspora

REMEMBERING THE LIFE OF KATIE DeRORRE

Caroline Waldron Merithew

There are three shrines in Illinois to heroes of the working class: one for the legendary Mother Jones; one for the Virden martyrs, who died for coal mining unionism, and whose memory is kept alive by labor organizers around the world; and one for Catherine (Katie) Bianco DeRorre. Katie's monument, unlike the others, draws few visitors today. But when it was dedicated in 1961, men and women—on the floor of the U.S. Congress, in the neighborhood where Katie grew up, at American universities, in union halls, on the streets of New York City, and in Milan—took notice and honored the woman who had become the "conscience" of "industrial wars."[1]

Who was Katie DeRorre? And how did she slip from the celebrated to the forgotten? My interpretation of these questions is consciously microhistorical. As Martha Hodes has shown, relations of power "can best be illustrated by exploring the experiences of particular historical actors in particular geographical settings."[2] Where historical actors and settings begin and end, however, can be complex—especially when we consider the realities of the majority of immigrants who move transnationally and leave scant records about their lives.

My answers to questions about Katie also challenge an array of historiographical assumptions about gender, the second generation of immigrants, memory, and the divergence of immigration, labor, and women's history.[3] In his work on the African American diaspora, Earl Lewis argues for understanding multipositionality as something more than identity shifting or privileging (e.g., race over class, gender over religion). "It is the interactive construction of identity—as child, lover, spouse, and so on—that requires fuller explication," Lewis contends.[4] A transnational immigrant's identity can move through large and small geographic spaces as well as take up the minds and hearts of men and women who make (or witness) global crossings. While the word "transnationalism" has been used to signify an array of meanings, my principle concern in this essay is to explore the term in a way that brings together Lewis's notion of the interactivity of public and private with what Donna Gabaccia and Loretta Baldassar conceptualize in this volume as the "diasporic private sphere."[5]

Memories of Katie come from those who knew her and, less often, from her own words. Each tells somewhat different stories, but together they reveal how arbitrary sociopolitical lines do not confine people's movements or experiences, and how individuals, communities, and social movements transcend global space. With some few exceptions, historical discussions of transnationalism have concentrated on either side of the 1924 and 1965 Immigration Acts.[6] This periodization has meant that the identities of the 1.5- and second-generation children who came of age between the Depression and the early cold war—a fundamental period for the immigrant story—have been missed.[7] The strength of Italian immigrants' transnationalism in its everyday form extended into the second generation, the members of which were raised in the post–Johnson Reed era, came of age during World War II, and defined their legacy during the early cold war. Memories of Katie DeRorre and her home were etched into people's minds and shared by them precisely at this time. This chapter begins with a conventional biography of Katie's life, which draws on both memories and her own scant writings and contextualizes the persistently transnational identity of a 1.5-generation female immigrant. The second group of memories highlights how cold war–era descriptions of Katie's home worked to domesticate transnationalism. The final section demonstrates how discourses of internationalism shifted from a political to a cultural form before and after World War II, hiding the transnational dimensions of immigrant life.

Memory, Biography, and Subjectivity

In July 1961, Giuseppe Prezzolini (an Italian journalist who had supported Mussolini's rise to power) devoted much of his regular column in *Il Borghese* to Katie's memory. Prezzolini acknowledged DeRorre's American roots—she had arrived in the United States at the age of eight—but he highlighted her Italianness. To think about how Katie lived her life was to be reminded of one of the great moments in Italian history: the "time when Italian socialism was in its pink phase, the epoch of Prampolini and Massarenti." These men "believed they could conquer the world with good," Prezzolini wrote. Katie's gravestone, which was engraved with the words "Good Samaritan of the Coalfields" and with images of a miner and child, also reminded Prezzolini of the ancient Mediterranean heritage they shared. Katie's tomb, he reflected, was like those of the "first Christians in the Roman catacombs."[8]

Prezzolini was not unique in "transnationalizing" the memory of Katie DeRorre. Gerry Allard, a French immigrant, socialist, and newspaper editor, also made connections between Italian and American pasts in Illinois' *Collinsville Herald*. "Two elements" shaped Katie's "character and actions," he argued—first, Italy's Piedmont region, and second, her mining father. "The Turinos," he wrote, were "progressive" and "socially minded." In their villages, the "teachings of Cavour, Mazzini, Garibaldi, and Modigliani took deep root." For readers better versed in American Civ. than Italian history, Allard helpfully explained, "These Italian thinkers and leaders are to Italy what Jefferson, Lincoln, Tom Paine, and Gene Debs are to America. That part of the world is now one of the bulwarks of democracy."[9] Jack Battuello, a coal miner and anarchist, remembered a different side of DeRorre. Before post–World War II Italy was remade, as Allard suggested, Katie had created a type of domestic democratic "state" of her own. "Katie's home was her cathedral," Battuello reminisced. "Through it passed people from all walks of life. They came; the atheist and the pious; the progressive and the conservative; the radical and the reactionary; the white man and the black man. None was shunned. None was turned away. None was segregated. They sat at her table and supped, and they left forever touched by her graciousness and nobility."[10] Such praise songs for Katie were repeated by others, too, including Frank Zeidler, the longtime socialist mayor of Milwaukee, and Roger Baldwin, the founder of the ACLU.

That these men—with markedly different politics, class backgrounds, cultural bearings, and standings in the world—would describe an immigrant homemaker in such international terms, especially at that moment in the twentieth century when immigration had fallen to its nadir, is puzzling unless we invest in deciphering biography, memory, and the material reality of an immigrant life. This biographical section focuses on that project.

Catherine Bianco was one of the thousands of poor Italians who immigrated to the United States during the late nineteenth and early twentieth centuries. She experienced the same type of emotional and physical hardship that many of her working-class female contemporaries did—she chaffed against "Old World" parents, she married in her teens, she gave birth and tried unsuccessfully to prevent one of her children from dying young, she found her political voice by picketing on the streets before she voted at the polls, and she fought for a pluralist American dream in which the rights of the underclass would be recognized regardless of race, class, religion, or national origin.[11]

Katie was born in the village of Canischio in the province of Turin in 1895. At the age of eight, she immigrated with her grandmother and sister to DuQuoin, in the southern part of Illinois.[12] Her mother and father had moved six years earlier to the small mining town in an area known as "Little Egypt." Their personal story reflected the larger demographic contours of this Italian region's diaspora as well as the industrial pull that brought immigrants to the United States. As Donna Gabaccia has shown, the "Europeanized north of Italy actually had lower rates of female migration . . . than most of the supposedly patriarchal south."[13] Until 1900, when new techniques were developed to efficiently extract coal, "Little Egypt" was agricultural and populated by farmers from the southern United States and Germany. In the next decade, new immigrants from Italy, Poland, Lithuania, Russia, and Hungary arrived.[14] After World War I, mining companies recruited African American men to work in the pits. Both her Italian upbringing and the changing demographics of the region shaped DeRorre's activism in later years.

Katie's childhood was trying. Like most mining households, the Bianco family was often in dire economic need, even though they were what a local newspaper called "one of the most highly respected Italian families in the city."[15] According to Katie's daughter, Catherine "Babe" Mans, Katie's emotionally abusive mother (Babe's grandmother) compounded the hardships of poverty. Though it is unclear what led to the abuse, we do know that Katie dealt with the trauma as many recovering victims do—by bearing witness, which the 1970s oral history that she undertook with her daughter Babe suggests. Babe's recollections in that interview encompass two layers of memory, which help to sketch out the way Katie coped with and constructed meaning in her life. The first layer is the testimony of Katie, told to Babe as a child. The second is Babe's own memories of her mother. In both cases, the narrative articulation follows a pattern that explains how Katie overcame childhood hardship and worked as an adult to avoid repeating it. In Babe's remembrances, there are three elements in many of Katie's stories: hardship and female labor, lack of recognition for this labor, and the presence of a loving kin member who recognized the unjust treatment. For example, Babe told stories of how Katie and her sisters took care of the family's boarders. They did the "heavy work" of household chores while "the boys . . . got all the privileges," Babe remembered. Despite the fact that the girls milked the cows, washed, and baked everyday for the houseful of men, they were not given much in return. The sisters had to wait for the boarders to finish before they could have their supper. "And if there was nothing left, why, they would get a piece of bread." Katie's grandmother (Babe's great-grandmother), who lived with the Biancos, tried to ease the strain on her granddaughter. The disagreements between generations of women must have given Katie hope of escape. And these were the recollections about which Babe remembered her mother telling vivid stories. Babe said: "My great-grandmother had many an argument with my grandmother because she didn't let the girls eat along with the boys." Katie's grandmother "would go sneak some crackers or a piece of bread or a piece of cheese [to] . . . my mother because she was crying." As an adult, Katie separated her nuclear family from her extended kin, as Babe's memory indicates. "I can't say too much about my grandmother," Babe said. "That was the only house that we never went to."[16] Katie's distancing of her childhood family from the family she created was a product of her 1.5-generation position. Language and cultural skills (acquired in the United States) made it possible to reject certain ethnic kin while still embracing Italianness.

On Saturday, 15 May 1915, Katie's wedding made front page news in the town of DuQuoin. Katie married Joseph DeRorre in the parish of Sacred Heart at seven in the morning. Katie's sister Angeline Casaretta was her bridesmaid, and Joe's brother, John, stood up as the best man.[17] Eight years her senior, Joe had been in the United States since childhood, migrating from the province of Belluno, Italy, to southern Illinois at the turn of the century. Like his father, Joseph was a coal miner. There is no evidence of how Joe and Katie met or about their courtship. Unlike many new immigrant couples, Katie and Joe immediately moved into their own home—the house on Walnut Street later remembered so fondly by visitors. Like many mothers, Katie told her children about her wedding day. Babe's memory suggests that even on that special occasion, Katie felt oppressed by the family matriarchy. Babe remembered her mother's story. "The day she was married, she had to go make sure that she milked the cows before she went to church." Katie and Joe began a family immediately. They had three children—Felix was born in 1916, Antoinette in 1918, and Catherine in 1921.[18] In 1931, Antoinette died.

According to Babe, the death of her sister changed her mother. Katie's world, her emotional well-being, and her frame of reference were altered. The loss of Antoinette opened up relationships with family members and friends but closed off institutional links that connected her to an immigrant past. Like many northern Italians, the DeRorres had a tenuous relationship with the Catholic Church. Though they were married in the church, religion was not a central component of their lives. Their marriage and their children's baptisms may have been their last acts of devotion. When Katie requested a funeral mass for Antoinette and a place to bury her in the Catholic cemetery, the local priest said no. There is conflicting information about how and why this happened. Babe's memory was that she and her siblings had not been baptized. Their baptismal records, however, are still at Sacred Heart Catholic Church. It is possible that a rift had developed between the DeRorres and the church or that another family member (Katie's mother, perhaps) took the babies to be blessed.[19] Regardless, Babe remembered that Katie never had anything else to do with Roman Catholicism after Antoinette's death, and others corroborate this claim.[20]

The cutting off of those religious ties—ties that were for so many Italian women important because the church provided a public space of activity outside the home that did not challenge the sacred role of women that was the key to the ideology of the private sphere—did not reflect a retreat for Katie into traditional domesticity. Katie did not grieve the loss of her daughter in a vacuum. Nor did she experience the sexism, racism, and class oppression against which she struggled in isolation. Her life was filled with family and friends she loved, as well as allies and enemies, to whom she responded. Raised in a home where authoritarianism and poverty were inescapable, she learned much about the dual oppressions of sex and class. She strove not to repeat them. The death of their daughter brought husband and wife closer together. Moreover, the DeRorres seemed to have eschewed some of the trappings of matrimonial patriarchy. The spirit of the DeRorre home had always been different from that of the Bianco household of Katie's childhood. The couple understood each other's strengths and, after the death of their daughter, needs as well. They both joined and supported a dual union struggle between the United Mine Workers of America (UMWA) and the Progressive Miners of America (PMA), which began the year Antoinette passed away. But with young children at home, they needed to make practical choices. Only one parent (at a time) could do the organizing, attend the meetings, and walk the pickets. Katie and Joe decided together that Katie would be the one. Babe offered an explanation. Her father "believed in the labor movement, and, I mean, he, he had no reservations about my mother being so active. He knew that this was an escape to her grief, and he was glad that she was active. But he stayed at home with us kids, and . . . oh, occasionally he would go, but Mom would go. . . . Mom was always gone, so somebody had to be home. But no, he was the quiet one of the family."[21]

Katie became homemaker and union activist while Joe was a coal miner and husband. Friends commented on the way Joe and Katie balanced union activism and family life. Thyra Edwards, an African American student at Brookwood Labor College who came to Illinois to help the Progressives, recalled the first time she visited the DeRorres' home. "Katie was out. . . . Her husband told us Katie is always out now, busy with the Movement. 'She can express herself better than I can so I'm glad to have her go.'" While waiting for his wife's return, Joe made supper for the guests.[22] Katie and Joe had a loving and respectful relationship that challenged gender roles and was a comfort to her.

Katie also took in boarders.[23] Starting in 1923 and continuing for over three decades, an Italian immigrant named Charlie Rovoletti was Katie's boarder. Born in 1896, he had migrated from Italy in 1912. Rovoletti was a "well-read" immigrant intellectual and "a self-taught scholar" who was "very interested in the labor movement and took an active part in it." Daughter Babe remembered that "after my sister died in 1931, my mother took it so hard that when the miners' struggle started, and Charlie being home . . . my mother got interested in it. . . . That was one of her escapes from her sorrow. And that's how she got so involved" in organizing and community work.[24] Charlie, Joe, and Katie were all close. The two men mined together for most of their adult lives. They shared a home, and it is clear that they both loved and respected Katie. The daughter of a friend of the family who spent a lot of time at the DeRorre home remembered Charlie as a brother rather than as a boarder.[25] Though we can only speculate about the details of each one of their relationships, fragments of letters refer to special connections and demonstrate a great closeness between them.[26]

Katie's involvement in the labor movement was not only driven by immediate personal tragedy. One of her first acts of organizing was both quintessentially feminine and reflective of her industrial feminist ideology—an ideology that Annelise Orleck has described as "deeply imbued with class consciousness and a vivid understanding of the harsh realities of industrial labor."[27] In March 1933 DeRorre and her activist "sisters" in DuQuoin opened a "lunch kitchen" for hungry children, and within weeks they were serving 100 to 150 children per day.[28] Katie opened her doors to all despite the fact that the community was divided between the dueling unions (and Katie was on the board of the PMA's Women's Auxiliary). "A hungry child is a hungry child to us . . . whether its father is Progressive or hasn't any more sense than to pay big dues to keep [UMWA president] John Lewis' family in luxury," Katie told a crowd at a rally in Belleville, Illinois.[29] In a report to the *Progressive Miner,* the DuQuoin women reinforced their lunch kitchen commitments: "No discriminations are made by the Auxiliary. . . . No matter whether they are American or foreign, negro or white, children of P.M. of A. miners or U.M.W. men, they are treated alike."[30] While it is likely that her abhorrence for racial discrimination was formulated before the PMA's organization, Katie's work with the Progressives gave her a means to work against the racial status quo in her southern Illinois community by welcoming both African American and white men and women into the new union. That's what many of Katie's female friends remembered most about her, and the issue that divided her from many of her new immigrant cohort.

The dual union battle was a violent one, and as it grew bloodier in the mid-1930s, Katie expanded her work without completely leaving behind the Women's Auxiliary. She joined the Illinois Workers Alliance and helped to organize the unemployed. "I am proud to have been a founder of the Auxiliary, although I devote most of my time in behalf of the unemployed," she wrote in 1936.[31] For the rest of the Depression, Katie picketed city officials for bread, justice, and better pay for WPA workers. She also demanded relief for victims when the Mississippi River flooded in the spring of 1936. The flood was an environmental catastrophe for communities already reeling from economic disaster. In one of her few published writings, Katie called for "conservation of America's vast natural resources."[32]

Katie was nevertheless shy about public speaking and even about writing. She preferred to communicate through action and "outside the sight of vast audiences."[33] She spoke to friends and allies privately, and they, in turn, spoke publicly for her. Her good friend Agnes Burns Wieck, whom Katie met while organizing in Illinois, could turn a phrase well—as one man remembered, if Agnes wanted "to say a fighting four-letter word, she says a fighting four-letter word. '[J]ust like that,'"[34] Katie could not. But Agnes was relentless in her effort to push Katie into public eye. In 1935, Wieck (by then in New York) received letters from two mutual friends in Illinois. The letters filled her in on local news and gossip and shared her friends' thoughts on politics and their anxiousness about surviving another year of the Depression. Each also told Agnes about how Katie was doing. "She made a splendid talk," wrote one. "Much improved in her speech. I commented [to] her on it. Yes if we had a few more like Katy we would get along fine." Echoing this thought, the other wrote, "Katie sure is working hard. . . . Now she sure looks fine too."[35]

Despite others' positive assessments, speaking and even writing for an audience made DeRorre nervous. We get a glimpse of her anxiety through letters that Agnes and Katie exchanged. Katie ended one missive abruptly: "Well, I must quit as I am so nervous for I had the story to write so Babe could type it."[36] There were even times when Katie could not muster the necessary commitment to write a letter (even to a close friend). "Received your several cards . . . but there's no other excuse as not answering them but just being too nervous to write."[37] Katie explained that she had been "so upset for the last two months that I had never sat down to write."[38] In another letter, Katie wrote in a postscript, "Excuse mistakes as I have several things on my mind." Katie apologized for "bad writing as it is written in bed and can't do much."[39] In one instance, she asked Agnes to write a newspaper article that she had been asked to compose. "I wonder if you could draw it up providing your health and time approves it."[40] DeRorre seems to have preferred political and strategic conversations in her home to speeches onstage at rallies and marches or even writing her thoughts for friends on paper. At home, Katie was the center of power and it was in the domestic realm where she most effectively honed and directed her skills.

Katie's political chameleon qualities made her a good mediator. As her daughter Babe said in a 2005 interview with me, Katie was "a socialist with anarchist friends." As the memories of Prezzolini, Allard, and Battuello suggest, she had admirers with a wide range of political perspectives. Katie worked against fascism in her community (though her association with Alpina Dogali Society—an organization that was seen as subversive and sympathetic to fascism by the military draft board during World War II—complicates matters). In an undated letter to Agnes, she wrote, "I have not yet seen where the men['s] convention went on record to adopt the resolution against fascism. Scottsboro boys, Mooney, Billing on a special program to educate the young miner."[41] Katie's mediation skills were a political reflection of the ways she reconciled the private and public roles that she lived and her embodiment of multiple identities. She may have observed these powers in early life from her grandmother, who fed her "under the table." It was obvious from her friends' and families' memories that she had a talent for making people feel welcome and bringing them together. She "not only excelled in the women's world, but was equally at home with the problems of the men," Jack Battuello said.[42] She was part of the Italian community but felt comfortable as an intermediary between immigrant and native-born Americans. In a place where racial tension was severe, she promoted "social mixing" despite the fact that this would be "offensive to certain people" within the union.[43]

If Katie had so much anxiety about writing and speaking, what caused her to continue her work in public? Why not instead retreat to a more maternal domestic sphere?

"It's mighty hard for the poor worker to forgive and forget," Katie told Agnes in 1937.[44] At that moment, DeRorre was exasperated by something a WPA administrator had told young men who had been shortchanged by their paychecks. The determination not "to forgive and forget" explains DeRorre's life choices and public activism. She was angered by injustice, and she was stunned when others did not see or work to change oppression. "The people here are just as other places," she told Agnes. "The left wing scares them an[d] those that don't believe can't say nothing." She kept working at it, despite her questioning. "I wonder if these people will ever wake up."[45]

Katie's vision of the world included male and female activists and a liberationist domesticity in which male and female tasks were not separated by biology. Katie even found cross-dressing a means of justice. Babe recalled that her mother—who had a car and so often drove her friends to union meetings through unfriendly territory—wore men's clothing to escape notice.[46] Just as Katie slipped between traditionally masculine and feminine roles in her working-class community, she did so between her Italian and American communities as well. DeRorre's 1.5-generation transnationalism was fluid. Katie's subjectivity (the ways in which her perceptions and experiences shaped her worldview) came out in her letters to Agnes, a woman of German and Irish roots. Katie mediated ethnicity as she did politics. By 1937, the majority of the Italians in DuQuoin had dropped out of the PMA's Women's Auxiliary. These women were her ethnic and political kin, yet Katie would not follow as they exited. "They think I too should leave such an outfit for it is only a disgrace to me," she told Agnes, "but I look it at [*sic*] a different point of view as I have always done before, we have an obligation to try to fulfill." Not only did she remain in the PMA, but she also joined the Alpina Dogali Society Auxiliary. Babe and Katie wrote the bylaws for this organization. "Peace on Earth" was their password.[47]

The documentary evidence on DeRorre's life falters with World War II. We know only that Katie worked for her local rationing board and was still hosting meetings of the Auxiliary in her home in the 1950s. In the postwar years, the Auxiliary raised money to help members who were in need or had lost loved ones. It used its treasury to send the children of coal miners to Washington, D.C. Though Auxiliary meetings often started with the Pledge of Allegiance and the Lord's Prayer, elements of Depression-era working-class Progressivism lingered. In 1957, for example, Katie supported a resolution lambasting the Taft-Hartley Act. The Auxiliary promised to use political force, and the women pledged to vote only for candidates who went on record against this anti-labor legislation.[48]

In 1959, Katie was diagnosed with cancer. She passed away in January 1960. Union members, politicians, friends, and DeRorre's large "famiglia piemontese" came together to memorialize their friend and comrade. Regardless of their background or standing, "All remembered this woman as one who gave comfort."[49] And they began to collect the money to erect a monument to her—"the third shrine the miners of Illinois have erected to their members."[50] Many of those at the funeral had recently been together to celebrate Katie's life in another way.

Sister Katie Day, 1956

On 3 June 1956, family and friends in Springfield, Illinois, paid tribute to sixty-year-old Katie DeRorre by declaring it Sister Katie Day and naming her the "Good Samaritan of the coalfields." Celebrants heard speeches by Milwaukee's socialist mayor, Frank Zeidler, and newspaper editor Gerry Allard and enjoyed a picnic lunch at the VFW hall. The organizing committee had solicited cards, letters, and photos beforehand—"a review of our younger days"—and pasted them in a red leather "souvenir book" to present to Katie at the festivities. Celebrating an individual woman's life in this way was a strategic choice. By 1956, radicals in the coalfields of southern Illinois had had time to regroup and redefine themselves. Taft-Hartley's restrictions on unions were almost a decade old; McCarthy was dead; the cold war was changing. In February of that year, Nikita Khrushchev had delivered his Secret Speech, which was leaked to the West. Allard and his wife, Irene, expressed their hope about all these changes. In their card to Katie, they wrote: "It would seem that this [Progressive] group lost practically all the battles but they may yet win the war." The organizers assembled a political event intended for the public around a single person, her life, and the personal loyalty many felt toward her. They chose Katie because her "heroic spirit . . . exemplified the career of thousands of others" but also because, as Tillie and Jack Battuello put it, "*We think Katy is just perfect.*" University of Chicago economics professor Maynard Krueger also emphasized the importance of this woman: "You may not know it," he told DeRorre, "but whenever as many as three . . . ex-miners in Chicago get together to chew over old times the name and the deeds of Katie DeRorre are sure to come into conversation."[51] The party-throwers had rehearsed all this beforehand, of course. But Katie played her part impromptu. She cried when presented with flowers, a watch, memorabilia, and the scrapbook. She "wondered why" all this fuss was made for a "common housewife," as the *St. Louis Post-Dispatch* reported.[52]

Sister Katie Day embodied the collective memory of a transnational Left. This memory was narrated as a feminization of the struggle that both revealed and masked the role that women like Katie DeRorre (and their homes) had played in the uprisings of the 1930s. John Bodnar understands immigrant memory as a marker of both past and present. He writes that people "inevitably recall the past in ways that best serve their purpose in present time, and they erase or revise facts and interpretations that they consider antithetical."[53] The crowd of Progressives "with Italian, French, German, Scotch, and English names" who gathered for Sister Katie Day were honoring, remembering, and rewriting the history of a quarter of a century at a moment when the Left, though decimated, realized it had survived the cold war.[54] But it was emerging cautiously with the celebration of an individual life, and a female one at that.

To call DeRorre a "Good Samaritan" was itself a sign of cautious times. During the struggles of the 1930s—in which Katie had been deeply involved—she was most often referred to as "Sister," not a "Samaritan." By the 1950s, "Sister," with its associations with subversion and communism, may have seemed too provocative a term. "Good Samaritan," on the other hand, both depoliticized and repoliticized DeRorre.[55] A Good Samaritan often did religious work. And while this allusion scarcely reflected Katie's hostile relationship to institutional religion, comrades claimed that her deeds were done in the true spirit of a Christian ethic. "Among her intimates, she often expressed perplexity at the immense division which exists among the religious denominations, and their failure to practice in the way of their doctrinal teachings," Battuello remembered.[56] The mayor of the city even read from Proverbs about the virtuous woman.

Others linked Katie to Mary and Joseph: "A Mississippi poet wrote that Southern Illinois . . . had never produced a Joseph, alluding to Joseph leading Mary to Bethlehem. That is true but it produced a Katie."[57] The soup kitchen work DeRorre did was also called saintly. She had helped to feed children regardless of their race, creed, or national origin or their parents' union affiliation in a way that would be familiar to "Jesus in Israel and St. Francis in Romany," reported the *Collinsville Herald*.[58] In his card, ACLU leader Roger Baldwin waxed eloquent about Katie: "If courage is the essence of freedom . . . and if compassion for your fellow men is the virtue which makes life meaningful, yours is blessed beyond most."[59]

During the cold war, "Good Samaritan" had become an expansive label for America in light of its new internationalism and imperialism. Diplomatic historian Emily Rosenberg has written insightfully that multiple components of Henry Luce's "American Century" had reinvigorated an international outlook, including the belief that the United States was "becoming the Good Samaritan to the entire world in times of hunger and need."[60] Calling DeRorre a Good Samaritan allowed 1.5- and second-generation transnationals to connect their radicalism with the emerging Americanization of the world. The organizers of Sister Katie Day might have had this in mind—they certainly knew the 1950s rhetoric and used it as they emerged from the Red Scare of the immediate postwar years.

The memories pasted in the scrapbook and read aloud at the party combined a sense of immigrant identity, the role that women played in the radical movements of the past, and American patriotic ideals about the present. Attorney L. P. Harris had mined coal with Katie's father, Felix Bianco. Harris's card to DeRorre paid "my deepest respects and fondest and best wishes to that girl who deserved the respect and esteem of the coal miners of Illinois." Harris wrote the note as much for Katie as for the audience and the public, who, he knew, would hear about the event through media reports. He found it important to emphasize both Italian heritage and American values. Katie's "father was a fine Italian immigrant to this country," Harris remembered, "a conscientious hard worker. . . . And no immigrant from any country was ever more deserving [of] the respect of the American people than was Felix Bianco." In particular, Baldwin echoed the sentiment of assimilation: "I have cherished the memory of you as one of the rare pioneers . . . in the good fight for our American freedoms." In May 1956, when Representative Melvin Price entered Sister Katie Day in the *Congressional Record,* he noted, "Mr. Speaker . . . Mrs. Catherine DeRorre . . . wife of an immigrant and daughter of immigrant parents . . . is a legend." He reminded others on the House floor that day that miners were a "special breed." "In every nation of the western world, even in the nations behind the Iron Curtain, miners have been in the forefront of every struggle for social justice. The men have not maintained their spirit without help and encouragement of women." Master of ceremonies Zeidler described Katie as exemplifying the American work ethic. He told the group that "'Sister Katie' . . . is a symbol of the pioneer woman of the industrial age. . . . She is 'one of the least of these, my brethren,' who along with inventors and builders and statesmen, bring the changes that make a kinder, fairer world." [61] The committee also spelled out its hopes. They were "proud to have participated in such an affair. . . . May our children and our children's children build a better world!" John and Betty Williams felt that remembering Katie was about both past and present. They wrote, "How wonderful it is . . . to have a friend who remembers—and who's not too busy to sit and speak of the past, and plan the future, and make him feel again that he is part of the things he loved so much."[62]

Though most of the Progressives (well versed in organizing tactics and the art of persuasion) wrote a single narrative for the times in which they lived, some of her comrades interpreted Katie in different ways, even in 1956. DeRorre's friend Craig Easton from Andover, Massachusetts, told a story that stood apart from the new vision of cold war internationalism and Americanization. "Just a few lines to salute you in this, your day," Easton wrote. "You stood up and was [*sic*] counted in the never ending battle to eke out just a nice bit more from our Oppressors. I am proud to have been associated with you and the others of the *left wing*[,] the best group in the USA. Persons who knew what *Nationalism is and was.* They thought along International lines."[63]

The celebration for Katie allowed friends and family to fortify the memories of their political heyday. These memories also reflected a reevaluation of women's labor in the movement. The planning committee that conceived of Sister Katie Day was all male ("Gerry and the rest of the boys," according to Krueger). These men had imbibed some of the cold war rhetoric, which, according to Elaine Tyler May, connected "ideology and the domestic revival" in the 1950s.[64] Women like Katie, "who throughout the turbulent lives of the miners, have stood by their side, have kept the faith, women who have kept the hearth of home warm and secure, held the brood together, and fed and clothed and nursed and bedded and schooled the children, and when the going was tough, real tough, they were to take the battle lines to uphold the right of the men to work not as vassals but as freemen."[65] As they recalled the roles their wives, mothers, and daughters had played in their lives, they glorified women in the past. But their praise songs did something more. Scholar Chiou-Ling Yeh has traced the feminization of Chinese New Year celebrations in the 1950s. Just as Chinese American men highlighted female subjectivity in this festival, Katie's male comrades chose to emphasize the domestic realm of their movements at the same time.[66]

Katie at Home

A month after Sister Katie Day, the *East St. Louis Journal* featured DeRorre in a story titled "Mostaccioli Her Specialty."[67] With a photo of Katie in her kitchen, the article framed her life in domestic terms as part of a diasporic private sphere in three ways.

First, the article's telling of Katie's past feminized the labor movement by highlighting the role of women in the miners' struggle. Standing in her kitchen, DeRorre recalled the fight between the United Mine Workers and the Progressive Miners of America. "There were things that had to be done, so I helped do them," she said. Katie hinted at women's importance: "Someone had to get things started—things couldn't go on as they had been."[68]

Second, the story focused on her home as the site of her politics. Some of Katie's recipes were included in the article, which seemed at first to downplay Katie's radicalism. But perhaps Katie herself intentionally highlighted the recipes. Read another way, the recipes actually show the domestication of the radical diaspora. Was Katie asked by the reporter to give recipes? Or did Katie include them as a means of underscoring how important her home had been in feeding her politics? Either way, the journalist echoed the words of Representative Price in the *Congressional Record,* noting, "Her home was always a haven for the afflicted."[69]

Finally, the piece drew attention to the transnational links that Katie continued to have with Italy. *Mostaccioli,* "her most popular dish," was served to the PMA Women's Auxiliary's Executive Board "in her home." She did not prepare *bagna calda* (a hot dip made with anchovies, garlic, and olive oil) for the board, but that too was an important component of her cooking. "Now that's a Dish!" Katie laughed, and the journalist reported further that "Mrs. DeRorre said that one must acquire a taste for this dish, but one may be assured that almost all Italian families serve it at least once a year." Cooking Italian meals for her guests and writing letters to her husband's family in Italy (because she was the one who knew how to write in Italian) was the way Katie, like other 1.5 transnationals, maintained links in the diaspora.[70]

In his perceptive equation of American identity with cultural ownership, David Roediger uses the image of "white houses" to unravel the complicated racial assimilation of the second generation.[71] Immigrant homes—boardinghouses, single-family dwellings, apartment flats, company shacks—were the nexus of family life and intimate relationships, and the place where ideas about America and the world were formed and rejected. Katie DeRorre had made her home a center of working-class community. It was in this setting where she wrote letters to kin in Italy, where she held meetings for the Women's Auxiliaries of the Progressive Miners (which welcomed African Americans) and the Alpina Dogali Society (which required all members to be Caucasian), where she fed people, and where she fashioned her American identity as a self-proclaimed left winger.[72] Relatives and friends who visited found refuge, political activism, and love. They, along with Katie, made the domestic into a political site, albeit in complicated and contradictory ways.

Katie chose not to separate domesticity and activism, and that is what many highlighted when remembering her. By the 1950s, the shifting public and private spheres that May views as part of middle-class life were emerging in working-class communities as well. In neither case was the 1950s home, with all its security, a reproduction of the Victorian private sphere. Memories of Katie's home paint a picture of a kind of third sphere that was physical and psychic. The roots of this third sphere were planted during the Great Depression, when the unemployed could not always meet or organize on the shop floor but had to do so in living rooms and in the hobo camps and at public park benches that too often doubled as public domicile for the poorest.

Descriptions of Katie's home provided opportunities to link personal and political reflections. In the card that Agnes Burns Wieck sent in 1956, she wrote: "As I greet you on this gala day, my thoughts go back to the time when first we met—almost a quarter of a century ago. Late at night, but it was never too late for a special supper in Katie's kitchen in DuQuoin." She continued, "Do you remember how your house used to overflow with women fleeing violence from meetings where they were denied their civil liberties? Like refugees we came. The little house on Walnut Street was transformed into a mansion of hospitality."[73] From the mid-nineteenth century through the 1950s, the home was seen as a refuge—a place to escape from the world. But Katie's home was not simply an escape. It was also an alternative. Thyra Edwards told Wieck in a letter that "the recollection of 'Sister Katie' conjured up the most thrilling experience in my life. I always have a feeling of deep gratitude to you and Tom Tippett for making it possible."[74] Agnes explained the meaning of the thrill in her greeting card to Katie and the partygoers.

> Do you remember the night I arrived with a Negro woman to help win the wives of our colored brothers? I hadn't asked you, and it could have proved disastrous. Somehow we all knew that Sister Katie was ever ready to go beyond the call of duty . . . . Soon you were visiting the DuQuoin schools, colored and white, to welcome every child who wished it, to a hot lunch those cold winter days. I can still see that ramshackle house your Auxiliary made into a soup Kitchen. To me it was like a shrine. For a little while, in labor's history, white and colored families shared true equality.[75]

In a newspaper article, Edwards remembered the food and solidarity of the DeRorre house too. "Katie's dining room was crowded with Negro miners and we talked P.M.A. as we lunched [on] French endive salad, Italian spaghetti, dolci paste and pickled wild mushrooms." Later on, "Katie's front parlor was full past capacity, with the wives of Negro Miners. And over cups of Katie's steaming coffee we talked Woman's Auxiliary."[76] In her role as an activist, DeRorre served as an example. She made her home a union hall that became part of the struggle for interethnic and interracial working-class justice, and she hoped others would follow her lead. For Battuello, who described the DeRorre house as a "cathedral," "her world" was a place where "there could be neither surplus [n]or surcease as long as there was one hungry child or one exploited miner."[77]

People experienced an alternative possibility to capitalist patriarchal authoritarianism in Katie's home that started with relationships between family members. In Katie's domestic world, the maternal was not necessarily the core. And motherhood was not sanctified (as in earlier generations' cult of domesticity and maternalism). What made good mothers was the same thing that made good workers—not biology but fairness. DeRorre believed that women should not focus on penny-pinching to help their households but rather "better their conditions to fight for more relief and a higher budget, not to pinch them down to show how far the dollar can be extend[ed]. The point is to point out the necessities of life in the growing children, pregnancy and nursing mothers."[78] To be sure, DeRorre was conscious of her role as a homemaker. But she was also a radical, and the work she performed in the third sphere bridged the private and public spaces that structured coal towns around family life and industry. In "Mostaccioli Her Specialty," she was adamant that the special relationships of her family had helped her define who she was and how she acted. "Family life has not been neglected," the *East St. Louis Journal* told its readers. "It is with deep pride, that she tells that it was the children and her husband who made possible her service to others."[79] Norman Thomas, associate editor of the *Nation*, shared DeRorre's viewpoint, noting, "I shall never forget the night I spent at your house and the extraordinary impression that you and your family made on me."[80]

Katie consciously rejected the model of the authoritarian family while at the same time retaining her Italian identity and ties. That embrace of Italian identity pushed her to refine her racial, gender, and class identities.

Conclusion

The identity of transnationals such as Katie DeRorre might be described as slippery. Their lives encompass the territoriality of immigration and the emotional ties of immigrant homes. They slip in and out of identities, highlighting and hiding different pieces of themselves at different moments and in different places. In the 1930s, the immigrant Left openly expressed the "culture of unity" at the workplace, making internationalist commitments part of an American identity. By the 1950s, their children relied on a domesticated version of their parents' diasporic community. The domestication of the diaspora highlighted a feminized radicalism in which the home, rather than the workplace, was at the forefront. Katie (and the memory of her) became an embodiment of that domesticated diaspora.

Despite the fact that historians have failed to find her—no scholarly work mentions her existence—DeRorre is significant.[81] Her life underscores how women have brought the public, private, and international worlds together in their homes, communities, and identities. The circumstances of DeRorre's migration and settlement offer an alternative narrative to the dominant urban immigration histories, which tend to ignore the realities of rural industrial settings and the middle years of the twentieth century. Katie's life also allows us to piece together how Italian radicals continued their work in the interwar period by melding Italian networks with expanding racially and ideologically diverse communities; by accommodating the increasingly restrictionist, conservative, and nationalist tenor of the cold war years; and by making the home a place where politics could live even in hostile times.

While the shrines to Mother Jones and the Virden martyrs are well-known sites, the one for Katie DeRorre has remained unknown even to labor historians. DeRorre cared about such shrines, and we should too. Pat Ansboury, a union "brother," remembered that on one occasion Katie (who did not have a phone in her home) came to his house at five o'clock in the morning, accompanied by her children in a car full of flowers. DeRorre invited Ansboury "on a trip to the graves of our brothers in southern Illinois who gave their lives for the cause of the Progressive Miners of America." Ansboury wrote, "It was a sad occasion, indeed. At each grave Katie laid a beautiful spray of red and pink roses. . . . Katie read the union obituary as she placed the flowers on the graves. . . . As Katie looked back when we were leaving she said: 'Good bye, our heroes. We will never forget.'"[82]

"Italian" Motherhood and Marriage through Oral Narratives

Calculating Babies

CHANGING ACCOUNTS OF FERTILITY DECISIONS AMONG ITALIANS IN MELBOURNE, AUSTRALIA

Pavla Miller

> "The Pope says: 'Multiply!' But no one understands mathematics in Italy."
>
> "The young people of today don't make sacrifices."
>
> "I think that the young people of today are more intelligent than all of us. We worked hard before; why should they?"

This chapter approaches the diasporic private sphere from a particularly intimate angle: discussions about making babies with three generations of Italian Australians.[1] In both Italy and Australia, fertility behavior signifies a much larger complex of issues concerning civility, security, respectability, and honor (see Pojmann's chapter). Among Italians themselves, "breeding like rabbits" has become associated with the past, with the south, and with poverty and improvident loss of control. Among Australians, these features were for a long time attributed to *all* Italians and helped justify disdain of "wogs."[2] More recently, the fact that fertility rates in Mediterranean countries have fallen below reproduction, and those of first- and second-generation Italians in Australia appear to be below those of other ethnic groups, has inspired a rethinking of mainstream demographic theory.[3] In reflecting on these changes, one of the core tools that scholars, professionals, and laypeople all tend to reach for is the concept of altruism.

Notions of altruism and property transmission between generations, so significant to demographic analyses, are also among the core conceptual tools in anthropology: Some of the classic publications in this discipline have charted culturally specific structures of social relations through in-depth analyses of giving.[4] This capacity to provide insights into wider social arrangements through analyses of personal lives helps account for the recent resurgence of theoretical interest in altruism and gifts and overlaps with the focus on transnational intimacies and the diasporic private sphere, which are the subject of this volume.[5] Both theoretical perspectives provide useful approaches to questions tackled in this chapter: Does reciprocity in the exchange of gifts and services provide a counterpoint to the uneven development of welfare states and the neoliberal emphasis on individual responsibility? Is it the mainstay of informal economies? Are different positions on these issues at the core of cultural differences between Italians and their Anglo counterparts, women and men, different social classes, different generational cohorts, or Italian residents of differently organized welfare states? How can changes from more communal and family-oriented notions of self to more individualistic ones be understood within this larger social context?

Although fewer than one in twenty Italians who left their country between 1946 and 1975 found their way to Australia, at 5 percent of the population, people of Italian descent today represent the largest non-Anglo immigrant group.[6] The fifty people I spoke to were not selected with statistical accuracy in mind but are broadly representative of postwar Italian immigrants in Melbourne. Around a quarter were grandparents when interviewed—women and men who came to Australia as single young adults or married couples with small children in the 1950s and 1960s, and who now have adult grandchildren. Most came from regions of severe unemployment and underemployment, many from villages devastated by war. Almost all were from peasant-worker backgrounds, participated in chain migration, and took on a series of blue-collar jobs after arriving in Australia. Over a third were parents at the time of the interviews—mostly people who came to Australia in the 1950s and 1960s as children or who were born shortly after their mothers' arrival and now have established families of their own (although four arrived as middle-class adults at the tail end of Italian immigration to Australia in the 1970s and 1980s). Over half of this group worked in blue-collar jobs; the rest were teachers or other white-collar workers. The remaining interviewees were adult children, mostly unmarried second- or third-generation Italian Australians under twenty-five, nearly all of whom worked in white-collar jobs or were studying to enter the professions. For a number of reasons, my sample did not include those who remained in Australia but were considered to have failed in their immigration project—although they did figure in most family stories.

In the 1950s and 1960s, Australia offered something simply not available in Italy: an abundance of work, however arduous and badly paid; expanding suburbs; and a banking system that facilitated home ownership. It was what is best described as a breadwinner welfare state and had a polity intolerant of cultural diversity. An English-speaking man was generally able to earn enough to support a wife who worked only in the home. Social services were built around housewives' full-time devotion to housekeeping and child care and made little allowance for those who did not speak English. Like most other foreigners, Italian men and women were recruited to fill the menial jobs that native-born Australians and immigrants from Britain vacated. Here, men's pay was below that required to maintain a family with three children in "modest comfort." But if men took two jobs rather than one, and their wives another, even people who came only with their suitcases could purchase a home—and with it the security and dignity they dreamed of.

Among the grandparents and parents I spoke to, these constraints provided a clearly articulated framework for the way they lived and recounted their lives, and a straightforward recipe for achieving security. This shared recipe, most believed, had a lot to do with Italian traditions. Because not all proved equal in following the recipe, a number of respondents qualified their references to tradition by identifying it with particular families and individuals. Illustrating anthropologists' routine distinction between valued norms and actual behavior, stories of the remarkable altruism of some relatives were counterposed to the selfishness of others, accounts of success to those of wasted resources and opportunities, luck to misfortune, the frugal and sensible customs of one's own town to the ridiculous and slothful practices of another. Importantly, one measure of the success of such working-class familist strategy was abandonment of many of the practices that made it possible. What was, in effect, the migration of children into a different social class entailed a number of risks, systematic changes of everyday practices and attitudes, and logical shifts. One of the most marked changes—and contradictions—entailed the calculation of how many babies to have, and when.

Grandparents and Calculating How Many Babies to Have

> "What reason is there to marry if you don't have kids?"
>
> "If there is no fruit . . . a family is nothing."
>
> "The family's like . . . if you take something . . . like a garden . . . without flowers. . . . The children are like flowers. That's it."
>
> "Having no children is like burnt-out candles."

To the grandparents, born and socialized in Italy, there was no question about whether to have children—that, after all, was the purpose of marriage. However, control over the number and spacing of babies was an inseparable part of the migration process. Not one of the grandparents I interviewed claimed to have had access to reliable methods of contraception. Nonetheless, a form of thinking best described as Malthusian calculus, a meticulous concern with balancing people and resources, with mobilizing and channeling all available energy to the greatest effect, permeated all conversations about establishing a family in Australia. Women and men did not always agree on the precise number of children to have, and there was much bitterness about some husbands' carelessness, but all agreed that too many children, at the wrong time, could completely undermine their life projects. Back in Italy, many noted, it used to make sense to have many children, because they would begin to pay for their keep and perhaps bring in extra money or food by the time they were ten or twelve. This, after all, was what many of the informants themselves did when they were young. But even there, things began to change in the 1930s and 1940s; the emigrants were making the same choices regarding family size as the pioneers of the demographic transition at home.[7]

The grandparents explained that it was desirable but not always possible to delay having the first child and to space the second and third. But all agreed that it was necessary to stop when the right balance between children and resources was reached. In a Sicilian village in the 1950s, one grandmother recalled, people would say: "Oh, be careful, don't have too many kids, because they'll cost money to have them, and there's a lot of responsibility [that] goes with having children"—although "no one really told you what to do." For emigrants, the concerns were arguably more acute. As sixty-eight-year-old Mrs. de Torre explained, "I came from a big family and I thought two were enough because I remember the poverty. . . . When there was a big family they didn't go to school. . . . [In Australia] if there wasn't the help of the wife . . . you couldn't get ahead. . . . My husband worked for the railways . . . so we thought two were enough."

Similarly, Mr. Trioli, turning to his adult daughter, recalled: "Well, at that time, as you remember, we had two of you. We had a lot of problems because we had to go to work. You by yourself go to school. When you consider all this . . . you say: 'Better we stop.' We got to sacrifice. . . . They got to sacrifice." His daughter chimed in: "We had to grow up on our own." In another interview, Mr. Trioli went into greater detail:

> We start with nothing, as you understand. Most of the people come with a suitcase. . . . And when you start with a suitcase and you buy house, wife, kids, car—how are you going to do all of this? Gonna work and save. . . . The wife gotta work. And I got to work. We have three or four kids. My wages wouldn't be enough to buy a house. Not today, not yesterday, never. . . . If she can't go to work, we got to live on my wages. And my wage won't be able to do that. That's why we stop. Okay. First of all we know what a bigger family means because I come from [a family of] six, she comes from [a family of] five.

His wife emphasized their lack of child care: "In the beginning here . . . we suffered, things were hard because . . . I needed to go to work. We had to leave [small children] with other people. And it was because of this that I stopped having more children."

For young immigrant couples in the 1950s and 1960s, not only the number but the timing of births was crucially important. For several women with two or three children, a husband's clumsiness or failure to exercise adequate self-control in the timing of conceptions still rankles—and occasionally startles their adult children. One grandmother declared with feeling to a group of acquaintances in the presence of her daughter:

> The first night I became pregnant. I didn't have a chance to think if I wanted it or not! . . . The second came because he came. . . . I didn't want him. And the third came because she came and I didn't want her either. . . . Not because I didn't like children . . . not because I didn't love them—and I still love them. Because I only just arrived from Italy, I didn't even have a spoon to eat with and I wanted to go to work and then I was going to have my kids. But phew, phew.

Since the child care costs for three toddlers made wage work uneconomic, seventy-year-old Mrs. Paventi supplemented the household income by caring for up to ten children of other working mothers: "I used to go crazy sometimes," she recalled, "but I did it and that's all."

In other families, the husband's decision to stop making babies, taken some three or four decades ago, remains an issue. The women asserted that while they themselves were ready to meet challenges head on, the men were fearful of added responsibilities. As eighty-four-year-old Mrs. Lucchesi put it, "With the first [child] I felt like a queen. . . . The second came along and the third—I didn't regret it. I would have liked another but my husband didn't want any more, so. . . . He's the boss." Asked for his opinion, her husband gave an indication of the harsh choices he faced:

> Nothing to reply, because . . . if I were to, the reply would be so long. . . . In reality those that I had for me was . . . the grandest thing—better than that. . . . Because my possibilities weren't enough to enable me to have a big family . . . because I knew what I was going up against, which I was proven correct in the end. I emigrated on my own. . . . So if I had

had [the responsibility of] a family of seven children on my shoulders, of course, I would not have been able to emigrate. . . . I would not have been able to change our way of life . . . to give a better way of life to my children. . . . Instead in this way we were okay.

In virtually every conversation regarding babies, parents and grandparents noted that it was a sin to "refuse a child" once it was conceived. Not one respondent mentioned anyone who had an abortion. Yet, as anthropologists and historians routinely stress, the frequency of proscription often indicates the persistence of forbidden social practices. Three forms of evidence support this speculation. Some respondents mentioned the desperation of their mothers and grandmothers when confronted with an unwanted pregnancy. Others described, with great intensity, circumstances in which such a pregnancy represented a calamity for a family. Finally, there is evidence that in the 1950s and 1960s many immigrant women did resort to backyard abortions. As the Italian interpreter in the largest maternity hospital in Melbourne recalled:

I had a lot of migrant women begging me to ask a doctor to terminate a pregnancy. That was heartbreaking too—because they had four children. And the idea was for her to go to work in a factory to be able to help her husband put a deposit on a house or pay off their fare. Terrible—so much debt! And all of a sudden she was expecting and she'd kneel down and beg the doctor. Nothing doing. Absolutely no. So what happened? Because of that I was forever at emergency department with miscarriages. They'd never admit they'd interfered or it was interfered God knows where—backyard abortions. They all denied it—they push a table, they lift a mattress, they had a fall, but in fact they were abortions.[8]

While the grandparents with whom I spoke had tended to calculate how many babies to have in light of limited resources, some also valued small families as a mark of progress and civilization. As Mrs. Paventi put it, "No . . . it's not dependent on the money. It depends on your thoughts about this. Why do we need to have a lot of children? When you have two, three, that's plenty, isn't that so? Not to have eleven kids as used to happen. Because those of past generations didn't use any preventatives, that's why they had so many." The respondents underscored their success restricting their family size by mentioning less successful contemporaries who, it was repeatedly pointed out, "bred like rabbits."

For a generation without reliable means of contraception, success in limiting pregnancies tended to be a matter of pride; those who mastered the art of withdrawal regarded it as a valuable skill worth recommending to others.[9] Asked how they managed to stop having more once they decided two babies were enough, seventy-one-year-old Sam recounted with relish:

Simple. Very, very simple. . . . We find the way not to do it and that's it. . . . If I got land and I put a seed in the land, anything could grow. Wild grass. Okay? If I go in the backyard there and put seeds of the tomato, what'd come up? Tomato plant, yeah. If I don't put tomato seed in the backyard, nothing will grow. The same thing man and woman—if no seed, nothing will grow. That's it. . . . Easy to solve. Easy. Years ago, I don't know why they can't work it out.

A friendship group of older working-class Italian women broke out in bawdy hilarity when discussing how to stop having babies. "If you always leave it inside," fifty-five-year-old Rosa declared, "then you will always be pregnant, and every nine months you will have a child." After giving the whole group a stern lecture on the fact that not only abortion but contraception was a sin, because "if you do *marcia in dietro,*[10] that is the holy spirit of God who gives you the child," seventy-five-year-old Adriana made a point of saying that she herself had only two children. Asked how she and her husband managed, she made a gesture suggesting that they too used *marcia in dietro*—upon which the whole group broke up laughing.

Today, some grandparents' pride in their success in family limitation is mitigated by their sense of regret that they did not, after all, make more children—for company, for support, and because "the children are the respect of the parents." According to Angela, a first-generation grandmother, "Our generation didn't have more kids because of the work, because, at least in my times, women had to work; you know, we came here with the suitcases, and we had to work. But back then you didn't think about those things, you only had one or so. I regret it now not having made four, because now I am alone, my kids got married and I am alone now."

Children, Money, and Time

Today, Italian Australian parents and children agree with the grandparents that family planning remains all important (and many express profound gratitude that they now have access to reliable contraception). However, their calculations start from different premises and are based on subtly different logic. In the first place, the flow of resources between parents and children is perceived to have changed. Laura, a second-generation mother of three small children whose family came from Rome, put it succinctly: "Back then they believed that if they had lots of children that in their old age they would be looked after. However, these days, I, for example, have three children and I'm always thinking about what I can and can't give them. I could never have nine children because I could never give them what they needed." Fifty-year-old Rosa, a mother whose family came from the Abruzzo region, agreed. Her family were country people who worked the land.

> The more people, kids, they had to help out, the easier it was. They led a very simple life, there was not a question of which school to send their children to. . . . The only thing you had to worry about was feeding them, and just clothing them. . . . In Aunty Maria's case . . . she told me that when she was ten, her parents would go and work on the fields and she would be in charge of her three younger brothers. She would cook, clean, do everything for them. And I think that's why a lot of people had a lot of kids too, because the older ones sort of took charge.

Similarly, sixty-one-year-old Sam, a grandfather, explained that "once upon a time when you had a child who was ten years old, you sent him to work, not to school. . . . The children were sent to work because . . . the boss would give the children something to eat—not because he would have given them a wage to take home. For the father, it was sufficient that they got a plate of spaghetti and something to eat at night." Today, he concluded, "it's all different. Everything is changed. Today . . . the children work, they help the parents, but they don't give." In all, this amounts to "a radical change, a very radical change," in attitude. Had he considered the situation of elderly grandparents,

Sam himself would have qualified his statement. All the parents and grandparents feel that once they become frail and old, they are entitled to—and to some extent receive—their children's care and assistance.

In addition, while living standards have vastly improved, the cost of children has risen even faster. As a result, much wealthier parents calculate that they can afford fewer babies. As fifty-four-year-old Sandra (first generation, mother) put it, "It's not that people don't want to have children because it doesn't please them to have children; it is too expensive to have children. You need to send them to school. You need to dress them. You need to give them sport, exercise, restaurants—all of these things that they want. And if I go to work and I don't have enough money to give them all of these things? And so, this is what I think. I have five children, but if I had to have children today, I'd only have two. Maximum three—but no more."

Education assumes particular significance in these calculations. Those who cannot afford private school and university fees, some of the grandchildren argued, simply should not have kids.[11] As twenty-one-year-old Amanda put it, "You'd want to be able to give them opportunities in terms of school. . . . If you can't afford it, then . . . that's my view anyway. I'd like to send my kid to [private] school and try and give 'em a head start sort of thing." A friend added, "Yeah, that's pretty much a general kind of view, isn't it?" "No conflicts there," she concluded, after everyone in the group of young adults agreed. Among those I interviewed, the only people who felt that their children and grandchildren did not need to attend private schools, and indeed actively condemned the contemporary expansion of the private school sector in Australia, were a university-educated couple who emigrated from Italy in the late 1960s to escape political developments they disliked, and whose own abundant cultural capital supplemented the lessons of state schoolteachers. This couple had a more relaxed attitude about material possessions, and a keen sense of the value of time. As Mrs. Bardini (grandmother, first generation) put it, "They say to bring up kids you need a lot of money—for me that's not true. . . . For me to give to a child my time is better than giving money." Noting that, with education, "you don't need a symbol to show what you are," the Bardinis used a sort of handy reckoner: "You judge . . . the ignorance of the people like a tree. . . . You count the number of rings."

This relationship between money and intergenerational distribution and experience of time constituted the second core theme of interviewees' stories. Whether grandparents, parents, or children, none of the people I interviewed had any illusions about intensive mothering in the past. Their own parents and grandparents, they noted, were brought up by the oldest sister, an aunt, a grandmother, or else the nuns. In many cases, their own children were brought up by grandparents. Similarly, while a successful strategy of limiting the number of children in a family facilitated the path to economic security, it made little allowance for intensive child rearing. As Mr. Trioli's Australian-born forty-two-year-old daughter pointed out, most children of immigrants had to grow up on their own. Asked whether she and her siblings were able to spend much time with their parents when they were young, a fifty-year-old teacher explained that her mother had worked the evening shift and her father a morning shift in the same workplace, and her father in addition had a job at a truck farm on Saturdays and Sundays. As a result, "we'd go out sometimes and stuff, but we weren't really close knit. . . . We ate our meals together, we worked together. But not as close as . . . I would have liked." Yet many believed that urgency and difficulty strengthened family bonds. As fifty-three-year-old Franca (first generation, mother) put it in her characteristically blunt fashion, "poverty brings a family closer together because it means you need one another's support. . . . These days children go out and they don't give a fuck."

Many of the parents and grandparents interviewed set concerns about time in the context of an intense bodily experience of the flows and depletion of emotional energy. As one grandfather put it, "my father's father had thirteen. How did he have thirteen children? He must have had a lot of time on his hands! You need time to have children. To educate them, see them being born, wash them, feed them." Asked whether she would have had more children if she "inherited a million dollars," his Australian-born daughter explained: "The money wouldn't have made any difference. No, children take a lot of your time. They drain you! It's very tiring. . . . Some people are strong and they can have more . . . but . . . no." A family friend, a forty-five-year-old office manager (second generation, mother), agreed. "You wouldn't be able to give that time . . . that attention . . . dedication. I think that I would expect to be able to give to my children." This was in part because of the difficulty of balancing career and family life, but mainly because "you need a lot of energy, emotional energy, to be able to have a lot of children because every child has its . . . individualities, its problems. . . . And the more kids you have, the more bad times you have . . . the more emotion."

After Chiara's third child was born, she too decided "there was no way I was going to have any more children. . . . And the reason . . . you can't give of yourself to so many children." Her husband, who came to Australia as a teenager, a teacher like his wife, agreed: "Not in these modern times. Perhaps in another time," and, against his mother's vociferous opposition, "went to the doctor's" for a vasectomy.

Lucia (second generation), the mother of two and a teacher, agreed with her husband that the most important thing to give children is time: "The biggest thing I think you spend, you can give your kid, is your time. . . . The time that you give them, you can teach them things, you can do all sorts of things . . . develop a relationship. But the most important thing, you can guide them along the path—and I don't think money can do that." Paying others to care for one's children, both spouses agreed, "defeats the purpose entirely." "I wouldn't have anymore," the husband concluded. "I would rather just do the job properly with these two." Asked how they mixed paid work, marriage, and children, Lucia responded without hesitation: "It's called grandparents. . . . If we didn't have grandparents and the twins had to be put in full-time care, you would seriously have to think about the viability of returning to work." She added that most of the people in their Italian Australian friendship group also "basically rely on grandparents."

Quality time, it turned out, was significant not just for the children but for the parents as well. As Lucia explained at length:

> I think that, given your education, you basically become more aware of yourself as an individual and the importance of personal responsibility, like, you know, when you have a child, and you've had a life before becoming a mother, you can't negate the fact that you were once a teacher, a social worker, a psychologist, a lawyer. . . . And so when you

> have a lot of children . . . and you have to basically do away with all the activities that you once . . . partook in . . . that sort of creates resentment because you've lost a whole portion of your life.

Asked what advice she would give her own children, she responded: "Don't have six kids. . . . You're exhausted, you're stressed, and, you know, you don't have any quality time for yourself. . . . Because, just as you have parental responsibilities, you've also got a responsibility to yourself."

Significantly, a busy part-time teacher and mother (second generation) who found her own company difficult to cope with saw children as one means of alleviating a focus on oneself and the "problems associated with a kind of selfish sort of lifestyle." The good things about having children, she explained, is that "your days are very full. You don't have time to think about yourself very much and your own little problems and your depressions. . . . And I like being kept busy. . . . I'm the type of person who cannot sit through a movie, you know, because I get irritated, let alone, you know, sort of staring at four walls. No . . . I couldn't imagine a life with no children."

What Price Altruism?

According to the grandparents' stories, successful settlement in Australia was impossible without selfless striving toward family prosperity. Certainly, some were said to succeed through rapacious exploitation of their compatriots as slumlords or sweatshop owners. For most, however, not only did a life of hardship and sacrifice bring material possessions and a better life for the children; altruism was ennobling in itself. Made meaningful through the Christian virtues of charity and sacrifice and a subaltern ethic of mutual interdependence, both the process of settlement in Australia and its results brought respect to a family. Yet altruism was not simply an attribute of women, Italians, or grandparents but had a clear class dimension. Seventy-five-year-old Giuseppa Di Caluzzi (first generation, grandmother) described the landowners in Italy as so harsh and unfeeling that "they were like traitors." She attributed her father's altruism to a stint in America, her husband's to practical religion, and her own to a knack for finding compatriots jobs and sticking up for their rights. Her brother-in-law (first generation, grandfather) extended the logic of mutual help and interdependence: "For every success . . . any person have to have help. Someone to help you. The other way you get nowhere. . . . Doesn't matter how intelligent you are . . . doesn't matter how strong you are . . . you won't. Oh, you get somewhere, but not where you should be."

An additional shared dimension of the logic of altruism was revealed in the Lucchesi family's discussion of backbreaking work made possible by the right attitude and mutual assistance of friends and relatives that establishment in Australia entailed. "How many days," fifty-year-old Nello (first generation, father) pointed out. "I did two days in one from 6 A.M. to 3:30 P.M. and then until 11 P.M." "With a good attitude—everything depended on a good attitude," his wife confirmed. "Nothing was too difficult—you just kept on going," the grandmother, also a first-generation Italian, joined in. "Because you were younger?" a friend asked. "No," she replied. "There was the right attitude . . . for the love of your family. . . . And it didn't weigh on us." Her Italian-born daughter Luciana added, "Here was much insecurity and it was important to have a home—that's why work didn't scare you." In Italy, she went on to explain, people could fall back on family support—however humble—when in need. In Australia, lack of power, recognition, and rights made it necessary to assemble an alternative form of capital:

> There was a great necessity to have a form of capital which you could call your own because . . . we have an identity but we don't have a power. . . . Here in Australia we had to work for it. . . . That's why work and family were the same thing. . . . That's what gives you the strength to combine work and family—giving them the same level of importance. . . . That's the strength which allows you to work twenty-four hours.

In complete agreement with her parents and friends, Luciana explained: "The reason's simple . . . there was no choice. You didn't have security; that's why you did it." Her friend Maura added another common theme: "And then the language was the difficulty." Several others continued: "It wasn't our homeland." "It wasn't our home at that time." Now, in contrast, "it's our home. . . . We have laid our roots." Luciana concluded by restating what this means in the specific context of Australian immigration policy and welfare system:

> There's a certain security because you have created your home. We have our home. You have some money in the bank, which allows you to . . . be more secure. You have a bit of English. . . . The system is more accommodating. . . . There's an interpreter. . . . You can ask [for] information. You are no longer in the dark. . . . The rights, for we Italians, were not there. They were only for the Australians because they had access to that information. We didn't have . . . no one made an effort to tell you your rights. Instead today you know you have them. You're better educated.

Measuring Success

Whether they explained their hard work and the assistance they gave and received as individual peculiarities or collective attributes, the grandparents' strategy of achieving economic security would have been immediately recognizable to the diaspora of Italian working-class emigrants. In gross statistical terms, it has also been remarkably successful. Among those born in Australia to Italian parents between 1952 and 1961, 83.4 percent were living in their own home in 1986, 85.1 percent in 1991, and 87.5 percent in 1996. The corresponding figures for third-generation Australians were considerably lower: 63.4, 69.7, and 74.4 percent, respectively. If success is measured by educational qualifications, the results are more complex. An earlier pattern of investing in sons' but not daughters' schooling (alongside reliance on daughters' housework contributions) has recently given way to a strong emphasis on the education of children of both genders. For those ages twenty-two to twenty-four whose parents were both born in Italy, 20 percent of men and 33.8 percent of women held a degree or a diploma, as opposed to 16.4 percent and 27.9 percent, respectively, for third-generation Australians.[12] There is also far less class-based disparity in educational participation of twenty-to twenty-one-year-old second-generation Italian Australians than among their third-generation counterparts. In 2002, among third-generation men and women, 30.8 percent of sons and 40.1 percent of daughters of men in managerial positions and professional occupations, but only 6.7 percent of sons and 11.1 percent daughters of men working in "other (mainly unskilled) occupations," attended university. Among the sons and daughters of Italian-born fathers, the disparity was far smaller: 25.9 percent of sons and 36.4 percent of daughters of men in managerial positions and professional occupations were university students, compared to 18.2 percent of sons and 21.3 percent of daughters of those in "other occupations."[13]

The implications of these figures for strategies of family formation are profound: While the investment in educational qualifications for all Australians is increasing, that made by people of Italian background is increasing faster. In addition, while more women than men in Australia now participate in formal education among Italians, this trend in favor of female educational participation is even stronger. Rather than assist their mothers with housekeeping, child care, and helping grandparents, daughters, like their brothers, might well be becoming net consumers of domestic services. As Olivia, a first-year marketing student, explained:

> My grandparents . . . on both sides . . . they give anything, they don't want to bother you kind of thing. It's "I'll do it for you because I want to do it for you," you know . . . "Have this" and "You eat more." My dad also, like, . . . he doesn't want, like, my brother or I to get up [to help]. Like, actually, it's more—he will let me do a bit more but [he tells] my brother, "Stay," you know . . . and . . . my mom has sacrificed a lot—she has gone without a lot for us, and for my brother and I, and I suppose I would probably do the same for my kids as well, because I'd want them to have the things that I've had.

These changes acquire additional significance in a rapidly changing economic climate. The Italian peasant-worker grandparents who arrived in Australia in the 1950s and 1960s landed in an industrializing country with critical shortages of manual workers; their children entered the workforce at a time when unemployment was low. There were several stories of sons who dropped out of school, found menial jobs, and eventually worked up to positions of responsibility. For the grandchildren, the risks are greater. In a deindustrializing economy with high levels of youth unemployment, there are fewer possibilities for those who "fall in with the wrong crowd." In all, it seems that as the material and educational resources required to bring up children have increased, so has the amount of temporal and emotional investment needed to help children develop suitable characters.

To the chorus of "This is bad" and "This is the worst thing" from her friends, fifty-five-year-old Rosa from Trieste recounted: "I have seen many, many families in which children have been brought up in cotton wool.[14] . . . And then they reach the age of fifteen or sixteen years and they say to their parents, 'Shut up.' . . . These children who have been brought up in cotton wool, if they run into bad company, they end up following them." Interviewees seemed to have similar ideas about how to prevent such calamities. The refrain "They must not be given things on a silver platter" ran through most of the interviews. The most straightforward way to teach children the value of money, and of gifts in general, all agreed, is to get them to save up their money to pay for half of the cost of a toy, piece of clothing, or car and then give them the other half. When it comes to marriage, some shrewd parents similarly demanded that a young couple "prove their marriage works" before they agreed to contribute money toward a new house.

Everyone Is an Individual

"Does the Italo-Australian wife and mother see herself as an individual, or is she so deeply entrenched in her roles of nurturer that her own needs and aspirations have gradually lost ground to an increasingly demanding home environment?"[15] A study written in 1988 that typifies the approach adopted at the time by Australian professionals dealing with immigrants and is discussed further in the following pages suggests that at least for some women, this is the case.[16]

Altruism and reciprocity work best when underpinned by a dense texture of social sanctions, when they are seen as unambiguous social norms. Like anthropologists, those I interviewed made clear distinctions between valued attributes and people's behavior.[17] Some relatives—and especially mothers and grandmothers—gave without end. Other mothers gave but complained. Amanda, a twenty-one-year-old social work student from what she described as an unusually close and loving family, provided three contrasting examples:

> I look at my grandma and she's, like, sacrificed every single aspect of herself for her family so easily and so quickly, and I think it depends on the individual. . . . Some women are like that. But I look at my other grandmother and she's not like that. She's very materialistic . . . she prefers her money . . . but my mom, she's sacrificed heaps, like, she does, like, everything—she cooks meals, she spends all her spare time washing and ironing, and whatever, like, but she always whinges [complains] about it. She voices it more and if she's unsatisfied with something, she's prepared to voice it, and we help her and things like that. But I don't think it is something that my grandma would voice.

Amanda, who has held a series of poorly paid jobs in the hospitality industry while studying, declares she has absolutely no work ethic and would love to marry someone rich so she can stay home and be a housewife. She fully realizes this too involves menial tasks, but they would be for her own family, not for a boss. Asked what she herself would sacrifice for her children, she was certain that there were certain things but could not think of an example aside from her free time and hobbies.

When successful, grandparents' altruistic devotion to family welfare was repaid with the profound respect of children and neighbors and made it possible for their children and grandchildren to lead markedly different lives. This difference, repeatedly mentioned by all interviewees, involves new forms of emotional economy. For parents with professional qualifications, in particular, selflessness competed with a felt necessity to maintain a measure of healthy focus on oneself. Only in a couple of cases did women equate personal happiness and mental health with the ability to give of themselves to others; to a few, the "compulsory altruism" of mothers acquired the unmistakable marks of patriarchal service and exploitation. Not only did the grandchildren require greater material and emotional resources and appear more difficult to control, but they represented a riskier emotional investment. Many felt uneasy when receiving a gift, and both were perceived to be and stated that they were indeed less appreciative of generosity and self-denial—not least because many of them set out to lead markedly different lives from those of their elders. Indeed, the requirements of higher education, professional work, and business all make altruism less rational and individualism more appropriate. This dynamic is compounded by the desire of many young women to become professionals rather than housewives.

Whatever the cause, the younger people I interviewed have a more individualist notion of the self, experience themselves as more independent and less connected to others than their elders, and have a sophisticated understanding of the transactional problems this causes. As Amanda's friend Elisa, a twenty-four-year-old social work student, put it:

> My mother . . . who is the sort of person that gives until she's got . . . she keeps giving forever . . . and ever . . . and she doesn't have a limit. . . . That's her value system, and it works well for her. I mean, I don't know if I can make a judgment if it works well for her, but that's the way she's . . . understood motherhood to be. . . . And I come from a value where I think that, you know, you should have time for yourself and make time for yourself, and so sometimes I, when . . . I feel my mother's giving too much, I'll say, "Stop." And then she'll sort of, like, um . . . be upset by that—the fact that I won't receive. So it's weird, so then sometimes I have to take things even though I feel uncomfortable doing it because it will please her. So, it's a weird thing. I think we come from different expectations and values of what is . . . if I refuse . . . say, if she wants to buy me something and I say, "No, that's your money. You take it for yourself. I don't want it." We'll get into a huge argument . . .'cause she wants to buy me something. She wants to give me something . . . and I feel like, you know, "No, I can do it for myself. Look after yourself."

Understandably, many of the grandmothers who built their identity around a life of sacrifice wonder if their investment will be reciprocated. Mrs. Paventi raised children without any assistance from her husband. She also cooked, ironed, and washed for her brother and sister-in-law and her cousin. When her daughter got married, she cooked and ironed for the young couple, gave them money, and helped raise their children. She still makes special dishes for the whole family. Asked, "And have they done something for you?" she answered: "Up to now—no. Because I haven't had the need. Because otherwise they'd do it, wouldn't they? But for the time being, I still do everything for them. You know, sometimes I'll ask them to take me to the doctor. You know, this sort of thing they do for me. And that's all." Later, she added: "They haven't done anything for me yet. However, I think they'll do it if the need arises. I hope."

While the grandmothers and many of the mothers, born and raised in working-class families, tended to regard self-sacrificing altruism as both a necessity and a virtue, many of the helping professionals they encountered contrasted it unfavorably with what they regarded as a more modern, more individualistic, and healthier form of self. This reading of feminine altruism as a mental health issue comes out clearly in a report on interviews with sixty Italian-born middle-aged women living in Melbourne. Written in 1988, the report is structured around the contrast between different forms of identity. The first, individual and modern, characterizes modern Australian society and is necessary for mental and physical health. The second, characterized by self-abnegation and the absence of distinctive individuality, was at the root of the many problems of the women in the study.[18] The women, Gucciardo and Romanin concluded, "came across as generally unassertive and largely abnegating of their own individual needs and desires."[19] This, they believed, was influenced by a number of factors, among them an unclear and undeveloped perception of self, unresolved individual aspirations frustrated by the priority role of being a wife and mother first and foremost, a culturally negative judgment of women's out-of-the-family interests and activities, the encouragement of socially submissive and passive behavior in women by a traditionally conservative social environment, the deprivation in Australia of the more intimate woman-to-woman support network that the women previously experienced within extended family and village networks in Italy, daily confrontation with the freer and more individualistic behavior of women in Australian society, persistence of outdated beliefs that are no longer relevant in today's society, and an inability to resolve family conflicts by honestly asserting differing opinions and seeking a workable solution.

Most of the female participants in Gucciardo and Romanin's study described themselves as self-sacrificing, and when asked to give an opinion on the "average Australian woman," all answered that they regarded her as putting her own welfare before anything else and none wished to be more like her. Children, all agreed, "should respect their parents, because especially we Italians have done and continue to do everything for them. We work hard to give them a good future." Like my interviewees, the women felt they had a rightful entitlement to deference, obedience, and caregiving from their children. Many of the children the women invested in, it seemed, broke the rules of altruistic exchange and obligation. As Gucciardo and Romanin put it, "overall, the women appeared to feel threatened by their children's sense of independence, self-expression, and freedom of choice." Having endured a life of sacrifice, the women sought repayment—or at least explicit recognition—of a tangible debt. The authors recommended switching to an alternative form of emotional economy, one that emphasized "healthy individualism," and equated exemplary altruism with poor mental health.

Conclusion: A Time of Reckoning

In Australia today, one in ten of the general population is sixty-five years or older, compared to four in ten among immigrants born in Italy. Italian-born working-class grandparents, who incurred the physical and emotional injuries of a lifetime of strenuous work, now confront an underfunded public health system. While much has been done by government agencies and Italian welfare organizations to improve services for elderly immigrants, the public health and welfare provisions in Australia, as in most other OECD countries, have deteriorated over the last decade. Even where subsidized support, domiciliary, and therapeutic services exist, there is evidence that many elderly Italian Australians cannot access them. In addition, like their children and grandchildren, many object to the purchase of personal services.[20] Among the elderly Italian Australians I spoke to, daily visits and phone calls from children and grandchildren—or less frequent but far more expensive long-distance and international calls—constituted a shared and tangible currency of contentment and sacrifice repaid. Yet most explained that the success of their children's and grandchildren's *sistemazione* (setting up a home and family) as educated individuals makes such dedication less likely; daughters' professional lives in particular leave little time for intensive care of the elderly.[21] In other words, the very success of the Italian immigrants' life projects, marked by the migration of daughters into white-collar jobs (such as receptionist and nurses) and granddaughters into professional jobs (such as accountants and lawyers), entails complex contradictions. One of the most painful ones is the loosening of the bonds of altruism between the young and the old, whether through a "healthy focus on the self" or the dynamics of a busy professional life. Yet, particularly during a period of welfare state retrenchment, interviewees in all three generations still felt that their "Italian" propensity to pool family resources provided a comparative social and economic—and emotional—advantage.

In calculating the number of babies to have, Italian emigrants and their descendants deal with more than personal peculiarities and family relationships; they confront relations of altruistic exchange between dissimilar demographic groups, in differently structured systems of welfare. I opened the chapter with a quip from one of the second-generation mothers I interviewed. "The pope says: 'Multiply!' But no one understands mathematics in Italy." The problem goes further. There are different forms of calculus in the heads of family members, in learned discourses, and in polities—and no easy way of reconciling them. In comprehending and negotiating these issues, the people I interviewed in effect (and without using the technical terms) employed notions of transnational relationships and diasporic private spheres. They compare the logics of making babies in Italy and in Australia during different historical periods; routinely link ethnicity, political economy, morality, and sexuality; explain who they are with reference to a dense transnational network of kin and compatriots; and at times take part in long-distance relationships of economic support and care.

Mothering Contradictory Diasporas

NEGOTIATION OF TRADITIONAL MOTHERHOOD ROLES AMONG ITALIAN MIGRANT WOMEN IN IRELAND

Carla De Tona

Le mamme italiane have a privileged role in Italian culture: As humble and proud nurturers, they are powerful makers not only of the destiny of their children but also of their families and collectivities. However, Italian motherhood also represents an "ingenious system to maintain female subordination."[1] Motherhood involves contradictory forces for women—both gender constraints and gender opportunities—that in migration are differently articulated but remain essential to the construction of a collective sense of belonging. The feminist scholarship on the Italian diaspora stresses how Italian migrant women almost invariably take on the lion's share of care work and kin work for their families.[2] They do so not just as women but *as mothers*. Motherhood allows women to manage the very intimate politics of their migrant families, which implies gaining power and some degree of freedom. However, these same roles can disempower and limit women, as traditional female kinship networks of support are disrupted and additional expectations are placed on women to reproduce the symbolic and cultural boundaries of their collectivities.

Following from this, I want to explore in this chapter how in Ireland, Italian migrant women's roles as mothers are valued according to gender ideologies. Unpacking the often taken-for-granted roles of women as mothers helps us to grasp the gendered implications of migration, which, along with women's experiences in general, tend to be relatively invisible and marginalized. Motherhood functions in this sense as a magnifying lens that exposes the dynamics of gendered migrations, particularly the coexistence of gender empowerment and disempowerment. This is often most visible in the intergenerational conflicts that result from the changes that migration brings.

I studied Italian migrant women in Ireland for my doctoral research between 2000 and 2006. I conducted participant observation and individual and group open-ended in-depth interviews with twenty-nine Italian migrant women (between the ages of fourteen and seventy-five) of different regional, educational, and class backgrounds and with different histories of migration (first, second, and third generation). Their personal narratives revealed complex and meaningful realities that challenge the existing discourses and representations of Italian migrants and Italian migrant women in Ireland as passive and unproblematic. The question of motherhood emerged spontaneously during my discussions with Italian migrant women. The narratives of motherhood were central to the women's self-ascription and self-positioning during the interview process and highlighted the permeability of the "public" and "private" spheres as I want to suggest in the following sections, and the contradictory implications of motherhood and diaspora.

The Myth of Motherhood in Italian Culture and in the Italian Diaspora

It is not surprising that motherhood emerges as a central issue in Italian migrant women's lives in Ireland. Contemporary Western cultures conflate femininity and maternity, often to "idealize and denigrate both."[3] In the European context, motherhood seems universally a key identity for women in a way that fatherhood is still hardly capable of being for men.[4] Men's identities are less structured around their roles as fathers; women, on the other hand, are inescapably implicated by their biological destiny as child bearers in the impressive structural power of the myth of motherhood.[5] In Italy, this myth is fueled by "a giant collective wish for perfect mothering. It is bolstered by a religion that gave us the Virgin Mary, nursery tales that supplied us with fairy godmothers."[6] The ideology that accompanies the myth of the perfect mother conceives of "one way to mother, one style of exclusive, bonded, full time mothering."[7] The rigidity and one-sidedness of this model are inevitably a source of contradictions, and they clash with the "superwoman" model of the gendered expectations of modernity.[8]

Motherhood is particularly potent in Italian discourses and traditions. It is the center of interest of powerful institutions, including ecclesiastical hierarchies, state governments, science, and the legal system.[9] These institutions have influenced demographic politics and social representations of motherhood, competing for the primacy to impose their ideologies over women's bodies and their reproductive capacities.[10] Moreover, the popular and much-cherished stereotype of the *Italiani mammoni* (Italian mama's boys and girls) highlights not only the attachment of Italian children to their mothers but also how a collective nationalistic sense of belonging is intrinsically related to women as the makers of identity and the keepers of its boundaries (as argued by Anthias and Yuval-Davis).[11] With their heroic and self-sacrificing model, Italian women as mothers have come to embody the nation, its ethos, its future, and its cultural and symbolic boundaries.

Nationalism impinges on motherhood in times of crisis, when women's primary duty becomes motherhood—an agenda particularly explicit in Italy during the fascist regime with its "fascist maternalism."[12] However, motherhood is still clearly steeped in contemporary nationalist ideologies, functioning as a terrain for the articulation of a hegemonic Italianness—visible also in how sexuality and mothering models of immigrant women in Italy are monitored and controlled to conform to the Italian national requirements.[13]

Traditionally constrained in private spheres of action and limited in the expression they can give their subjectivities, women (especially those of a particular age or generation, as noted by Miller in this volume) are socialized to sacrifice their social personae, to become full-time, omnipresent, and devoted mothers.[14] Objectified as an ideological battlefield, motherhood has turned Italian women into "silent and powerless *mamme sacrificali*" (sacrificial mothers) who avenge their "social nullity [by] taking possession of their children."[15] However, women are not simply victims but also agents and may also be agents of domination, given that "we all have the capacity to act in ways that oppress, dominate, wound (whether or not the power [to do so] is institutionalized)."[16] These roles that women play are not merely imposed on them: "Women actively participate in the process of reproducing and modifying their roles as well as being actively involved in controlling other women."[17]

Therefore, it is not surprising that motherhood can become a tool of domination, and in fact, as Boneschi suggests, children are often held as Italian mothers' private property and remain dependent on them as long as possible.[18] Thus motherhood "lends itself to the enactment of a social drama" wherein other women's domination could easily occur as a means of exercising and maintaining control by women.[19] Within these "contradictory impulses" of motherhood lies the potential for Italian migrant women to practice a "politics of domination," especially over their daughters,[20] who are often socialized to perform "appropriate" gender behaviors that limit their own and other women's power and authority.[21]

The myths and contradictions of motherhood have a deeper resonance and a stronger resilience in migrants' lives because of the ways that national stereotypes of Italy—and the role of women in performing and enacting them—figure in the genesis of ethno-national and diasporic identities. At the same time, motherhood arises as the foundation for public activism for Italian migrant women and as a form of passive resistance to the hegemonic discourses of womanhood.[22]

I turn now to analyze how the "social drama" of motherhood manifests in the lives of Italian migrant women in Ireland. The Italian migrant women to whom I spoke experience *as mothers* many pressures and constraints because they are expected to reproduce, biologically and symbolically, the boundaries of their ethno-national community at a time when such boundaries are under threat and most fragile. The "proper" behavior of migrant women is seen as central to the integrity of the migrant group's identity,[23] and in order to keep the group's boundaries intact, women are generally under strict social surveillance. Moreover, mothers are usually given full responsibility for their daughters' education, and for controlling them and passing on to them knowledge of traditional gender models.

At the same time, *as women* they are empowered in the liminality of the differing gender normativities that they come to experience. Discrepancies among differing sets of gender norms of the migrant group and of the country of destination create a space in which to negotiate women's emancipation while new modes of gender identification become possible. Inevitably, migrant women's empowered gendered positions overlap—and often clash—with their role as mothers and its collective implications. It became evident during my research in Ireland that motherhood is a source of often irreconcilable conflicts between how women are expected to act and behave and how they are enabled to behave in diaspora, both as mothers and daughters.[24] How are the tensions of these contradictory forces of motherhood played out? The discussion and extracts of narratives presented in the following pages reveal the nuances of gender and motherhood in the context of migration.

The "Long" and "Silent" Italian Migration to Ireland

A consistent presence of Italians in Ireland dates back to the turn of the twentieth century and is characterized by a continual proliferation of chain migrations and transnational networks. The number of Italian migrants living in Ireland in 1981 was 1,351,[25] and in 2002, according to the Irish census, was 3,770, of whom 2,145 were male and 1,625 female.[26] The limitations of these figures are demonstrated, however, by the data in the Italian Embassy in Dublin, which in 2006, on the eve of the first vote by Italian emigrants in Italian political elections, showed a much higher figure of 10,767 Italian migrants (5,857 male and 4,910 female) registered in its lists.

Although not large compared to other migratory groups in Ireland, Italian migrants are exceptional in several ways. They arrived in and continued to migrate to Ireland at a time when Irish people were emigrating en masse. Their migration has been singularly long term, continuing for over a century. In addition, a single origin and occupation dominated among the earliest waves, resulting in the formation of a village-based diaspora[27] from the Frosinone province, a region located between Naples and Rome. According to unofficial sources, in the late 1980s people from Frosinone formed 70 to 80 percent of the total population of Italian residents in Ireland. These migrants imported and literally monopolized the business of fish-and-chips takeout shops in Ireland, which, anecdotal evidence suggests, they learned during their diasporic wandering in Great Britain. Notably, in Ireland, fish and chips came to signify Italianness par excellence. It still does today, even though in the 1990s, new and numerically more consistent waves of Italian migrants arrived in Ireland, taking advantage of the social and economic changes of the so-called Celtic Tiger economic boom. These waves of Italian migrants differed in regional, class, social, and occupational backgrounds. In the last decade, in particular, IT and finance professionals, service- and third-sector workers, food industry entrepreneurs, and students have been numerous.[28]

Most of the limited accounts about Italian migrant women in Ireland focus on the families of the early migrants and depict them as silent and passive followers of their men, subjected to and objectified by masculinist ideologies. More recent representations focus on the entrepreneurial qualities of Italian migrant women, which in part resonate with the strenuous efforts of Irish hegemonies to present Ireland as a successful multicultural society.[29] In both cases, these representations are limited. My research shows that Italian migrant women have interesting and more complex stories to tell about themselves. An analysis of their gendered experiences can also tell us a great deal about the migrant groups at large.

In this chapter, I focus on three groups of migrant women. The first group comprises recently arrived, mostly young, professional women (between twenty and thirty-five years of age) who migrated to Ireland between 1990 and 2006—at the time this research was conducted. These women left Italy independently and most are prepared to move elsewhere but do not necessarily wish to return to Italy. The second group is that of the long-settled migrants, made up of women who migrated to Ireland between the 1960s and the 1980s. Typically, these women either are semi- or highly skilled professionals who initially arrived in Ireland to study English and often married Irish men or are linked to the Frosinone chain migrations. The third group, the village-based diaspora, comprises families of the early waves of migration generally originating in the Frosinone province; these families arrived in Ireland at the turn of the twentieth century and later and include first-, second-, and third-generation migrants.

"Until I Became a Mother": Italian Mothers in Ireland

In my open-ended interviews with these three groups of Italian migrant women in Ireland, motherhood emerges as the most relevant of all female social personae and pervades women's lives independently of their actual biological status as mothers. This is evident, for example, in the narrative of Elena, a sixty-year-old second-generation Italian migrant whose family belongs to the Frosinone chain migration. When I asked Elena to talk about herself, she explained that she endured many constraints and, as she put it, "wasn't allowed to go out until further mother" (until she became a mother), but "well, I have never been a mother, but these [her friends and relatives who took part in the group interview] are. . . . What else? How can I say, I don't know, I have no children of my own, so I don't know."

Elena equates female independence with being a mother, even though, notably, she is not a mother. Motherhood is here a metaphor for womanhood that signifies a rite of passage that grants Elena, *as a woman*, independence and authority. However, this status has a high social price, as womanhood is in turn largely bound by mothering roles. Widowed and with no close relatives in Italy, Elena explained in fact that she spent her days caring for her sister's grandchildren, and there was a strong element of pride and a sense of fulfillment in her stories about her role as a "shared mother."[30] She also noted that for her female friends, "The first thing is their children. Not that the Irish aren't—oh, they are very good, but maybe the Italians have their own way. . . . They spoil their children, spoil the babies."

Elena's narrative is dense with coded messages about Italianness and motherhood: Italian women perform a specific "traditional" motherhood and in so doing they create the boundaries of Italianness vis-à-vis Irishness. The boundaries can, however, also shift, as my doctoral research highlighted, and an attentive analysis of women's narratives further reveals how traditions are subject to innovation. Significantly, it is again women as mothers who have a central role in the transformation and transmission of a shifting Italian diasporic identity.

Elena's association of womanhood with motherhood was common among the Italian women who participated in my research. Miranda, a fifty-five-year-old first-generation migrant woman also from the Frosinone group, lived in the Irish countryside and recounted stories of isolation, hardship, and violence. She shared that her husband used to hit her even "when I was expecting the children" and she "worked till the ninth month." Miranda's emphasis on her pregnant self—in the absence of any other legitimized self—suggests that motherhood is conceived as the ultimate validating status of her social persona. Violence is condemnable because it violates her not merely as a person but as a mother.

Many early-wave migrant women like Elena and Miranda are occupied in the fish-and-chips shops family business. This activity has deeply constrained the lives of both men and women as they work long hours together and late into the night. However, for the women, it directly affects their traditional domesticity, which expands into the back kitchen of the fish-and-chips shops—usually located adjacent to their family homes. The women complain in fact that they work too much and that they were, as Sara put it, "recruited as staff" in Italy by their husbands.

In the early migrant women's families, which were most acutely defined by social class and economic hardship, motherhood assumes even more strongly a totalitarian role: Women's narratives stress that their primary duty is to be mothers, at the cost of their own personal development, education, and careers. Women of the early waves of migration spend a lot of time with their children, and they often lament having little space in which to express their subjectivities outside the context of these relations. For example, Monia notes that "I was in the house most of the time and again through my days and years just looked after the kids and [took] them to school. . . . I just sat quiet there . . . but one thing I regret: I should have learnt English, go[ne] to school, . . . but no! Now I feel so stupid, because my kids have been to college."

The dominant and powerful role of motherhood is present also in the narratives of recent and long-settled migrant women. These women, among whom are many professionals, have had more opportunities to be active outside the sphere of domesticity. However, motherhood is still a primary role that dictates the course of their lives. Consider Franca, for example, a forty-year-old recent migrant who married an Irish man and became an "ethnic entrepreneur" in the Italian food industry. She shared that her life changed once she became a mother. She recalled that when her children were born, "a new course of life started. Everything became more solid. It became more solid, the initial instinct I had, that the most important adventure for me was to build a life in which both my children and I, and after all [my husband] as well, we all could have found, created, a bridge between two cultures [Italy and Ireland], between two lives. . . . In one way all I did afterwards was directed towards this end."

Concetta, a long-settled fifty-year-old professional migrant, also recounted how becoming a mother drastically influenced her life choices, and her children became her "roots." If earlier she was migrating from one country to the other,

> When the children started to come along, and you put them into school, that's what—the children that are born in the new country—what creates the root system. When you are single or you are a couple, you have always that sense of freedom: I can go back to my own land, I can go back to Italy any time I want, but when the children start to arrive, and they are born here, and that's their reality. . . . And by the way they only have a sense of your Italian reality by extension, because of what you teach them, because of what you show them. Because again, the stories that my mother told me, the prayers, the rhymes, the little songs and *dialetto*, I would say [that] since my children are born I would recite the same ones to them. So it was passed on. But by extension, it wasn't as real as it would have been between my mother and myself.

This interview extract sheds light on the power that mothers have to shape the contents of Italian identification largely through practices of narrativity and storytelling, a modus of identity building that is of primary relevance in the context of migration. As Nunzia, a long-settled fifty-year-old migrant put it, while telling stories to their children, women transmit the "origins" and "roots" of their ethno-national groups, but these roots are not "real"; they are changing at every intergenerational act of storytelling. As I have suggested elsewhere, Italian migrant women's practices and acts of narrativity allow for the construction of the shifting boundaries of the diaspora.[31] This capacity, as I want to stress here, is largely based on women's gender roles as mothers. In the intimate spaces of their motherhood, spending more time with their children and being their first acculturating agents, women socialize the future generations of Italians. Their families invest women with power as the main intergenerational transmitters of the family traditions, stories, and sense of identity. Nunzia observed,

> Because it is the woman who is going to bear the child, and your child is born in a country that is not your own, that's away from your own country, . . . your sense of origin is much stronger . . . But I think women are more sensitive to these things; men are more practical. [Men think,] "We are going to live in a foreign land and set up our own lives, and I will work, I will look after the family." We will make this move and then the children are born in the new country and go to school locally, and I think the mother is the one that perhaps has had more time, traditionally, I suppose, to spend more time with the children.

Like Nunzia, other women describe themselves as having a major influence on their children and as powerful actors in relation to their motherhood. However, the power that women gain *as mothers* can signal a loss in relation to other determinants of selfhood *as women*, such as personal freedom, confidence, and educational and career opportunities. These constraints are faced by all the women in my research, whether they are working at home, in the fish-and-chips shops, or elsewhere. The women spoke about a strong sense of guilt about being "too busy" (Franca, Marisa, Giulia) and unable to "care full time" (Livia, Mary) for their children. For example, Giulia regretted that she had no time to help her children with their homework because of her long shifts in the fish-and-chips shop.

A lack of self-confidence was common among the women from the earliest migrant waves; this can be linked to the disempowering roles of women as mothers. Paradoxically, it is against the achievements of their children and particularly of their daughters that these migrant women find a referent for the evaluation of their own limitations. Their children's achievement and the social mobility that comes with it are a source of pride for the women, significant in relation to the working-class ethos that characterizes many of the early waves of migrant groups. However, this intergenerational mobility can simultaneously be a reminder of the older women's own personal constraints and can inflict class injuries[32] on them. When comparing themselves to their daughters, some women revealed a sense of resignation and lack of self-esteem, while others spoke forcefully about the power they hold over their daughters. For example, Mafalda, a forty-five-year-old first-generation migrant from the Frosinone group, explained that she did not like her two adult daughters "to go too wild. Maybe it's because they are girls, you know? . . . I think I am a little bit old fashioned with that. . . . They go to college, they get what they need, whatever, but they have to work, they have to help me. Because they have to see where all this [economic success] came from as well . . . and I am stricter than my husband."

Mafalda seemed proud of her "strictness" and revealed that although she was very generous with her daughters, they had to live under her control. As with other women, the power of motherhood seems to function as a form of compensation for the social invisibility inflicted on Mafalda, who, unlike her daughters, was prevented from receiving an education and getting a job, a lack of opportunity she remarked bitterly on. This very social mechanism of compensation arguably explains the many narratives that emphasize the "strictness" of mothers. Franca, for example, observed also that there is a lot of "pressure on Italian women to be serving, like their mothers, and Italian mothers can be really tough."

The gendered intergenerational tension between mothers and daughters is further complicated by migration. Mothers' authoritarian attitudes are a cultural investment in women's key roles as educators and transmitters of the group's culture and traditions. Several early-wave migrant women spoke about the strong collective pressure to be strict educators, especially of their daughters. Women (mothers as well as daughters, who complain frequently about their mothers being stricter than their fathers) are aware of the ways that women's "proper" and "traditional" behavior embodies the very boundaries of the Italian migrant collectivity. During a group interview, Simona, a second-generation migrant woman from the Frosinone group, talked about this with her aunt, Silvia, who was living in Belgium at the time of the interview.

> Simona: If we wanted to go out, we always asked Daddy; if we asked Mummy, she always said no. [According to her mother] girls have to stay in the house, so we always asked Daddy. Daddy would always say, "Yeah, yeah, yeah."
>
> Silvia: I know, but if something happened to you, whose responsibility is it? Of your mum! Then you understand why she does it, 'cause I am sure that Father has said to Mother sometimes, "Be careful, don't let anything happen to her! Don't let anything happen to her, otherwise it's your fault!" My mother once told me this, after my father had died. . . . Then of course, women have more responsibilities for their daughters.

Daughters of all ages remain under strict social surveillance, which is mostly carried out by powerful mothers and older women acting as shared mothers. These women are required by Italian culture to be responsible for their daughters, and they are assigned authority to do so.

The narrative of Silvia and Simona also suggests that the conflict and ambivalence in mother-child and especially mother-daughter relationships depends on the generational gaps that intersect with the migrant conditions. In Italy, the revolution of moral customs and gender norms of the 1970s created deep generational gaps between mothers and daughters.[33] However, the implications seem most poignant today for the migrants who left Italy before or during those years and are now settled in Ireland. Migrants tend to idealize how things were at the time they left, and they invest in preserving the cultural traditions they left behind as a hallmark of their identity. This cultural defense exacerbates the differences between migrant women and their daughters, who grew up "emancipated" in Irish society.

Recent migrant women are differently implicated in the ambiguities of motherhood. For migrant daughters, the Italian mother is an indispensable "guardian of tradition," keeper of the home, and bearer of language.[34] However, the model of the mother also represents and actualizes the reality from which migrant daughters wish to be distanced. Migration is often a gendered project of emancipation for Italian migrant women in Ireland, a choice that inevitably ends up clashing with the role of their mothers.[35] Marianna, a thirty-year-old Sicilian woman who had recently moved to Ireland, elucidated the complexities of her own case.

> It was always my mother who has always something to say or complain about. Now my father is happy that I moved to Ireland, he is very proud that I work for IBM. My mother still sometimes tries to ask me, "When do you come back? When do you come back?" . . . But when I go back, I am always her little daughter for her. I must stand under the house rules—if I go out I must go back home early and all that. This has left such a mark inside me, because I am a bit unsure, I am not someone with a lot of self-confidence. . . . I always try to be more confident, to trust myself, but then I arrive there, and my mother, in one day, two days, destroys it all! From a psychological point of view, I prefer not to go back to Italy. I prefer to talk to her on the phone, even if on the phone, it's a different story than being there.

In the case of recent migrant women such as Marianna, migration represents a constructive distance from a possessive and powerful mother. Yet the distance is lived with a sense of loss and guilt, an urgent need to return for visits or to keep in touch by phone. Daughters love and respect their mothers but also challenge them in order to break away from gender constraints. If the loss of the daughter to the mother and the loss of the mother to the daughter are the essential female tragedy,[36] then this loss is particularly tragic for migrants. For migrants, the tragedy is that the daughter, who loses the mother, loses also a means of continuity with the past and a keeper of the home in the diaspora.

A linked issue that emerged in the women's narratives is how during migration, female kinship or quasi-kinship networks are disrupted so that women cannot rely on traditional gendered forms of support. The women complained that they feel isolated, and as a result, their mothering roles become a greater challenge. At the same time, as a result of the ease of travel and the relatively short distance between Italy and Ireland, transnational gendered practices of support develop that facilitate their mothering practices. Several women spoke about having to send their children home to Italy (and occasionally to live with relatives in other European countries) alone for a few months or a few years. In several cases, female relatives, often mothers who have retired or remained in Italy, traveled to Ireland to care for their relatives' children. In addition, some of the women claimed to return often to Italy to care for their ailing relatives. Men were almost never mentioned in these narratives of networks of care.

A diasporic motherhood develops along transnational chains of care (as discussed by Baldassar and her collaborators)[37] and involves female relatives almost exclusively. As the main family caregivers, migrant women actualize a form of transnational "shared motherhood," following the blueprint of the migrants' transnational networks. These mothering practices entail other sets of both gendered struggles and gendered opportunities. On the one hand, shared motherhood allows migrant women to find "possibilities for escaping oppressive social codes and a basis for solidarity with other women."[38] Shared mothers' transnational networks allow gendered resources and social capital to flow and be shared among women. For example, women in Italy learn about the lives of women in Ireland and their gender models, and vice versa, and exchange news, information, and the like, practices that allow them to overcome the boundaries and limitations of their ethno-national groups and in many cases allow the women to resist and be subversive. Consider Livia, for example, a seventy-year-old long-settled migrant women who recounted that when Ireland prohibited the sale and importation of contraceptives (the sale of condoms in Ireland was legalized at the end of the 1970s),[39] her grandmother in Italy would send Livia's mother in Ireland letters with news about their family, Italian newspapers, and packets of condoms!

At the same time, transnational shared motherhood reveals the continued presence, "albeit in a transformed way, of gendered social relations that serve to subordinate women."[40] Like many other women, Marisa, a sixty-year-old woman from the early migrant wave, was expected to leave her young children behind in Ireland in the 1980s to go to Italy to help her ailing mother. She felt "split always in half . . . devastated each time I left either Mum or my children alone." This practice continues today, unchanged, as in the case of Cinzia, a twenty-five-year-old recent Sicilian migrant. Cinzia explained that when her father fell sick, she had to leave Ireland for a few months—and put aside her career aspirations—to go to Italy to assist him even though her brother actually lived in her father's hometown in Sicily.

Conclusions

In this chapter I focused on the question of motherhood in the narratives of Italian migrant women in Ireland. Looking at the most intimate of all women's roles, the chapter aimed to analyze migrant women's experiences of motherhood and to unpack the gendered contradictions and tensions of migration (both its enabling and disabling outcomes).

The analysis of women's personal narratives showed that the essentialized acceptance of motherhood functions simultaneously as a protective shelter against the vulnerabilities and changes of migration and as a source of conflicts for women, which is apparent in both how the older migrants (the early-wave migrants and the long-settled migrants) interact with their second-generation migrant daughters and how the more recent migrants interact with their mothers back in Italy. In both cases, the generational gap between mothers and daughters is lived with urgency and intensity; only in the first two groups (the early-wave and long-settled migrants) is the gap actualized in Ireland, while among the most recently arrived migrants, it is lived transnationally.

Looking at the intergenerational tensions associated with changing gender and motherhood roles in the context of migration, I argued that while migration holds the potential to be an emancipatory force for the Italian women in Ireland, simultaneously it works to constrain them. Motherhood plays a key role in the enactment of both the gendered constraints and the gendered opportunities of migration.

While giving power to the migrant women as mothers (especially in the construction of transnational female networks and of a collective identity that offers the Italian families a stable sense of belonging), traditional motherhood roles also signal a loss for the women in relation to other determinants of selfhood (such as personal freedom, education, confidence, and opportunities). At the same time, the Italian migrant women invest in traditional motherhood, seeking commonalities and connections in terms of Italian belonging, but also achieve emancipation and undergo transformations based on the very nature of their gender roles and relations. In other words, Italian migrant women experience conflicts and contradictions (which epitomize the collective ruptures of the diaspora) but also manage to resolve the tensions, particularly through practices of relationality, connectivity, and reciprocity.

My analysis of the intimacies of Italian motherhood in Ireland shows that the tensions between the opposing forces of migration are largely played out between women, and particularly between mothers and daughters. The mother-daughter intimacy creates support and conflict for women, not in a single place (Ireland) but transnationally. This shows also that intimacy (and conflict) across borders holds the potential for transforming notions of motherhood (and gender ideologies) in both Italy and Ireland.

Love Crossing Borders

CHANGING PATTERNS OF COURTSHIP AND GENDER RELATIONS AMONG ITALIAN MIGRANTS IN GERMANY

Yvonne Rieker

Italian immigrants to Germany experienced radical cultural and social changes as a result of their migratory moves. One consequence of these events was a significant change over the course of a generation in attitudes toward romantic love. Perceptions of love and marriage, especially concerning young women, and of gender relations among couples became the subject of serious reevaluation, often characterized by uncertainty and sometimes painful estrangement from traditional values. These attitudinal changes were by no means a linear development following clearly discernible models of modernization. Rather, the highly complex and fragmented process of acculturation to German industrial society was both shaped and limited by the migrants' negotiation of class, gender, and educational structures, through which certain aspects of the host society culture were embraced or transformed while others were not. Still, this settlement process continues to be influenced by Western discourses of romantic love that are usually understood as characteristic of modernity.

Courtship and Marriage in Postwar Italy: Customs and Constraints

Alfredo and Rosalia Giordano started to laugh when asked about their first encounter.[1] "That was really wonderful," Alfredo said, smiling.

> It was Easter 1960. I had migrated to Rome then, where I found work, and I was in my home village for a holiday. I had regular work then including holidays. I would never have been able to find this in the village. I stayed with friends of mine and they were invited to a wedding. I was not invited, but at that time people were not so strict with invitations. Today everyone has a list of guests, but then it was different. I put 500 lire in an envelope and said, "Congratulations, I want to join you," and there I met my wife, who was a guest there too. It worked well between us, but we also had to overcome some difficulties. I had to leave the village two days later—that was the worst thing. But I wouldn't have been allowed to see her anyway; there were strict regulations at that time. But I appreciated that, because if a girl in the village was merely seen talking to a boy, she had a bad reputation, not like here. And then I had to leave; that was hard, I was sad—for three years we only met once a year.

Alfredo Giordano was born in 1941, his wife, Rosalia, in 1946, in Acerenza, Provincia di Potenza. When they first met, he was nineteen and she was fifteen. Their behavior toward each other reveals that the affection they seem to have felt some forty years before has passed the test of time. What to a contemporary observer might seem like a somewhat commonplace romantic tale of an elderly couple's first encounter is in fact rather extraordinary. This was indeed a kind of transgression. They met and talked in public without the permission of the girl's parents and as a result had to cope with some difficulties. But since they were from the same social and geographical background, their families finally agreed to allow them to marry in 1963. Soon afterward they had to migrate from the southern Italian region of Basilicata to Germany in order to earn a living for their young family.

But not all marriages followed this "modern" and transgressive script. Salvatore Palumbo was born in 1932 in Monte S. Angelo, Provincia di Foggia. He worked as a shepherd on unfavorable terms after completing only four years of primary school. In 1957 he and his brother migrated to Germany.[2] When I asked him how he first met his wife, he answered simply: "My wife? I met her when I was eighteen years old. We lived in the same town. We got married in 1955. There is no more to say about it." He seemed a bit surprised by this kind of question. When asked about his life, he concentrated on the harsh living conditions of his youth and the changes brought by his emigration.

Also in contrast to the Giordanos, Nunzia Rivarola, who was born in 1939 in Petralia-Sottana, Provincia di Palermo, told me, a little plaintively, that the man who would eventually become her husband had come to their Sicilian village looking for a wife during his vacation.

> I was married in 1966. In 1965 I became engaged. My fiancé grew up in my village too; we knew his family. I was always obedient to my parents, I agreed to whatever they told me. I was not willful or stubborn. My grandfather knew him, and he told my mother, told my parents, "I am able to give her a piece of bread," meaning as a dowry for me and my husband. We became engaged. After a week he went back to Germany and after a year we celebrated our wedding. A fortnight later we went to Germany. I have been here since then.

The relationships described here were all subject to strict rules governing the meetings of teenage boys and girls. The parents usually took the lead in arranging marriages, especially for their daughters. At the time, it was difficult for romance to develop, and the situation was particularly problematic for women. In the absence of any viable alternatives, they were obliged to marry for economic as well as social reasons. Lack of employment and norms surrounding honor and shame were additional constituting factors. Thus, the narrative of Nunzia Rivarola can be read as indicative of a social pattern. It is, with some minor variations, the story of many women living in southern Italy in the 1950s and 1960s. The interviewees usually interpreted the regulation of women's opportunities at that time as normal. This does not mean they did not harbor ambivalent feelings about these social mores. Nunzia Rivarola, for example, told me after the tape recorder was switched off that she was "already" twenty-seven when she got married and that she had very few opportunities to make a living for herself in the village. She emphasized rather sorrowfully that she had always *belonged* to someone:

first to her parents, then to her husband. She made no further comment on this, aware as she was that changes in social rules had come too late for her. She wanted me to understand this, but it was too painful for her to allow it to be recorded.

Caterina Rivarola was born in 1940 in Alimena, and her husband, Danilo, in 1939 in the neighboring village of Petralia, Provincia di Palermo. When I asked them how they became acquainted, Caterina said, somewhat defiantly, "Well, I only saw him once before the wedding." Danilo related calmly: "Yes, in 1961 I came from Italy to this place . . . and it was here that I met her uncle, her mother's brother. . . . He told me he came from Alimena, a village about twenty kilometers from mine. We shared a room here; he told me about his niece and said: 'If you think you would like her, you can have her.'"

Caterina, who until now had spoken Italian to me, interjected in German: "Men are stupid, aren't they?" She was clearly aware of the fact that by contemporary standards of behavior her experience seemed to be an extremely humiliating one. I asked Caterina whether she had been asked for her opinion. She replied: "Well, at first I wasn't asked anything. I had to wait until I saw him. . . . In those days things were not the way they are now."

Caterina came to a halt and seemed to ponder how best to explain her feelings. "He was on holiday, and I had to decide quickly whether to say yes or no, but I did not actually want this, which was only natural, but then as time went on, of course . . ." She stopped again, and I asked her whether she would have preferred not to marry. Caterina again tried to answer in a way that would allow me, and perhaps herself, to understand this difficult decision:

> Well, in principle, I did want to get married, but you know, it's only . . . not . . . how can I express this—I did not want to be forced to make a decision in such a hurry. I wanted to take my time. . . . He is from another village, you see, he did not live together with me in my village, and you didn't know anything about this person. Who he is, you had to have correct information about him. . . . And then we agreed, and in the following year we got married, but we hadn't had a chance to get acquainted, to get to know each other better. We had only known each other for three weeks.

During the course of the interview, some tension developed between the couple, and Danilo finally left the apartment to work in the garden, where, as he informed me, he spent a lot of time. After awhile Caterina returned to the subject of her marriage, describing the void between herself and her husband and deploring the fact that she had married someone she had not gotten to know well beforehand. After her father's death, she related, her brother had to take responsibility for the family. He wanted to get married himself, and so he had to ensure that both of his sisters were placed in the care of other men. For a number of reasons he was not able to maintain two families.

"It is like this," Caterina explained to me:

> In those days, people said, "This man works, he doesn't drink, he isn't a gambler, he doesn't loaf around." My mother said that if I liked him . . . well, in fact, it was my brother who told me. . . . This is the way things were for me because I had no father. If you are a man, you can go and work. But where could women find jobs? There were no factories

> in our villages, and anyway we were only allowed to work at home. And so my brother told me that it would be much better if I would agree to marry, better for my mother and for me. Afterward he would be able to get married himself. . . . I didn't say yes at once. I said, "We will see," and then people said, "He is an ordinary guy." . . . I wanted to talk about it—but never mind, whether it was this man or another one, it would make no difference.

It seems obvious that it was distressing for Caterina to tell me about the circumstances and the first years of her marriage. But she spoke quite frankly, especially after her husband left the room. She had probably told the story to her friend Rita, because it was Rita who had urged me to speak to Caterina, insisting that she was a woman who "knew" things that would be important to me.

Rita Giordano, Rosalia Giordano's sister-in-law, was also born in Acerenza in 1939, the daughter of a destitute day laborer. She told me that keeping her honor and respectability became extremely difficult, mostly because of the loss of her mother early in her life. The rules for unmarried women, she explained, were rigid. Everybody would talk in a critical and deprecating way about a girl born to an impoverished family, growing up without respectable female supervision and with a father who was often away for work. She was regarded as an outsider in the village. Even today she is still enraged by social rules she describes as unjust and prejudiced.

> Yes, we lived outside the village in the countryside, and although I was a very little girl, I had to take care of my mother, who was very ill until she died in my arms. She had a heart defect, and so I was able to attend school only for one year, there was no alternative. . . . There were so many things that I could not cope with. My sister, for example—it was even worse for her than for me. . . . My father went to Africa for awhile to try and earn some money. We children were left alone at that point.

After she had been silent for a long time, I said: "That must have been very hard!" She continued:

> Yes, and it was such a small village, everybody stared at you, because you had no mother and you were not allowed to speak. . . . You know, you always have to walk straight and upright; if you appear crooked, everyone will say, "Look, she has no mother, she isn't careful about the way she conducts herself, she talks to men." That was awful and that's why I got married so young. In those days people thought, when she's married, she's off the street—you cannot comprehend this today, but that's what it was like then.

Again Rita stopped talking and was visibly upset. After awhile, I asked her: "Did you feel better then, coming to Germany?" She answered: "Yes, I felt better . . . on the other hand I always told my children, 'Don't marry so young.' Because in those days, you understood nothing, nothing at all. I did not understand what happened, really, I didn't know anything."

Rita was interrupted by her husband, who showed me pictures of their village, and after talking for awhile about the sights and the landscape, I asked both Rita and Antonio how they had come to know each other. Antonio explained: "Well, you go out on the street, a small village, we didn't even have a cinema, everyone knows everyone else.

Yes, I would like to put it like this, people talk." Rita interjected: "Everything happened very quickly, all his relatives said, 'Oh, so you will take her, will you,' and so on. This is normal, and you are not allowed to see each other or talk to each other. . . . We have been married for forty years now, I was seventeen when I got married, and at first it was, . . . it was really . . . really . . ." After a long pause she continued: "But that is how it was. And all in all it was a nice time, too."[3]

Rita grew up in poverty and as an outsider. She was low in the village's social hierarchy and she took the first opportunity to flee these conditions. She stressed that she never wanted to return to live in Italy.

Migration and Marriage: Increased Freedom for Women?

Anthropological studies of southern Italy emphasize the fact that in the 1940s and 1950s, male honor was extremely important.[4] The balance of power in relations between the sexes tended to favor men. Female behavior—defined on a continuum ranging from shameful to obedient—was strictly regulated in order to maintain male honor. Male and female spheres were separated. A woman was not permitted to engage in private conversation with a man, not even her fiancé. Women were seen almost as property belonging to their fathers and husbands.

The worshipping of the Madonna as a female ideal in religious terms found its secular equivalent in the mother-son relationship, unlike the relationship between wife and husband, which had no such enhancement in the symbolic value system.[5] In order for a woman to gain a respectable position in the social hierarchy, it was necessary for her to get married. Although it was hardly possible for a man to maintain a close relationship with a respectable woman without marrying her, his social status was not vulnerable if he engaged in any shameful behavior with women. His reputation might be damaged, and he might be criticized by family members or acquaintances, but the reaction to real or alleged misbehavior among women was most likely to result in social isolation or even violence. Men could decide to stay unmarried, to go to brothels, or to migrate alone and seek their luck in a new country because of their economic independence. In fact, a rather high percentage of Italian male immigrants were unmarried at the time of their arrival in Germany. Some of them migrated to escape not only social conditions perceived as intolerable but also unhappy marriages or engagements. Once husbands emigrated, their wives in southern Italy were rarely able to force them to provide financial support.[6]

In comparison with overseas immigration, Italian migration to European countries was possible even for impoverished day laborers, for hardly any financial resources were necessary to travel to France, Switzerland, or Germany. Living conditions were harsh and even hunger was not unknown in the Mezzogiorno in the postwar period. According to a micro-study on a village in Calabria in the 1950s and 1960s, European migration enabled the poor to get married.[7] Previously women without any means usually had to stay unmarried and often had a hard time, as they were entirely dependent on their families and were often perceived as an unwelcome burden. In addition, emigration provided opportunities for those on the margins of society, such as illegitimate children. It was also an alternative for those who rebelled against the still almost feudal southern Italian system of land ownership.[8] After riots and bids to occupy land that left the population of the Mezzogiorno without any hope for social change, the long tradition of emigration once again came to the minds of many.

Migration was an option for women, but only as wives of male emigrants, which enabled them to escape antiquated social rules and to extend their personal freedom, primarily through access to the labor market.[9] Partly as a result of these newfound freedoms, the solidarity of the migrant couple, in comparison to the traditional distribution of power, albeit unequal, became significant among extended family in southern Italy. In the closer relationship of a married couple resulting from the experiences of migration and settlement in a new land, the balance of power could change, enhancing the position of the woman. Emigration in many ways led the way toward individuality, a capitalistic economy, and mass consumption. This process took place in southern Italy years later and—in respect to the change of the family structure—in different ways. Individuality even in today's southern Italian society is restricted by an economically based need to maintain extended family structures that result in more traditional gender roles.[10]

Some women in southern Italy were well aware of these possibilities and urged their husbands to emigrate. I was told such a story, for example, by Angela Ruggeri, who was born in Favara, Provincia di Agricento, in 1955. She came to Germany in 1974. Her father was not happy with her decision and wanted her to stay with her family, fearing what might happen as a result of a supposed lack of social control while she was in a strange country alone with her husband. In Germany she completed her education by completing the terza media (high school). As a child, Rosaria Lo Cascio accompanied her parents to the German Ruhr Area. The family returned to Sicily when she was fourteen years old. She eventually married a labor migrant and returned to Germany with her husband. She worked for years in a steel mill because she liked being financially independent.

However positive these examples might seem, traditional gender roles and family hierarchies persisted. Caterina Rivarola, who shared with me the difficult conditions of her marriage, also mentioned the absence of her female family members, which was especially painful in difficult times. She said that she would have preferred to stay in Sicily and see her husband only during his vacations. Today marital ties among migrants are, of course, associated with romantic love. But the women I interviewed did not need to travel to Germany to learn what romantic love is.

The idea of romantic love has long been circulated in southern Italy through folk songs and folktales, but most of all through the opera. In many descriptions of festivals, the interviewees emphasized the pleasure they took in the singers' interpretations of famous Italian opera arias. Films of love stories were also brought to the villages in southern Italy and were shown in public places. Notions of romantic love might have been harbored by many, even when marriage was most often planned and arranged mainly with regard to practical considerations. This behavior was quite common in peasant societies.[11] Love was thought of as belonging to the world of fiction, sometimes as wishful thinking, rather than reality. It was certainly not regarded as an emotion on which one would actually act. In spite of these conditions, love was present as an idea, or perhaps as a dream, and it could motivate what others took to be severe transgressions of social rules.

Asked how she became acquainted with her husband, Maddalena Battaglia, born in 1934, narrated in an impressive manner a tale of romantic love and outside interferences:

> My husband was from my village. Actually I got to know him through his sister. . . . At that time I was engaged to this mischievous big boy sitting next to me here; he was my first fiancé. And then [the man who would later become her husband and who died some years ago] came to me . . . , telling me that he wanted us to become engaged. I said no, I can't because you are younger than me. But to tell the truth, this didn't matter at all. That's how we got acquainted. But then this boy here left me. During his military service, we parted. For you know that in those days parents were more domineering and somewhat aggressive toward their children. When it was a man's father—how can I make this clear—he exercised his authority more severely, because his child was a son! Daughters were regarded as persons of minor value! And since his father was an office worker—well, in those days, life was somewhat hard for everyone. He wanted his son to get married to the daughter of another white-collar worker. By comparison, I was working on a farm, in the countryside, and for that reason his parents insisted that we should part. . . . We were engaged for about three years and in the last year he was doing his military service and then we had to part, and afterward I married my husband. I was forced to, and it was his fault. See, it's destiny. After forty-five years we met again.

She pointed at her former fiancé, sitting next to her.

In a system of arranged marriages, strict norms were mainly intended to prevent romantic relationships between partners who were socially unequal. Love in such cases would threaten not only the patriarchy but also the class system. As in Maddalena's case, emigration could effectively level out social inequalities and make the village's class structure seem irrelevant. Thus Maddalena Battaglia and her former fiancé could have a new beginning. Since Maddalena's family still believes that she transgressed the widow's code of behavior, it is possible that Maddalena's age as well as her economic independence give her increased authority and agency over her life.

Migrants' Children and Shifting Gender Roles

Arriving in Germany, Italian migrants often experienced mixed emotions, including hope, excitement, confusion, and fear. In 1971 Patrizia Lagana, the daughter of Maddalena Battaglia, came from Monteiasi, Provincia di Taranto, to Germany, where her father had already been working for a couple of years. She described her arrival as an adolescent girl filled with expectations. This worried her father, who responded by falling back on southern Italian rules:

> When I came to Germany I was thirteen years old, and the year after our arrival, I started to work. When we arrived here, my father was very . . . well, we had come from a small village to a big town. . . . My father never permitted . . . well, the only chance I had to go out was to attend Catholic mass once a week and to meet other Italians there. . . . All I

knew about was my work, our house, and the Catholic mission. . . . Well, my husband and I, we got acquainted like this: My sister, who is younger than me, wanted some ice cream. We went to a *gelateria* and when we went in, the man who would later become my husband, he was behind the bar. . . . That was the first time I saw him. About six weeks later I visited a friend of mine, and she said, "Look, we'll say we're staying at home, but we'll go to the cinema." And my brother-in-law told my father that I could stay with his family for the night and my father finally gave in. . . . I said to my brother-in-law, "Look, I feel really low, because I always have to stay at home. I'm not allowed to go out; my father doesn't allow me to go anywhere."

Patrizia's brother-in-law then invited her to go dancing with his family and friends. Patrizia knew she was only allowed to stay with the family at their home and was not allowed to go dancing, but she could not resist the opportunity. "When I entered the San Francisco Club I could feel my heart beating. I didn't want to betray my parents, who were very rigid. Anyway, we went there and after ten minutes some other Italians arrived and among them was the man who became my husband. . . . After awhile he said, 'I am shy too, like you. So will you dance with me?' I said, 'Okay.' We danced and that's how we got to know each other."

The couple met a few more times after Patrizia left work, and at her German lessons. They had only a short time together because she was expected home early. Finally he went with her to speak to her father. Patrizia told me her father was astonishingly friendly to her suitor. He had been concerned about her because she was so young and inexperienced. She was seventeen, she said; her admirer was twenty-six years old. Her father insisted she should not marry before her eighteenth birthday. Her boyfriend was allowed to visit her at her parents' home, but they were only allowed to go out if members of her family joined them. The time that they were allowed to enjoy alone was limited. Reflecting on this time in her life, she said, "Yes, I must say thank heavens everything went well and I found a sound and decent man. I myself had no experience at all, and I might have ended up with a bad man who was looking for a simple and unsophisticated girl just like me. That's how it was."

Livia Martino was born in Trapeto, a small fishing-village near Palermo. She arrived in Germany in 1963, when she was ten years old, with her mother and sisters. Her father had migrated to Dusseldorf some years before, looking for work as a hairdresser. She told me that she and her husband met when they were set up by one of her girlfriends. She and her friend went together to an Italian café where Italian teenagers met. There the young man who would later become her boyfriend was introduced to her. She was seventeen years old and was allowed to go out in the afternoon and early evening.

When I was older, I sometimes wanted to go to the city center, to a disco, but there was a problem. I was allowed to go to school alone, and my friends could visit me at home. I was seventeen and wanted to go out dancing, but I had difficulties. My parents didn't permit this and above all my mother was against it. . . . I was defiant, I had been living in Germany for years and I was well aware that my friends were going out and had boyfriends, but we had to have our morals. . . . Well of course I insisted on going out dancing, but I wasn't allowed to. Well, naturally I did go out in the end, somewhat on the

> sly, and in the end I was allowed to stay out until 10 o'clock in the evening. Very well, but what I missed in life was being allowed to enjoy my youth without being afraid.

Livia got married when she was just eighteen. I asked her if she married so young to become independent of her parents. She considered this carefully and answered in a very low tone: "I'm not sure. But in retrospect I think I would have been better off without such pressure exerted on me. I could have developed a personality and opinions of my own. I have to say that these restrictions were not good for me."

Emigration from southern Italy resulted in a number of important developments, including economic mobility, integration into the urban working class, and the acquisition of job skills as well as new and diverse life experiences. Over the course of time these novel events led to the reevaluation of internalized norms of behavior and the questioning of social role models, which often led to a more or less courageous breaking of rules. The changes in attitudes and behavior that accompany acculturation do not follow a linear course. Immigrant parents were uncertain about their children's education, particularly if they intended to return to southern Italy, which had a much stricter system of values. But mobility and urbanization made Italian immigrants more independent of their ethnic and family networks. Integration into the German welfare state also reduced the need for solidarity provided by the old networks.

Italians in the early years of postwar migration viewed their sojourns abroad as temporary; indeed, German society formally defined them as guest workers. As a result of this dual refusal to acknowledge an obvious pattern of immigration, the acculturation of Italian migrants in Germany could be defined as neither successful integration nor complete segregation. Researchers have described what they call *Zwischenwelt* ("a space in between"), a condition of no longer belonging to southern Italian society while not yet a member of German society.[12] As a result of these structural conditions, Italian migrants experienced their migration to Germany as an extended period of ambiguity. Conflicts and prejudices were commonplace. Italians were seen as communists (a stereotype quite often shared by governmental institutions) or thieves and, in general, as unreliable people. But even in the beginning of the Italian migration to Germany, there were also positive stereotypes that arose from middle-class Germans' experiences as tourists in Italy, for example, the idea that Italians would import *una bella maniera di vivere*—a distinguished and joyful lifestyle—to Germany.[13] Over time, Italian migrants became better integrated, often unintentionally, particularly the second generation. In addition, the general expansion of mass culture during this period had a significant impact on the modernization of cultural values in Germany.

Italy in the mid-1950s was—especially in the rural areas of the south—an underdeveloped country. The industrial sector, with all its repercussions for modern society, was mainly limited geographically to the northwest of Italy. In the south, land ownership remained the dream of the peasantry, but the terms and extent of ownership no longer offered a sustainable income. During the 1960s, *il boom,* or the "economic miracle," was accompanied by a social revolution that changed the way of life significantly. Nevertheless, these processes were less profound in southern Italy, and traditional family patterns and gender roles there changed in a different, more restricted way.[14] The more rigid roles defining the conduct of women were viewed with a certain rancor by migrant women returning to their villages of origin on holidays. This was explained vividly by Angela Ruggeri, who considers this female code of conduct a reason to stay in Germany.[15]

As a result of the more profound social and cultural changes in German society, immigrant families were forced to respond in one way or another. By the 1970s, Italian migrant integration into German society was made easier by improved public perceptions of Italians and more positive stereotypes, which by now were more prevalent. Notions of desire, love, affection, and passion were projected onto Italy and Italians.[16] As a result, the majority of second-generation Italians in Germany are well integrated socially, and this is particularly evident in friendship networks as well as intermarriage patterns.[17]

The Second Generation: Female Autonomy

"I do have my freedom. I went to school, completed my education, and now I am working as a nurse," stated Paola Tornatore, who was born in Germany in 1974. "I have an apartment of my own. It is close to my parents' house, and this is not bad. I have many friends who visit me more often now, and I have a boyfriend. We have been together for five years now." Her boyfriend, Marko, is a German student and her mother, Maria Elvira, approves of him and is delighted that he speaks some Italian and shows an interest in the Italian way of life. Marko's family invited the Tornatores to their home, which was very important to Maria Elvira, because it demonstrates the respectability of Paola and Marko's relationship.[18]

The children of Italian migrants in Germany today do not experience the same kinds of struggles that their parents did in their youth. However, perceived differences between Italians and Germans do remain. There is still a belief that Italians have stronger family ties, as well as an important symbolic emphasis on Italian "ways of life." Young Italians in Germany live more or less according to the cultural and social mores of Western modernity, meaning that they take their time choosing a marriage partner—while keeping in mind social restrictions, but without too much regard for parental influence. For them, the ideal that one must fall in love to engage in an intimate relationship or marry has become prevalent. In the course of only one generation, attitudes toward love have undergone a profound reevaluation, in keeping with changing living conditions. Despite its diversity and fragmentation, this process has gone relatively smoothly, and without grave estrangement between the generations.[19]

The Rise of Romantic Love as an Ideal

A number of sociologists and anthropologists have argued that romantic love is a universal idea, a "cosmopolitan passion."[20] Other commentators argue that there exists a specific European ideal of love that derives from poems about medieval courtly love, called *Minnesong*. Norbert Elias describes the *Minnesong* as the art of praising the lady of the court, practiced by knights in low social and economic positions to honor their lords or princes. These songs of love could be seen as a symbolic code of homage intended to help the artist improve his position in the court hierarchy and, ideally, to earn him a regular source of revenue. Elias points out that the transformation in the late Middle Ages from a society of warlords to a more centralized court produced a specific class of impoverished noblemen, of whom the famous poet Walther von der Vogelweide was a typical example.[21] Elias stresses that courtly love was an important part of the process of civilization.[22] *Minnesong* promoted sublimation, that is, the modification of instinctual impulses into a socially acceptable form of expression. These poems provided instruction regarding affect and violence control and introduced a socially acceptable form of behavior for interacting with an idealized woman. Such poems were addressed to women beyond the reach of the author; they did not imply the expectation of reciprocation.[23]

In late medieval society, which was characterized by the gradual development of a monetary system, the growth of a bourgeois class, and the undermining of the institution of knighthood and the practice of chivalry (the code of conduct of the nobility), the practice of courtly love distinguished an individual as belonging to the nobility. In the late eighteenth century the notion of romantic love was a distinction of an intellectual elite. To pursue the ideal of romantic love in one's life implied leisure and educational and financial resources as well as integration into urban society or the possibility of traveling to augment the circle of candidates for one's affection and passion.

Reinhart Koselleck points out that with the emergence of modernity, the space of experience and the horizon of expectations drift further apart.[24] Modernity can be seen as a period during which expectations became more remote from experiences. Until the late eighteenth century, marriage was seen as an institution intended to ensure the maintenance of a family's wealth and the production of succeeding generations. Marriage was determined on the basis of social and economic motives. The emergence of romantic feelings between young adults was regarded in this context as a threat undermining strict social stratification. Only in the nineteenth century did the institution of marriage undergo a fundamental change occasioned by the spread of the idea of romantic love across all social classes and segments of society. This implied a secular and enlightened understanding of marriage as the appropriate relationship of a couple united no longer by economic or social ties but by mutual love.[25] Although in the end marriages were still based on criteria like religion and social status, wishful dreams of romantic love and the fulfillment of a blissful relationship between two people gradually became prevalent in European societies.[26] Yet the bourgeois notion of romantic love remained an ideal that few individuals dared to follow.[27] Among the nobility, a couple that was deeply in love could threaten dynastic politics; farming families, too, continued to promote the unity of family life, upon which the practices of their peasant economy rested. For most of the working class, the ideal of a constantly doting housewife was not practical, because women's work both in and outside the home was an economic necessity.[28]

Over the course of the twentieth century, opera and folksongs as well as popular novels and movies made romantic love a major theme of mass culture in both Italy and Germany. This was enabled and furthered by industrialization, urbanization, and a greater focus on individualism and by emancipation from traditional family structures. The southern Italy of the mid-twentieth century was nevertheless still characterized by remnants of feudalism and the absence of industrialization.[29] My interviewees came from relatively isolated villages marked by an inflexible social hierarchy and severe poverty. People there were aware of romantic love as an ideal, but most of them thought this ideal beyond their reach.[30] Although transgressions occurred, restrictions regarding whom one could marry and with whom one could engage in a sexual relationship were widely accepted. Whether they were also appreciated remains open to speculation. Italians who immigrated to Germany experienced a radical social change. Their living conditions changed fundamentally, and as a consequence, their perceptions of marriage, especially for their daughters, became the subject of serious revaluation. Decisions concerning love and marriage, although still constrained by social and economic status, became a matter of individual choice for young Italian migrants.

Processes of modernization also took place in southern Italy. Beginning in the late 1970s, gender relations and traditional patriarchal and Catholic models of family were subject to significant shifts. The autonomy of individual family members increased. This was especially true for women and girls. Nevertheless, a considerable gap concerning these modernization processes between northern Italy, Germany, Switzerland, and France and southern Italy must be taken into account.[31] Goddard's field study of Naples described the enhanced freedom of movement for women during the 1970s and 1980s in contrast to the immediate postwar period. Girls were allowed to establish casual friendships called *fidanzamento fuori casa* ("engagement outside the home") with boys. These relationships were expected to be sexually innocent. Serious courtship, *fidanzamento in casa* ("engagement in the home"), allowed for more intimacy but was expected to lead to marriage. Virginity remained important for girls and women. It was considered ideal for a woman to marry her first lover. But marriages were no longer arranged by the couple's parents; instead young men and women were allowed to meet in public.[32] These changes in traditional southern Italian society influenced the Italian immigrants' perceptions of their villages of origin.

Nevertheless, differences between southern Italians and Italian emigrants to Germany are still evident, especially to the daughters of emigrants. Giulia Ruggeri, born in 1977 in Germany, for example, reacted with indignation when her aunts and grandparents in a village near the Sicilian town of Agrigento scolded her for going to the local beach without a family member acting as a chaperone. They demanded that she not show up wearing a bikini at the beach again without a chaperone. She explained that such incidents helped her make the decision to stay in Germany in spite of her feelings for her parents' village of origin and her relatives. Nevertheless, Giulia shares her parents' Catholic family values and hopes that she will find romantic love that will lead to a marriage lasting a lifetime. Her feelings about wearing a bikini at the beach are different from those of her southern Italian relatives. In her value system, a bikini is not inherently associated with flirtation, and therefore there should be no danger in wearing one. But in her description of love and marriage, some of the more traditional values of contemporary southern Italy were evident.[33]

As the sociologist Niklas Luhmann points out, in modern times, intensive reflection on love as a passion often leads to questions about the institution of marriage.[34] Marriage implies the impossibility of love, as love is not predictable in its temporal duration. The shift of romantic love from an ideal of little consequence for marriage to a real possibility involved, almost from the beginning, a certain sense of disillusionment.

The tension between the ideal and the reality of love has been interpreted in poems and novels, some drawing a contrast as stark as that between utopia and nightmare.[35] The feeling of being in love with someone is not dependant on those feelings being reciprocated. The discourse of romantic love is highly selective and is deeply rooted in contemporary social reality. Love is seen as a precondition to marriage; yet it tends to last only part of a lifetime. The consequences of this contradiction, including, for example, increased rates of divorce, have not yet reached the greater part of southern Italian migrants in Germany, but this may become a tendency even among them. Until recently, the notion of romantic love among the children of Italian emigrants to Germany has seemed to be closest to the original idea of marriage as the foundation for a lifelong bond between two partners. In the future, improved economic integration as well as changes in the discourse of love may open up new ideas about love.

Mothering across Boundaries

IMMIGRANT DOMESTIC WORKERS AND GENDER ROLES IN ITALY

Wendy Pojmann

In the past several years, international media outlets such as the BBC have reported on the phenomenon of *mammismo,* or overprotective mothering in Italy.[1] The stereotypical Italian mother is a woman who tends to her children's every need, makes sure they are well fed, and dresses them in high-quality fashions. The problem of *mammismo* arises when adult children renounce becoming independent for the comforts of being taken care of by their doting mothers. Representing another view of Italian motherhood is Monica Bellucci, the beautiful actress who appeared pregnant and naked on the cover of a 2004 Italian edition of *Vanity Fair* in protest of a new law that restricts women's rights to fertility treatments. Embodied in this image is the contemporary claim that it is possible to be alluring and maternal at the same time. Meanwhile, recent articles on immigrant mothers tell the stories of a baby abandoned in a sack in Verona by a young Romanian woman, and an Albanian mother held by police while her infant daughter awaited a liver transplant.[2] Depicted as mothers in crisis, immigrant women are clearly excluded from discussions of ideal Italian motherhood. So what do these media accounts suggest about the current state of motherhood in Italy? How are public discourses about Italian motherhood shaped by changes in the private sphere? Finally, what is the relationship of ideal motherhood (versus *mammismo* gone too far) to women's rights (represented by an Italian sex symbol) and to immigration (the representation of motherhood as tragedy)?

This chapter will attempt to respond to these questions through an examination of postwar ideals of middle-class motherhood, challenges to those ideals made by feminists, and renegotiations of motherhood brought about by the increasing presence of immigrant women in the Italian private sphere. Domestic labor migration and its associated class issues have contributed to the construction of categories of motherhood that contest Italian models based on both middle-class tradition and emancipated womanhood. By tracing the history of ideals of motherhood in Italy since the days of fascism, I argue that contemporary discourses on motherhood are actually dependant on the presence of migrant women. As Italian and immigrant women have begun to engage in new forms of mothering, distinctions between the public and the private spheres have become blurred. As labor, domestic work would normally be categorized as part of the public sphere. However, since domestic workers are employed in family homes, they actually work in a less regulated private space. This reconstruction of boundaries has serious repercussions for ideals of motherhood and demonstrates the complexity of the ways in which race and citizenship are implicated in the diasporic private sphere when women migrate.

My methodological framework stems from the fields of history, women's studies, and migration studies, while my sources include speeches and texts by Italian feminists and immigrant women, interviews, newspapers, statistical data, and participant observation. I look at the traditional serialization of events such as women's movements, which are generally interpreted through a national lens, as well as events taking place at the same time across national borders. In other words, in relation to the diasporic private sphere created in Italy, it is useful to understand the recent history of motherhood and connect it to immigration to Europe. For the purposes of this chapter I therefore focus more on what is happening in the homes of Italians than on what is happening in the homes of immigrant women, although they are sometimes the same residence. This suggests that transnational motherhood exists in multiple familial spaces, including those of household members who are neither relatives nor co-nationals. I do not intend to suggest, however, that the diasporic private sphere is simply an "imagined community" constructed exclusively by choice. Rather, it is the result of the simultaneous processes of Italian women's emancipation that began at the end of World War II and of international labor migrations that began in the era of decolonization.

Recent research has linked the increase of immigrant women domestic workers in Europe to globalization and the feminization of migration.[3] Scholars have noted the gendered component of migrant domestic work and how it has led feminists to reconsider such categories as public and private. As Helma Lutz has argued, analyses of female domestic work have upset clear-cut ways of considering the spatial dimension of salaried work: "Theories of labour location in the 'public,' separating the cultural from the political, the private from the public, reproduction from production, have to be revised; those notions have contributed to the academic invisibility of domestic workers."[4] The private sphere that is created through immigrant women's work in the homes of Italian employers has largely been forged outside the public gaze. Nonetheless, it is clear that Italian private space takes precedence over immigrant private space in the Italian context. As in other places in which global care chains operate, immigrant women's labor contributes to the successful functioning of Italian families, often at the expense of their own.[5] In the modern European nation-state, however, it is taken for granted that families are made up of citizens or immigrants who are directly related. Bryceson and Vuorela claim that "When the family is taken as a parallel and central metaphor for the nation, it remains unproblematized. . . . Imagining a family means giving it a definition that may conflict with the nation state's definition of legitimate immigrant families."[6] Since the families of immigrant domestics who are also mothers are rarely factored into conceptions of protected private space, until very recently, migrant domestic work has served mostly to reinforce ideals of middle-class motherhood.

Middle-Class Housewives

The success of the fascist state in setting back a nascent women's movement has been well documented.[7] Fascism forced Italian women into a primary role as producers of babies for the state and organized their free time through state-sponsored pro-fascist activities. Luisa Tasca has demonstrated that fascism produced two models of motherhood. One spoke to the middle-classes and was based on American home economics. The other, which the fascists came to prefer, was centered on the valorization of peasant life.[8] Although both models had a lasting impact on ideals of motherhood, another emerged and became dominant in the postwar period. The so-called average housewife of the 1950s and 1960s represented middle-class notions of what full-time work as a wife, mother, and housekeeper actually constituted. Kristin Ross has shown that in France "clean bodies" as well as homes were the obsession of French housewives.[9] Women's days were filled with tasks supposedly made easier by new consumer goods. These goods, however, really led to higher standards and expectations for housework. These same conditions existed in Italy, but greater wartime devastation delayed the economic boom there. Cleaning, cooking, and even gardening occupied most of an average housewife's time in the new urban model of motherhood that took hold. As Tasca writes, "The average housewife's work and image aimed to transform the Italians into a middle class. Such a process of 'uniformity' sought to transmit a standardized form of domestic labour, a family pedagogy, and a precise division of roles."[10] Clean floors, starched shirts, and well-fed children were proof of a woman's work well done. Although many Italian families still lived in extended households after the war, the nuclear family was idealized. Italian housewives were to be self-reliant, not counting on children, mothers-in-law, or paid domestic workers to assist in the home. This truly meant that wives and mothers also became full-time domestic workers. Domestic work, even more than the care of children, defined middle-class motherhood.

Domesticity was the preferred role of postwar middle-class Italian women, but it was not the only option available to them. Women had demonstrated their great courage and abilities during the Italian Resistance. They demanded a voice in the rebuilding and reshaping of a new democratic Italy. Part of that involved having more access to careers and direct participation in the government. Large women's associations such as the communist/socialist Unione Donne Italiane (UDI) and the Catholic Centro Italiano Femminile (CIF) promoted the idea of allowing women multiple options in their lives.[11] Now that women were full citizens with the right to vote, they should be afforded greater public participation. Although the UDI tended to support women workers over middle-class housewives, whereas the CIF privileged housewives, both organizations attempted to shape a new ideal of postwar womanhood. According to them, middle-class women could aspire to work outside the home and be mothers. The reality was, however, that this path was open only to a very few. Women who embarked on a university education and found white-collar employment in young adulthood often found themselves leaving careers once they married or had children. In fact, it was common practice to fire women outright when they married, on the assumption that motherhood and domestic life were close behind. The UDI and the CIF fought for legislation to end this sort of discrimination, but hiring and firing practices reflected widespread views about women's work and their position in the family. Despite competing discourses about motherhood among women's groups and working-class women, the dominant image of middle-class motherhood persisted through the 1960s.

Feminism and Motherhood

It was not until the social movements of the late 1960s were underway that a stronger challenge to middle-class ideals of motherhood moved to the forefront. Italian women, especially young university students, called into question a life of domestic devotion. They asked why marriage and motherhood were obligatory and why women had not made significant strides beyond the confines of the home. As Paola Bono and Sandra Kemp have explained, "For Italian feminists, increasing stress on the exposure of the middle-class ideology of the family was reinforced in the early seventies by the campaign in defence of the newly approved divorce law, and by the growing mobilization for the legalization of abortion."[12] Legal divorce, which became law by the late 1960s, meant that women could dissolve the family. Legal abortion, confirmed in a referendum in May 1981, gave women greater control over whether and when to become mothers. Some feminists suggested moreover that women's productive and reproductive labor be recognized and protected through salaries for housewives. Others questioned whether or not the home should be women's domain and proposed greater visibility of women in the working world. Still others rejected all notions of traditional patriarchal family structures and called for a new form of separatism. These feminists rethought the mothering role, this time in a symbolic space rather than in the home.[13]

Whichever perspective the feminist groups preferred, all had to confront the looming image of ideal middle-class motherhood. As politicians, public figures, and ordinary Italians grappled with the issues raised by feminists, women's groups met in their own centers to compose manifestos, draft desired legislation, and respond to criticism. Women's associations such as the UDI and the CIF had long recognized the importance of social services, such as day-care and after-school programs, to Italian mothers. The newer feminist groups, however, sought both theoretical and practical alternatives. On one hand, if the position of the Italian mother held such an important place in the minds of Italians, perhaps motherhood and power could be linked in creative new ways. On the other hand, the continued association of women with motherhood meant that they would never be able to be considered autonomous beings. These themes took center stage in the work of feminist authors such as Dacia Maraini. Virginia Picchietti has explored Maraini's writings on mothers and daughters in plays such as *I sogni di Clitennestra,* in which a transgressive mother is placed in a psychiatric hospital. Pichietti writes: "Maraini's examination of the complexity of the maternal discourse parallels the emergence of the women's movement . . . and fashion[s] a maternal discourse based on subjectivity, choice, and the rejection of the imposition of motherhood."[14] Women were no longer content with proscribed lives as mothers and homemakers, but upsetting well-established norms sometimes had serious consequences.

The momentum of the women's movement propelled many Italian women into the workforce. Ever-greater numbers of women held jobs outside the home. Employment outside the home, however, did not mean that women were freed from their responsibilities within it. Domestic chores, child care, and spousal duties all awaited middle-class mothers when they returned from work. Expectations of cleanliness and home-cooked meals had not changed. Husbands, fathers, and children were not likely to lend a hand in chores; if women wanted to work outside the home, they needed to be able to balance their duties efficiently. Many Italian women felt torn as a result. Another shift resulted from this conflict of public versus private life. Women who struggled to maintain a middle-class home while working found that domestic chores took up so much of their home life that they no longer had time to devote to their children and husbands let alone participate in an *autocoscienza* group or spend time with friends.[15] Was it more important to have shiny floors than to help Gianni with his homework? Was it more fun to spend the evening ironing your husband's shirts or strolling with him through the piazza? Was it not better to share your frustrations with other women than to curse at the mop?

Women now had some earning power, but they had not been freed from the cultural expectations of middle-class motherhood or the discourse of the integrity of the family. Even if they received help with child care through state-sponsored programs or could count on extended family to babysit, the state was not going to scrub the floors, and Grandma should not always be expected to do the laundry. Mothers wanted to be with their children—not overburdened with housework. The hiring of domestic workers provided one solution to the problem. Women were willing to commit part of their wages to be freed from housework and have more time for their families and for themselves. Prior to World War II, domestic workers were a regular part of most middle-class Italian homes. After the war, only wealthy families had domestic staff, often women from southern Italy who migrated north as the economy there expanded. The housewife of the 1950s and 1960s was expected to devote herself full time to housework, thus alleviating the need for paid help. During the 1970s, as more women adopted a feminist consciousness and entered the workforce, they came to rely increasingly on a new source of domestic labor—migrant women.

Migrant Women and Housework

By the early 1970s, southern European countries such as Italy and Greece had become attractive sites for migrant workers. As immigration controls to countries such as England and France tightened after the oil crisis of 1973, migrant workers increasingly sought entry to Italy, where immigration policies were applied more loosely. The most significant trends included the arrival of lone males from northern Africa in search of work in the agricultural and manufacturing sectors and women from countries such as the Philippines and Cape Verde seeking employment as domestic workers. In many cases, Italian women looking for help in the home sent notices to Catholic clergy and employment agencies in these countries. Local representatives screened candidates and made arrangements for the women to travel to Italy. The first women to migrate settled into Italian homes and then arranged work for female relatives and friends. Increasingly, Italian women turned to this new source of labor for an inexpensive solution to their domestic problems. Migrant women could keep the home spotless and do the laundry while Italian women went to work, tended to family members, or demonstrated in the piazzas.

Jacqueline Andall and Victoria Chell have argued that reliance on migrant domestic workers simply shifted the burden of household tasks to a less privileged class of women. Women's work outside the home failed to overturn traditional gender roles inside it.[16] Instead, Italian women were still responsible for maintaining middle-class standards inside the home. The difference was that they could now pay someone else to do this work. Chell has argued that "The incoming migrants, particularly the female migrants, have satisfied a demand for work that comes not from the productive system, but the redistribution of income where families from the 'middle-classes' have rediscovered a function for migrant labour not readily available from Italian nationals."[17] Southern Italian women continued for a time to meet the needs for domestic labor in central and northern Italy, but migrant labor came to be preferred because it was cheaper and more flexible. Italian women were also less likely to accept live-in domestic work. Filipinas and Cape Verdeans, among other migrant women, were willing to accept their employers' terms in exchange for the financial benefits they assumed awaited them.[18]

How then did the presence of migrant women in Italian homes shape perceptions of motherhood for Italian and migrant women? What impact has migrant domestic labor had on Italian, migrant, and transnational families? What sorts of intimacies have been created in the private sphere inhabited by immigrant and Italian women? Broadly speaking, from the perspective of Italian women, there was at first very little consideration of the impact of migrant domestic work on the families of the migrants themselves. Italian women saw these newly arrived women as a partial solution to their own difficulties within the home. The relationships the women constructed were primarily economic, with an Italian female employer paying her migrant woman employee for services rendered. The exchange freed Italian women from some of their domestic responsibilities while the migrant women earned much more than they could in their home countries. The perception was that migrant women were better off in Italy, otherwise they would not have chosen to go there. Italian women could be better, more emancipated mothers as a result.

When Italian women employed immigrant women, they entered into a complex realm where the lines between public and private blurred and living conditions determined their interactions. However, although migrant women have been employed in Italy for thirty years, many Italian women have continued to view migrant domestic workers in a purely professional manner and seldom engage with them in private conversations. There is very little intimacy, in fact, in interactions between migrant and native women. This is especially the case for Italian women with children living at home. In a study conducted by the Filipino Women's Council in Rome, researchers found that the private lives of migrant women rarely entered into conversations between them and their employers. Only 28 percent of Italian women employers between the ages of twenty-eight and forty-five had ever asked their domestic workers about their families in the Philippines, even though this age group employs Filipina domestic workers for the most hours per week.[19] Despite having more opportunity to converse, younger Italian women preferred not to learn the details of their domestics' lives because they wanted to uphold a wholly professional relationship. The same Italian women reported, however, that they were "interested in the phenomenon of Filipino migration, but get their information on these matters only from the mass media and the Internet, and are not interested in direct dialogue and 'personal' questions about the domestic helpers."[20] This suggests that perceptions of migrant domestic workers are shaped more by the media and popular culture than by interactions in the private sphere.

Nonetheless, Italian women are more likely to identify culturally with their domestic migrant workers on issues connected to the private sphere and motherhood than on issues related to education, class, or nation. Italian women list values such as "attachment to their families, respect for the elderly, [and] special capability in taking care of children" as common to both Italian and Filipina migrant women, for example, and as necessary traits for good domestic workers.[21] The overwhelming preference that Italian women have for Filipina and eastern European domestic workers is based largely on stereotypes of them being culturally similar in terms of their private lives and mothering skills. Jacqueline Andall and Amelia Crisantino's research shows that black African domestic workers have typically earned less than domestic workers from other migrant national groups.[22] Italian women trust African women less in their homes because they see them as culturally dissimilar. Stereotypes of large families and polygamous marriages lead some Italian women to believe that there is little structure in African households, and they therefore hire them only as a last resort. Thus the private lives of the migrant domestic workers (or at least perceptions of them) are taken into account.

Even when Italian women do not hire members of the most preferred national groups as domestics, they still privilege the private sphere over public services in caregiving tasks because of the intimacy the home grants their own family members. They believe that only the home environment can provide the familiarity, security, and love their families need. Italian mothers overwhelmingly express a preference to have their children cared for at home rather than in day-care facilities or after-school programs. If a family member cannot assist with this care, Italian women turn to migrant nannies and babysitters or rely on domestics to watch their children. Although the wealthiest Italian women are able to pay for the services of child care workers from other European nations or the United States, many middle-class Italian women do not have this option and so look to their domestic workers instead.

Furthermore, as the burden of elder care falls on a growing number of Italian women, they are employing migrant workers for this kind of help as well.[23] The nursing home conjures up images of filth, loneliness, and death in the minds of many Italians. Moreover, Italians view Americans and northern Europeans as cold and distant for sending away aging parents. However, since they do not have the time or resources to devote to elderly family members themselves, many Italian middle-class women hire migrant home workers to care for them. It appears to matter less that the migrant workers be trained for their jobs or have an interest in working with the elderly than that the family member is able to stay in a private home and the cost is not too prohibitive. In the tradition of the ideal nuclear family, it is better still if elderly parents can be cared for in their own homes. In an attempt to balance cost and intimacy, middle-class mothers have found a partial solution to the demands placed on them.

Access to public discourse favors Italian mothers as well. In the 1970s and 1980s, Italian middle-class mothers earned a place in the public sphere where they could engage in discussions about the rights and responsibilities of motherhood. They were able to use their leverage with the state to achieve some of the most generous maternity legislation in the world. The Italian government has long been aware of declining birth rates among Italian women and has used incentives to encourage population growth. Therefore, women who are regularly employed can take up to one year of maternity leave without risking their jobs, and many employers allow part-time work for up to three years after the birth of a child. A wide range of public and private day-care services are available to middle-class Italian mothers. Moreover, the fact that the Italian government has intervened to ease the regulation of migrant domestic workers, over other sorts of workers, indicates complicit approval of the ways this source of labor lessens demands on the state. Italian women have had a role in both supporting maternity legislation and shaping ideals about motherhood.

Migrant women's experiences of motherhood in Italy obviously have been quite different. Migrant women often leave families behind in the hope of being able to provide for them financially. Women who migrate with children have to find solutions for their own child care needs, and still other migrant women decide not to become mothers at all because of possible risks to their employment. In any case, when they enter the homes of Italian families, migrant domestic workers have to engage in many tasks associated with mothering, but for a family not their own. The majority of domestic workers primarily perform domestic chores such as cleaning, laundry, cooking, and shopping. However, migrant domestic workers also attend to the emotional needs of the elderly and children, even when these activities are not assigned as their main duties.[24] Rhacel Parreñas has written on the psychological consequences for Filipino women who mother their own children from a distance and look after other women's children on a day-to-day basis. She writes: "Taking care of children is not just taking care of children when, in the process of doing so, one cannot take care of one's own children. This contradiction accentuates the pain of domestic work and results in their simultaneous aversion and desire for this job."[25] From the first migrations of the 1970s through today, domestic work has been the main source of employment for migrant women. During that time, caregiving tasks, including watching children and assisting the elderly, have assumed an ever-greater role in the domestic sector. Migrant women first helped to free Italian women from cleaning. Italian women then came to rely on their domestics to provide a more affective role in the household. As more than one woman in Italy has wondered, "Maybe northern countries are now importing maternal love the way they used to import gold?"[26]

In addition to having ambiguous roles in Italian homes as caregivers and house cleaners, immigrant women have had far less ability to shape the public discourse on motherhood even when they are mothers themselves. Nonetheless, immigrant mothers are often the focus of a great deal of public discussion about the potential crisis of motherhood in Italy. While the birth rate for Italian women continues to hover around one birth per woman, immigrant women are statistically much more fecund.[27] The Italian public, especially the media, interprets this data in various ways. On one hand, it is clear that the combination of a rapidly aging population with a low birth rate will result in a population shortage. Immigrant mothers have the potential to ensure that there will be sufficiently large future generations of workers. On the other hand, a surplus of lower-income immigrant mothers may also result in added strain on public services, a loss of Italian identity, and even threats to national security.[28] In any case, migrant women's voices have been largely absent from public debates about motherhood even though they, too, have a stake in the future of public schools and social services. Access to citizenship often means the difference between having representation in the public sphere and not.

When immigrant mothers are citizens, their subjectivity changes, especially if they are married to Italian men. The Italian public is most tolerant of children produced by an Italian father and a foreign mother, the most common form of coupling between Italians and foreigners.[29] Since the child usually carries the father's surname and citizenship is tied in the historical and patriarchal imagination to masculinity, the child's Italian identity is ensured. An immigrant mother with an Italian child is therefore more likely to benefit from public participation than are immigrant mothers who do not have Italian citizenship. Since the Italian government does not recognize jus soli, the second-generation of immigrant children are denied the privileges of full citizenship. The concerns of these immigrant mothers carry less weight as a result.

Migration, Feminism, and Motherhood

Through the new model of motherhood described in the previous pages, globalization processes can be seen clearly. Middle-class Italian women engage in fewer mothering tasks on their own and work more on developing themselves professionally. This is in part due to an economy that requires families to have access to two salaries to maintain a middle-class lifestyle and in part because of individualistic goals of personal fulfilment. Meanwhile, poor economic conditions in one country lead women to immigrate to another country where their earning power is great enough that they can send money to families at home. Migrant women sometimes even pay for yet another woman to look after their own children. This pattern can be seen worldwide (e.g., global care chains). Women in wealthier nations work more outside the home and rely on migrant labor to assist them where the state and family do not. The same process is repeated in poorer nations. The result is that "this process of the globalization of maternity generates a transfer of affection and feelings south-north/east-west that does not enter into the calculation of salaries or budgets but produces, no doubt, material consequences."[30] It leads, moreover, to the perpetuation of exploitative behaviors between women. Rosa Mendes, an immigrant feminist from Brazil active in multiethnic women's associations in Rome, says she employed a domestic after becoming a feminist and finding work outside the home: "In the seventies, the Brazilian woman, like the Italian woman, left the house . . . but to do this she put another woman inside the house to do her work. I reflect on whether this is liberation."[31]

Since the late 1990s, a growing number of Italian and migrant women like Mendes have begun to directly confront the problems created by the imbalances of globalization. Italian women are asking themselves if the employment of migrant domestic workers necessarily means treating less privileged women as mere servants rather than as individuals with complex human relationships of their own. Mothering has been at the center of their discussions. Italian feminists now acknowledge the role migrant labor had in allowing women to enter the workforce. Ideals of emancipated motherhood of the 1970s and 1980s helped on the whole to overturn those of the middle-class housewife of the 1950s and 1960s. Emancipation, however, was won partly through the labor of another class of women.

Egyptian-born Italian feminist Sonia Tsvrenis has been working in Tuscan native-migrant women's associations such as Punto di Partenza and IRIDE (Innovate Relations Identity Desires Ethics) for many years. She argues that an important first step in building intimacy between migrant and native women is adequately acknowledging failures in the Italian women's movement. On this point Tsvrenis explains that "We Westerners in part resolved our familial oppression by going to work and making money—using the salaried work of immigrant women to free us from housework, child care, and elder care without fighting within our own families, against the selfishness and indifference of men, and, as a movement, against choices that result in an ever less favorable status for women."[32] Their choice not to be housewives led Italian women outside the private sphere and toward greater political and social advancements but without redefining what was actually taking place in the home. By not redistributing household tasks among family members, especially husbands, Italian women simply reinforced their own roles as domestics and mothers.

At the same time, Italian women, including feminists, had a part in contributing to female migration to Italy. Of course, some Italian women consciously sought migrant domestic workers by inquiring about them through their parishes or with employment agencies. However, most Italian women probably did not connect their desire for help in the home to the growing number of women immigrants in Italy. They simply noticed that there were more migrant women and fewer Italian women available to work as domestics, and they benefited from the new low-cost labor force. Globalization specialist and feminist Sara Ongaro says it is time for Italian women to recognize that their decisions about their homes and families have implications far beyond the domestic sphere of their own nation, especially when, as she puts it, "Our emancipation depends on the subordination of other women. . . . One cannot have a domestic worker without asking why today millions of women are forced to emigrate."[33] Rather than taking a complacent attitude and asserting that they are really helping migrant women by employing them, more Italian women are examining the pull factors of migration and are seeking to understand how they have contributed to such high numbers of women on the move.

In addition to their self-critiques of the division of labor in the home, Italian feminists are also beginning to recognize shortfalls in the development of feminist theories that failed to adequately address ethnicity and class from the perspectives of migrant women.[34] Multiethnic women's associations in Italy are just beginning the work of coming to terms with these omissions. In groups such as Punto di Partenza, IRIDE, and Trama di Terre, Italian and migrant women are searching together for new ways to value differences among women. This involves redrawing the boundaries between private and public space and reconstructing shared sites to create new conceptions of transnational intimacies. Within the walls of their centers, Italian and migrant women are establishing relational models that transcend those of employer and employee. Sandra Gil has noted how women's associations, in fact, help Italian and immigrant women to redefine relationships that are normally based on a monetary relationship and characterized by inequality and hierarchy. As she sees it, "the work of an association takes place in a public space, is based on cooperative links, and promotes autonomous relationships oriented toward the attainment of common objectives."[35] By choosing to work together in spaces that overcome the inequities of the domestic sphere and the exclusions of a traditional public sphere, immigrant and Italian women are forging alternate concepts of the transnational family.

Moreover, their work shows that meanings of motherhood are not fixed or stable and need to be contested continually as a means of preventing oppression based on gender, class, and nation. Sometimes this means that Italian and immigrant women have to examine both the discourses that circulate about them and their actual lived circumstances. After all, many Italian feminists rejected notions of ideal middle-class motherhood. Although they may regret having left in place the traditional attitudes about women's responsibilities that led them to seek the labor of other women, they do not necessarily reject the idea that women need to be freed from the limitations of motherhood and domestic work to be emancipated. In fact, Italian women express concern that immigrant women might fall into the trap of believing that motherhood is the ultimate marker of womanhood. As a participant at the University for Women in Florence noted, "The problem for immigrant women is that they are young and they have small children. We need to do something to take in these children and make the women understand the importance of realizing themselves as women, not only as mothers."[36]

Italian feminists view migrant mothers who make sacrifices on behalf of their children with compassion and sympathy. Yet there is often a gap between their assumptions about migrant women's backgrounds and experiences and the realities of what their lives are actually like. For example, Filipina domestic workers who were part of the first migrations to Italy in the 1970s and early 1980s were generally highly educated professional women.[37] Most fell into domestic work by chance, having no other options, rather than by choice. Migrant women are not always able to have their degrees and qualifications recognized in Italy and may not have a command of the Italian language. As a result, they are often underemployed and economically vulnerable. Realizing themselves as women, in the sense of following fulfilling careers or pursuing an education, is often out of the question. Since motherhood, especially providing for their children, was a factor in their migrations, immigrant women take solace in their maternal role.[38] They may connect their status as immigrants, rather than as mothers, to their oppression.

Differences in status between immigrant and native women are evident in debates over recent legislation on fecundity and immigration. The Italian government passed a law in 2004 limiting state support for artificial insemination to heterosexual married couples of "normal" childbearing age. Since a majority of Italian women postpone marriage and motherhood until they are in their thirties, infertility rates have multiplied. Lesbian couples and single women have also been turning to alternative methods for having children. By denying nontraditional categories of women the right to motherhood, the state has reasserted a conservative approach to what constitutes a family. Interestingly, debates on fecundity legislation were taking place simultaneously with debates on the Bossi-Fini law (Law 189/02), which put in place stricter immigration controls tied directly to regular employment.

Italian and immigrant women have had a difficult time mobilizing their communities to connect motherhood, globalization, and feminism so that they might work together on a more comprehensive approach to these matters. Nonetheless, immigrant women have noted the irony in the fact that, in many of their communities, they are still struggling to achieve greater acceptance of birth control and abortion. Meanwhile, Italian women have been looking for new ways to become mothers since their emancipation has contributed to the postponement of motherhood or led them to seek it outside the structure of the heterosexual couple. On the Bossi-Fini law, on the other hand, immigrant women have commented that the legislation does little to advance the image of immigrants as connected to families and other support networks. Instead, the Bossi-Fini law recognizes immigrants only as a source of labor to benefit the Italian economy. The legislation further narrows the definition of family for purposes of reunification to include only parents and their children under eighteen and directly ties legal residence to contractual, uninterrupted employment. As a result, despite the clear economic benefits of migrant women's labor, immigrant domestic workers have become one of the most vulnerable categories at risk of losing their residency since they are the most likely to work without a legal contract. Immigrant domestic workers have pointed out, moreover, that the legislation fails to recognize that it is usually the Italians, not the migrants themselves, who prefer to work around the law to avoid having to pay taxes and provide benefits.[39] Despite their best efforts, the Italian and immigrant women's movements have not been able to mobilize the public to overturn these laws; the legislation stands.

Conclusion

In conclusion, I return to the state of motherhood mentioned in the introduction. Stereotypes of overbearing Italian mothers can be just as damaging as those of young immigrant mothers in crisis. All images of motherhood—whether as emancipated, sexy, or essentialized—can be confusing. In any case, contemporary ideals of motherhood are not limited to the narrow parameters of the middle-class housewife that emerged at the end of World War II. Italian women, nonetheless, still find they must situate themselves in relation to the dominant ideal and defend the choices they make about work outside the home, domestic work, child rearing, elder care, and their leisure time. The women's movement of the 1970s helped Italian women assert themselves in the public sphere but it did not, in most cases, help them to overturn traditional gender norms governing mothering and housework. Instead, Italian women have benefited from the feminization of migration worldwide in the new era of globalization and have come to rely on immigrant women's labor in their homes.

Despite their close contact, immigrant and Italian women have not developed much intimacy in their relationships in the private sphere. In fact, Italian women have reasserted hierarchical relationships and have reflected very little on the impact of immigration on the lives of the women they employ. Although the Italian women employers are very much a part of these global care chains, the diasporic private sphere that is created in Italian homes is a space that remains largely hidden from them, and one in which foreign women feel very alone. Immigrant women perform the domestic and caregiving chores that are normally associated with mothering, but for other women's families. Just recently, immigrant and Italian women have begun to examine the implications of their unequal status and what it means for the future of feminism. Their analyses will have a broad impact for migrant domestic workers in Europe. This is because, as Italians and other Europeans continue to accept women domestics into their countries, they will have to confront more than just the economic or political consequences of migration. They will need to reevaluate the significance of deeply rooted social and cultural institutions like motherhood if they are to guarantee the liberal rights they espouse.

Ethnographic Studies of Family, Community, and Nation

Between Public and Private

THE TRANSNATIONAL COMMUNITY OF SICILIANS IN MONTEREY, CALIFORNIA

Carol Lynn McKibben

"There was always this feeling of continuity, of belonging, as Sicilians and as fishermen," said Elizabeth Grammatico, a businesswoman and president of the Italian Catholic Federation of Monterey.[1] Across cultures, fishing people tend to isolate within rather than integrate into larger regional or national groups.[2] In his study of San Francisco Italians, Dino Cinel noted that the fishermen "proved that . . . a group could isolate itself almost totally from the larger society, recreating patterns of economic and social organization almost entirely from the Old World."[3] For the fishermen of Monterey, shared activities, imaginings, and symbols allowed them to create a particularly self-sufficient community, albeit a transnational one, oriented toward the sea. These activities included sending money home to Sicily, visits home, participation in family/kinship networks, the invention of traditions, the sharing of memories, and cultural rediscovery. For Monterey Sicilians, home was no single place but "a concept and a desire" as well as both a public and private space, which was constantly replenished by new migrations, from Sicily to Monterey and back again.[4]

Members of Monterey's Sicilian community identified both as Sicilians and as fishers, whether or not their family actually fished. They also expressed a sense of belonging to Monterey, as well as to Sicily. This connection was more than just translocal, however.[5] While Sicilians have remained deeply involved in their home villages and consider themselves intimately involved in village affairs, they are acutely aware of and connected to events in Italy as a nation, especially with regard to the economy, political changes, and social issues. Similarly, although migrants clearly express a sense of an American political identity, many of the most recent arrivals struggle with the issue of citizenship, sometimes remaining for years in the United States without actually obtaining U.S. citizenship.

These practices have fostered an identity that has persisted over time and over generations, long after the demise of the booming sardine industry made it impossible for Monterey's Sicilians to remain fisherfolk. Sicilians sent home remittances and made frequent visits to Italy and Sicily along with their American-born children. They continue to strongly favor marriage within the community. Communication through mail, e-mail, and telephone keeps them in almost constant contact with family and friends in home villages. Both Sicilian dialect and the Italian language continue to be spoken and are taught to children. Sicilians in Monterey commonly tune into RAI, the Italian television channel. Meals celebrating both ethnic and fishing identities are part of Sicilian family life, especially around holidays.

Here is a transnational identity that fuses an occupational identity (as fisher people) developed in public with private rituals of family and Sicilian ethnicity in three interlinked places (Monterey, Sicily, and Italy). It was the women of Monterey who purposely constructed this identity for their community as they moved between the private world of family and marriage and the public worlds of work, church, and community organization. The invention of this identity began with women's waged work in sardine factories in the 1920s through the 1940s and was consolidated by the formal events of church and community organizations (such as the Italian Catholic Federation, the Italian Heritage Foundation, and the Sons of Italy) that made the identity public and visible. Sicilian women were uniquely poised to create this identity. As Sicilians, they were accustomed to managing the family economy. As migrating people, they participated actively in all decisions regarding the household and family migration, from destination sites and occupational choices to decisions about which family members should stay or leave. Most important, as fishing people, they enjoyed a level of independence and power that contrasted sharply with that of other women in their class, culture, and national group.

Sources and Methods

This chapter is based on eight years of research in Monterey, California, and in the Sicilian communities from which migrants there came. During that time, using a snowball sampling, I conducted oral history interviews with one hundred women and fifty men. I worked ethnographically, attending community events, participating in small gatherings of women's groups, and visiting several generations of each family. In addition, I conducted follow-up group interviews with ten families who migrated to Monterey after 1965.[6] Informants came from Isola Delle Femine, San Vito Lo Capo, and Marettimo, in northwest Sicily, which I visited in the spring and summer of 1998. About half of the interviewees were from working-class backgrounds (people without capital who worked either in the canneries or on the fishing boats but did not own either, although home ownership was common among all classes). I quickly learned, however, that working-class people often had extended kin connections with people who owned the fish canneries and boats. There was no rigid class divide within extended family groups.

Since oral history involves interviewees' memories and perceptions of moments long ago, I balanced the oral interviews with newspaper accounts from the *Monterey Peninsula Herald* (the major local newspaper in Monterey) and records in the special collections in the Bancroft Library, the Monterey History and Art Association, and the California History Room in the Monterey Public Library, as well as manuscript census records, tax assessors' records of property ownership for Monterey County from 1914 through 1960, Monterey city directories through 1965, and marriage license records from 1920 to 1980.

Migration from Sicily and Monterey

Sicilian migrants to Monterey represent only thirty-five family groups. According to oral histories, they came to North America in three distinct waves, beginning around 1880. Between three and four thousand Sicilians are claimed to have made their way to Monterey to fish for sardines, salmon, and other varieties of fish between 1880 and 1914.[7] Considering the population of Monterey—only 1,748 people in 1900, and 11,300 in 1910 in the entire county of Monterey, which included Salinas, Carmel, Pebble Beach, Big Sur, and inland communities—those estimates are probably high.[8] Public records do not note their settlement in Monterey until 1915, when tax assessor's records show a demographic shift and the appearance of Italian surnames.[9] Because they were people on the move, traveling back and forth among Pittsburg, San Francisco, and Martinez, California, as well as Detroit, Chicago, Milwaukee, and the home villages in Sicily, Sicilian fisherfolk were hard to count.

A second wave of migration to Monterey began in the 1920s, usually by way of San Francisco or Pittsburg or Martinez, which is confirmed by the census.[10] According to the oral histories, almost all these migrants had kin and village ties to the first settlers. In 1920 the Monterey population of 6,680 included 972 Italians, most of whom lived near the docks and proclaimed fishing as their occupation.[11] Most of their surnames originated in the three Sicilian villages identified in the oral histories. The population of Monterey reached 9,141 in 1930, and 10,084 by 1940. According to residents and recent scholarship, approximately one-third of this population was Sicilian in origin.[12]

A third wave of immigrants arrived in the late 1940s from the island of Marettimo, rather than San Vito Lo Capo or Isola Delle Femine.[13] The decline of the sardine industry led to some out-migration of Sicilians to San Pedro, California, and South America, but a significant and stable population remained in Monterey. Small numbers of Sicilians continued to immigrate to Monterey throughout the 1950s and up to the present day. Many came as a result of the passage of the 1965 Immigration Act, which favored family reunification. Although it is not possible to provide exact numbers for recent immigration, it is clear from the oral interviews and observation that Monterey's Sicilian community continues to grow, with fifty to one hundred new immigrants each year who marry into established Sicilian families in Monterey. Monterey sends at least the same number of migrants (mostly young people) for extended visits to Sicily, which also commonly result in marriages that revitalize communities on both sides of the ocean. This exchange arguably creates one of the most active transnational communities of Italian origin in existence. There is no empirical evidence of how many Sicilians are in Monterey today, but according to city officials, nearly one-third of Monterey's population of 30,641 still identifies as Sicilian.[14]

Monterey in Transition

In 1915, Sicilians entered a city in the midst of transformation and fraught with social conflicts over identity. Monterey residents once envisioned their city as a mecca for tourists and a vacation destination for the wealthy. By the end of World War I, however, Monterey had become a working-class industrial town focused on the mass production of canned sardines. At the height of the sardine boom in the 1930s and 1940s, the fishery supported a canning and by-product industry worth $50 million a year, making it the single most valuable fishing industry in the United States.[15] Industry drove the population expansion of Monterey. Sicilians made up about half of the 350 fishermen in 1920, and 86 percent of the fishermen by 1940. They also made up one-third of the sardine cannery workforce.[16]

White, middle-class residents of Monterey objected strenuously to the rapid growth of industry, and in 1939, the Monterey City Council adopted a master plan recommending that the "fisherman's wharf be removed [and that] booth's Cannery be removed entirely." It claimed that the entire downtown area was in need of "reinstatement of [its] original scenic conditions."[17] None of these recommendations were realized. Instead, the wharf area expanded, the population of working-class migrants increased, and even more canneries were built. Monterey's working class seemed to overwhelm the city socially and economically.[18] In 1949 there were thirty-one canneries and reduction plants in Monterey.

By 1961, however, only five remained. The sardines had abandoned local waters. The last big sardine catch of 1948 marked an abrupt end to nearly three decades of economic expansion and population transformation. After 1948, Monterey again turned to tourism.[19] The development of the Monterey Bay Aquarium in 1987 at the site of Hovden Cannery epitomized the completion of this changeover.

Service industries that supported tourism gradually replaced fishing but made room for the Sicilian families, who had moved from focusing on home ownership to investing in Monterey's restaurants and commercial enterprises. Once ethnicity and industrialization no longer threatened tourism and scenery, Monterey began to celebrate its Sicilian and Italian heritage, and even the industrialization of the past. At the same time, Sicilian migrants became aware of their American political identity and their stake in Monterey's success. They turned their attention to the streets, neighborhoods, and businesses that made the city attractive to tourists. They slowly transferred their ideas about development and modernization from factory building to housing development and the opening of small businesses such as restaurants, shops, and service-oriented enterprises. Gender had everything to do with the successful transition of Sicilian families from transient fisher people to promoters of the tourist city of Monterey.

Fishing People, Identity, and Gender

With their origins firmly entrenched in the traditions of fishing, Monterey Sicilians share an historical understanding of gender that values women as decision makers, workers, and the very foundation of their families and communities. Many cultures attribute power to women in their roles as mothers, but the peculiar lives of fisher people gave females exceptional power. Cross-culturally, women (especially married women) in fishing communities adapted to long stretches of time spent away from men by becoming key community and family leaders. Important decisions had to be made, and were made, without the participation of males in the household. Fishing environments are, and were, overwhelmingly female spaces. Males come and go as they pursue their livelihoods following migrant fish. The marine anthropologist James

McGoodwin has summed up the scholarly consensus on gender among fishing peoples: "The life situations of fishermen's wives and their central role in the economic and social affairs of their communities contribute importantly to the distinctive character of fishing cultures. . . . Many fishing communities manifest tendencies toward matriarchy and matrifocality."[20] Sicilian women generally controlled the family purse, increasing their power as men participated in the huge out-migrations of the early twentieth century.[21] In Monterey, local informant Theresa Sollazzo reached the same conclusion as McGoodwin, telling me, "The families were almost matriarchal."[22]

When asked about women's involvement in family finances, Anita Ferrante, whose family came to Monterey in 1934 from Marettimo to become prominent commercial fishermen, was equally clear. "You bet your life we were involved. Definitely. After my father died, especially, everything was free and clear. There were four of us, and I was in charge of investments. I took equity out of one property and put it into malls, shopping centers. I made it grow. It still supports my mother, my family. I run the show here."[23]

Monterey Sicilian women used their power to control their marriages as well as to make important financial decisions. Peter Cutino explained, "What is family here? I will tell you what it became. It became this interlocking network of fishermen. There was this intensive activity, intermarriage, so that the community is truly linked by blood. Family was the entire group. We were put together by age groups. Children were raised together as cousins. We had the same values, traditions—we even had the same thing for dinner every night—right down to material possessions. Everyone had the same thing. Everyone is related to everyone."[24] The intensity of a kin-linked community meant that public-private boundaries were unclear. They remained unclear on both the local and international levels on both sides of the ocean down to the present. As late as 1962, Anna Sardina arrived in Monterey from Sicily at the age of twenty to marry her first cousin. It was a marriage arranged by the two mothers to ensure that Salvadore, Anna's prospective husband, did not marry an outsider.[25]

Even today it is difficult to draw a line where family ends and community begins in Monterey. Women still gather in communal rosary, sewing, and embroidery groups to talk together, eat together, and share their lives. In the past, Sicilian women drew strength from the freedom they had with husbands away on fishing trips in ways that most working-class women in other places did not have the time for. "You couldn't talk much at work; you had to keep going. . . . But our husbands were never around. They would go to Alaska and they would stay three months. It was terrible, but it was great too. We needed a break. We had plenty of freedom. We'd meet every day and crochet or [do] embroidery while the children would play. We couldn't have done that if our husbands had been around. Your mind is at ease when you crochet," Nancy Mangiapane explained.[26]

The socializing was obligatory. "We spent all of our time visiting, visiting, visiting people, bringing food, going to homes, and them coming to see you," recalled Rose Marie Cutino Topper, whose parents immigrated to Monterey in the 1930s from Isola Delle Femine by way of Pittsburg.[27] It was these gatherings that built the Sicilian fishing community. It was, and is, in these casual meetings that women decided everything from what to make for dinner to whose children ought to marry. According to Janet

Russo, "Women were in charge of everything. Our mothers used to cook, clean, do all the finances for the family. Then they would pack us all up and take us camping in Big Sur. We have all these pictures of the women in aprons scurrying around, putting up tents, doing everything. They made us all close. And we still are. Even today."[28]

The community bonding did not end with the men's return. During the full moon, for example, the men could not fish for sardines. Men entered the Sicilian community that the women created. Cannery workers and fishermen of other ethnicities were excluded. The monthly parties celebrating the fishermen's return with the full moon were exclusively Sicilian events, organized by Sicilian women. According to Janet Russo, "It was a big celebration. . . . We had huge dinners [where] everyone contributed their favorite dishes, sausages, and card games, where people would go from neighbor to neighbor for dessert and coffee. All the families got together and everyone stayed up all night, fried sausage, then got up in the morning to go to church."[29]

Sicilian immigrants to Monterey managed to communicate with and visit family members and remain connected to village life in Sicily, even during the period between 1915 and 1948, when they were poorest. Anita Ferrante recalled her family's connections with family in Marettimo: "We stayed close to them. You have no idea the packages we sent [in the 1940s] that my mother made me drag to the post office every week. Sugar, flour, canned goods. They had no food. They needed to have food. Then [in the 1960s] my father went back and bought a boat for his brothers. We always sent money. My mother used to send $200 or $400 a month."[30]

Sicilian migrants who arrived later, after the demise of the sardine industry, described their lives in surprisingly similar ways. JoAnn Mineo came to Monterey from Trapani, in Sicily, in 1970. She recalled the difficulty her mother had leaving family behind. "My grandmother was old and sick. We wanted to come here, for work. But my mother didn't know what to do. We went back and forth. Then we finally came. My grandmother—she died. Then we had to go back. We paid for everything—flowers, coffin." She and others who came in the decades after 1965 described almost constant contact with family and households and remain involved in each other's decision making even over the smallest matters. "We talk almost every day, sometimes twice a day. When someone needs a doctor, hospital, we give our opinion. Everybody gives their opinion. That's what it's all about."[31]

Communities forged by women through kinship and female socializing soon also extended into public domains. Sicilian women worked in the sardine canneries, where they formed a conspicuous and formidable ethnic bloc. The organization of public *feste* rooted in Sicilian village practices was also a female-driven initiative. *Feste*—events through which they performed decidedly transnational identities—marked the public spaces of Monterey as Sicilian. The *feste* in honor of Santa Rosalia and Saint Joseph organized by women reminded the fishing people of their Sicilian origins but also required the residents of Monterey to acknowledge the Sicilian fishing people as critical actors in Monterey's economic and political life. The Santa Rosalia *festa* remains the single most important identity marker for Sicilians—who still call themselves fishing people even though they no longer fish for a living—in Monterey today. It functions to integrate newcomers, and especially women, to the community. Anita Ferrante recalled her mother's experience as a new immigrant from Marettimo realizing the importance of the *feste* in bringing her into the community of Sicilian women in Monterey: "They were going back in their minds to the warmth of their country and bringing that feeling here. It united us. The first thing my mother did was ask to join the *festa*. That's how we were incorporated into the community—through the *festa*. That was truly how it worked. She wanted to become part of the community. And she wanted us to become part of the community too."[32]

Identity in Public: Confronting Citizenship

Sicilian women first used Santa Rosalia to express in new and more public ways the identity of the Sicilian fisher community they had created by the 1930s and 1940s. The nationalist and ideological passions of World War II inevitably challenged their efforts. National citizenship became a controversial issue for Monterey Sicilians as they became "enemy aliens" during World War II. Sicilian women were the most vulnerable members of the community, for they were the least likely to be citizens. Pearl Harbor Executive Order No. 9066 (which defined some Italian immigrants as "enemy aliens") disrupted community building and demanded a response. Much of that response came from the men of the community.

Prior to World War II, Sicilians in Monterey had avoided American politics and dismissed formal ties of national citizenship as unimportant and irrelevant as either a marker of identity or a way of achieving economic goals. "My father really believed that Italians needed to have [political] power, but they weren't that interested in voting. They were fishermen," said Mary Brucia Darling, whose father, Antonio Brucia, a bar owner, sought to marshal Sicilian political power in Monterey even before the controversies of World War II. Mrs. Darling remembered the efforts of her father, who organized a political association called the Sons of Italy in 1928. She explained: "My father believed in the vote, in citizenship. He was responsible for more than five hundred Italians becoming American citizens. He filled out their citizenship papers, acted as their witness, and took them to the county court in Salinas to pass their test and take their oath."[33]

The Sons of Italy remained a small entity, however, as it struggled with the political indifference of the female-dominated community. No mayor or member of the city council, board of supervisors, or sheriff's department or any of the hastily organized citizens' defense groups in Monterey, Pacific Grove, or Pebble Beach had an Italian surname at the time of the bombing of Pearl Harbor. Despite the economic predominance of Monterey Sicilians in the 1930s and 1940s, and the strength of their female-dominated community, they had no political visibility whatsoever. The public world was not off limits to Monterey's Sicilian women, but the public world of politics was.

While uninterested in American politics, Monterey's Sicilians, especially its men, paid close attention to politics in Sicily and in Italy. They were aware of Italy's transformation under Mussolini and generally supported it. Mussolini appeared to be a strong leader who had a vision for Italy that would modernize, industrialize, and unify the country. Monterey Sicilian migrants felt especially hopeful for the changes Mussolini promised. "Most people thought he was a pretty good guy," recalled Albert Mangiapane, who immigrated to Monterey in 1925, three years after Mussolini came into power. "Some people were afraid of him because he made so many changes, but he brought law" to Sicily, he said.[34] Others remembered their mothers sending their wedding rings to the Italian government to support Mussolini's war effort. "Most thought Mussolini was a hero," said Peter Cutino.[35]

In June 1940, the Alien Registration Act (Smith Act) required the registration and fingerprinting of all aliens age fourteen and older. Aliens had to fill out an extensive questionnaire that asked for their occupation, address, marital status, organizational affiliations, and means of entry into the United States.[36] Then, on 7 December 1941, the Japanese military bombed Pearl Harbor and the United States declared war on Italy as well as on Japan and Germany. Monterey men remembered this as a significant moment. "When Italy went to war against the United States, their faith in the Old Country was destroyed," said Peter Cutino in reference to his parents and older relatives.[37] His mother, Rose, remembered the outbreak of hostilities between Italy and the United States as a family issue. "Everybody had families [in Italy]. We were torn and very, very sad. We were American but our heritage was there. People were disappointed. No one could get letters, packages; everything stopped. We didn't know what was happening to them. It made us feel funny that Italy was at war with us."[38]

Suddenly, national security became paramount at the federal, state, and local levels, forcing Monterey Sicilians to reconsider their largely apolitical and female-dominated communities. Like the Japanese, whose population totaled 2,247 in Monterey in 1940, the Italians had formed an increasingly visible and public if apolitical and female-dominated community, symbolized by the *feste*.[39] With the outbreak of war, suspicions were harbored of any member of a migrant group from any of the Axis Powers—anyone of Italian, German, or Japanese descent—belonging to a traitorous "fifth column."[40]

The first order of forced evacuation of enemy aliens occurred on 29 January 1942. It was followed on 19 February by Executive Order No. 9066, signed by President Roosevelt, which allowed the military full discretion in evacuating from the coast anyone suspected of being an enemy, whether that person was a citizen or not. It began to look more like a fatal error than a simple oversight to have neglected so obvious a statement of loyalty to the United States as the acquisition of official citizenship. In the months after the bombing of Pearl Harbor, there was a flurry of activity and conflicting information reflected both in the pages of the local newspaper and in the narratives of my informants that made it imperative for Monterey Sicilians as "suspect ethnics" to make their political allegiance clear, as well as to assume a place in the dominant population.

For Sicilian women, most of all, the acquisition of legal citizenship was a detail often overlooked. Citizenship was regarded as a trivial legal nicety. Joe Favazza described his mother, Providenza, as a "good American" but indicated confusion over the meaning of citizenship. "She loved America. She was devoted to the United States," he recalled. "She didn't even give her ring to Mussolini when everybody else did. She was a good citizen even though she didn't have her papers."[41] According to one local observer at the time, "Among the Italians, there are a great many families in which one of the adults, usually a husband, has become a citizen, while his wife remains an alien. Because of the new restrictions, the entire family . . . will move."[42] Rosalie Ferrante's personal experience confirmed that observation. "The ones who had to leave were the non-citizen grandmothers, so the whole family went too."[43]

Monterey Sicilians did not pursue a strategy of organized resistance. But they quickly realized that they had to rethink their community-based identities to adapt to a new political reality. Elite men in Monterey's Sicilian community played a crucial public role in making that transformation. In their very public displays of donations to the war effort, they emphasized the essential contributions of fishing people to the local and national economy and the loyalty of the community to the American government.

The experience of alienation during the war years transformed an identity rooted in female-dominated community and public religious displays into an ethnic identity as American citizens. Years later, that identity still carried with it a memory of the trauma of World War II. Because migration to Monterey continued to occur even after the war, there were no clearly defined first, second, or third generations in this community. And once the most intense period of international warfare ended, the newer arrivals quickly forgot the importance of acquiring American citizenship. As migrations to the United States from Southeast Asia, Latin America, and the Caribbean increased, Monterey Sicilians began to enjoy a sense of themselves as welcome European immigrants. They did not feel the urgent need for American citizenship as protection in a nation that might turn hostile at any moment. Since marrying into the Marettimare family in Monterey thirty years ago, JoAnn Mineo has traveled continually between Sicily and Monterey. When asked about acquiring citizenship after so many years in the United States, Mrs. Mineo, like other postwar migrants, declared, "No, no—I don't have citizenship. When do I have time? I have to work. It is not that important to me. It wouldn't change anything. I have my green card, so this is enough. I love America. I love Sicily too. Both."[44] For this transnational community rooted in Sicily's fishing villages, entering a public world of politics and national identities tied to citizenship seems a temporary response to the mid-twentieth-century crisis of global warfare.

The St. Joseph *Festa* and Postwar Identity

The Santa Rosalia *festa* was also transformed in the aftermath of World War II. No longer a paean to a Sicilian patron saint, or to the "sardine men," it became a cultural extravaganza, a tourist attraction, and—in becoming far more nationalized than in the past—an Italian Pride Day. It allowed participants to perform an ethnic identity that fully incorporated American political allegiance based on ethnicity. John Steinbeck described it as "the biggest barbecue the sardine men had ever given. . . . The speeches rose to a crescendo of patriotism and good feeling beyond anything Monterey had ever heard."[45]

With the demise of the sardine industry, another *festa,* this one honoring St. Joseph, gained prominence among Monterey's Sicilian families. While the Santa Rosalia *festa* celebrates a patron saint popular in northwestern Sicily, St. Joseph, the patron saint of friendship, is commonly honored with special rituals throughout Sicily and southern Italy. The St. Joseph's *festa* in Monterey celebrated not the Monterey community but links to Sicily and particularly to the island of Marettimo. Today the St. Joseph *festa* in

Monterey rivals the Santa Rosalia *festa* in terms of its importance within the community. It began exactly as the Santa Rosalia *festa* had begun—as one woman's impulse and many women's ritual.[46] "I started this whole thing in my kitchen," said Vitina Peroni.[47] "We talked about it and we said, 'We should do St. Joseph's here too,' just like we did in Marettimo," recalled Josephine Arancio.[48]

Women migrants from Marettimo dominate the planning and execution of the St. Joseph *festa*. Unlike Santa Rosalia, however, St. Joseph's does not take over the streets of Monterey or attract tourists. It is limited to a church service and banquet at the Elk's Lodge in Monterey. The St. Joseph *festa* is focused mainly on the ritual consumption of special foods, specifically desserts and other sweets made for that occasion only. The Italian language, and Sicilian dialect, is the dominant, if not exclusive, form of communication at the celebration of the St. Joseph *festa*. Sicilians plan vacations to Monterey to coincide with this celebration, and many of Monterey's Sicilians plan visits to their villages of origin, particularly Marettimo, to coincide with celebrations of St. Joseph's there.

Although no longer dependant on fishing as a livelihood, Monterey's Sicilian fisher people continue to express their identity as Sicilian fishers through their celebration of the *festa*. According to sixty-three-year-old Anna Sardina, who migrated to Monterey in 1962, it is the essence of identity, and Sicilian women are responsible for making it happen. "St. Joseph's is small, simple. It is our faith, our belief. This is how we bring the culture to our families, our children. This is the main thing. This is the beautiful thing. For St. Joseph's we gather together in Bea's house and make the *pignolo* and the *cubaida*.[49] It makes me remember the days when I was young—my grandmother. It is like being at home with all of the women together like that. The gathering—it makes you feel like you're not even here. You're there. [At St. Joseph's] everyone speaks our language."[50] Mrs. Sardina's narrative reflects the symbolic connection to home in the celebration of the *festa*, and that women were its driving force.

For JoAnn Mineo, the St. Joseph's *festa* is a critical symbolic connection to Sicily. As she rolled out the dough for the *pignolo* in Bea Bonnano's makeshift garage kitchen for the 2005 St. Joseph's *festa*, she reflected on "home." St. Joseph's is far more private an affair for Sicilians in Monterey than for Sicilians in Sicily. "It's closer here," said Mrs. Mineo. "We get together for a mass, lunch, and then a dinner dance. There are about 150 people who come. Everything is well organized, small, religious. We are new and old [immigrants]. Both. It is a time to be together."[51] That sense of togetherness in private is critical to Mrs. Mineo, who enthusiastically participates in the group baking and organizing that the Sicilian women do in the month before the *festa*.

Transnational Identities and Female-Dominated Community

The sense of transnational community—again maintained by women—is alive among the newer migrants as well. When I visited JoAnn Mineo, she was watching the Italian-language news on television, a common practice among Monterey Sicilians. She did not attend school in the United States but is fluent in English. Still, she is most comfortable speaking Italian, specifically Sicilian dialect. She and her family have made countless long and short visits to her native Trapani in the years since 1970. Her son was born there. Once, they stayed for a three-and-a-half-year sojourn. "I should own Alitalia," she said, "We go back so much! Every year! We own land [on] Marettimo. It has a view of the sea. We will build there, maybe in a year or two. We sold one house and I bought a[nother] house. In ten years I paid it off." Yet Mrs. Mineo considers Monterey her permanent home. "When I am there, I miss here. I miss the freedom, the shopping, the going out, the working."

Migrants like Mrs. Mineo expressed ambivalence about the kind of transnational identity they have forged. "Who am I? A little of this, a little of that. I'm an American, sure, but in my heart, I feel that [Marettimo] is my home. We go back in the summer, most of the summers. Sometimes I feel a little strange there too," commented Anita Ferrante.[52] Her ambivalence was echoed by other interviewees, who also expressed a strong sense of connection to Italy, to Sicily, and to Monterey. One recent immigrant and native of Trapani, Maria Tringali, said this of her sense of identity: "I don't know. I guess I am a little bit of both, here and there. I live here now [in Monterey] but we go home every year for a month, two months. I feel like I am at home [in Sicily], but I feel different too."[53]

It is possible to decide not to choose a permanent home site in the twenty-first century. One woman interviewed operates a small inn with her family on the island of Marettimo during the summer months but spends much of the winter in Monterey, working in retail shops on the wharf. She lives with cousins while she is in Monterey in order to economize, and because it is more comfortable for her to be with family, not because she might commit a cultural faux pas by living alone.[54]

One young mother of three in her early thirties now makes her home in San Vito Lo Capo, a village her grandmother left in the 1920s. On one of her summer vacations to San Vito in the 1980s, she met her Sicilian husband, fell in love, and decided to remain in Sicily rather than returning home to Monterey. She now divides her time between San Vito Lo Capo and Monterey but spends the bulk of the year in San Vito Lo Capo, which she considers her primary home, although she identifies herself as an "American girl." Hers is an unusual but not unique situation. As families increasingly enjoy the luxury of travel and descendants of migrants spend summers with extended families, there is continual migration back to Sicilian villages by younger generations.[55]

Identity for such people means a sense of genuine, lived attachment to Sicily and to Monterey, only intermittently troubled by the demands of nation-states for loyalty, taxes, or, during times of war, military service. Their family and marriage ties and long histories of movement allow them to navigate relatively easily the limited demands that nation-states such as Italy and the United States make on their citizens, so long as peace reigns in relations between the two nations their lives link. The life of Marielena Spadaro is a case in point. She is the granddaughter of women and men who migrated from the island of Marettimo, Sicily, in the 1920s. They never intended to return to Sicily. "My grandparents had bad memories of Marettimo. They wanted to make a new life here from the beginning," she explained. The family thrived in Monterey. They took advantage of the boom years of sardine fishing in the 1920s, 1930s, and 1940s. "My grandfather paid back an $80,000 loan in a year. They worked hard, saved, and really prospered here. No one ever thought of going back to live in Marettimo. But our family sent a lot of money back there, bought homes, boats" for the Marettimare relatives.[56]

Marielena married a fisherman from Marettimo while he was visiting Monterey. Her husband continues to identify as a Sicilian. His intentions as a migrant were to fish recreationally while finding work in Monterey and to return home to Sicily. With his marriage to Marielena, that changed. The couple purchased a home next door to her parents' home in what is known as Fisherman's Flats in Monterey. They have two children. They visit Sicily often for periods of a month or more but have no intention of living there permanently. Marielena's husband appeared to be the typical sojourner who came to look for better economic opportunities in Monterey but identifies strongly as a fisherman. Marielena's family history demonstrates that the migrations to Monterey were largely family enterprises and meant to be permanent movements, even from the beginning of settlement. When families came to Monterey, they came to fish, and although they moved into other businesses as new opportunities in tourism arose, they continued to identify as fishing people while making economic decisions that cemented their presence in Monterey. Women in the family participated actively in both the migrant stream, in cementing identities as fisher people, and in the business enterprises that followed the economic dependence on fishing. Women primarily kept connections alive, which led to a constant migration flow. Sicilians maintained a conscious attachment to the culture of Sicily and the customs of their villages of origin, as a matter of course, but these attachments were intensified when it became possible to visit the island frequently enough to make the connections real. And yet it was Marielena who determined the home site and the family's place of primary residence. Both Marielena and her husband feel strongly attached to Sicily, an attachment they express through everything from menu items in their restaurants to the language that they speak. The family home is Monterey because Marielena made that choice, but that did not imply a loss of connection to Sicily.[57]

Rose Ann Aliotti, a travel agent and a member of one of Monterey's fishing families, emphasized the frequency of visits by migrants at every economic level to Sicily and Monterey. "It is common for honeymoon[ing] couples or people who come to visit families or to work for a few months to come to Monterey." It is the continual influx of new migrants, temporary or not, that adds ethnic vitality to this community.[58]

The scholarly literature on Sicilian immigration recognizes women as important, even vital, to the migration and settlement of families.[59] However, this study clearly shows that Sicilian women in Monterey played a pivotal role in the process of continually reconstructing the community's identity. A reassessment of identity requiring an incorporation of political identity as Americans occurred during and after World War II, but this reassessment—largely accomplished by men—proved temporary. Over time, Sicilian women and men maintain important ties to the villages that keep connections alive and allow for the formation of both the active and symbolic transnationalism so commonly noted in scholarly literature on Mexican, Dominican, and Southeast Asian immigrant groups in the late twentieth and twenty-first centuries.[60]

The sense of transnational connection that Monterey Sicilians feel extends beyond the local on both sides of the ocean. Travel to regions of Italy beyond Sicily is just as extensive as travel to home villages. Italian popular culture and news about politics and economics are readily accessible to residents of Monterey through widespread access to Italian television. Sicilian Monterey reflects a deeply rooted transnationalism that is persistent, continual, and felt at all levels, from family and household to village, region, and state.

State-Imposed Translocalism and the Dream of Returning

ITALIAN MIGRANTS IN SWITZERLAND

Susanne Wessendorf

Emigration has been part of everyday life for the poor in Italy since the nineteenth century. At first, Italians primarily went to the Americas and later, during the first half of the twentieth century, to northwest Europe and Australia. These migrations were undertaken in the context of harsh economic and social conditions, and transnational families were a widespread phenomenon all over Italy.[1] Thanks to shorter distances and swifter means of transportation, postwar Italian labor migration to northern Europe was characterized by particularly lively transnational relations. Although earlier studies on Italian postwar labor migration did not conceptualize these relations as "transnational," already during the 1970s and 1980s, researchers were looking at the connections that Italian migrants maintained to their homeland.[2]

In line with more recent studies that look at postwar Italian labor migration in Europe from a specifically transnational perspective, I focus here on the long-standing connections of Italians living in Switzerland to their home villages, and on the continuity of such connections through the generations.[3] It could be argued that these relationships are translocal rather than transnational, since migrants travel back and forth between their villages of origin and the towns of settlement in Switzerland, and their connections to the homeland are based on nostalgia for the place of origin rather than the nation-state.[4] I examine two main factors reinforcing such connections. The first is what I conceptualize as "state-imposed translocalism," referring to Swiss state regulations regarding migration across national borders. The second relates to Italian families' own plans to return to Italy as soon as possible, even as they simultaneously extend their stays from year to year for economic reasons. I describe how the combination of national public policies regulating migration and Italian families' own plans to return have led to what Italian migrants have long regarded as "provisional settlement" in Switzerland, with migrants staying in Switzerland for several decades, while continuing to dream of returning.

I begin with a discussion of how Swiss immigration policies affected the private lives of Italian families during the first years of their migration in the 1950s and 1960s. These policies led to repeated and prolonged separations of migrant families and to strong connections with their villages in southern Italy. But even after receiving permanent residency permits in Switzerland and after the reunification of their families, Italian migrants continued to maintain their connections to Italy because they dreamed of returning. However, economic obstacles prevented the realization of their return for many years.

The second part of this chapter describes how as a result of the long-term separations of families because of restrictive policies on family reunification and migrants' repeated extensions of their stays in Switzerland, Italian migrants have developed a somewhat idealized notion of the united family, viewing family solidarity as a primary element in Italian culture. This family solidarity becomes particularly strong over the annual summer holidays in southern Italy, when the united family can be celebrated and can enjoy each other's company. Summer holidays are the principal way of celebrating connections to Italy, and the whole year is organized around these holidays. I describe these kinds of engagements as "holiday translocalism." Holiday translocalism has persisted over several decades and has changed from provisional extensions of families and households across long distances to continuities of cross-border activities and intimacies to form an integral part of many families' everyday lives.

Despite these continuities, fifty years of emigration and the divergences of life experiences between migrants and non-migrants make it difficult for many migrants to imagine a life in their homeland. Furthermore, with the second generation entering adulthood and the birth of the third generation in Switzerland, many Italian migrants' family relationships have become increasingly localized in Switzerland. While for several decades life in Switzerland was perceived as a provisional phase that would eventually lead to a definitive repatriation, this shift of family relationships from translocal (between Switzerland and Italian villages) to local (in Switzerland) has brought with it the awareness that the dream of returning and of living as a united family in Italy may never be realized. The parallel existence of kinship networks in both Italy and Switzerland and the distribution of family members across borders are thereby increasingly accepted as a fact of life rather than seen as a provisional life phase.[5]

The Background of Postwar Italian Labor Migration: State-Imposed Translocalism

Postwar Italian labor migration to Switzerland was part of the European labor migration, during which tens of thousands of southern and southeastern Europeans moved to western Europe to help build the booming postwar economy. By 1970, more than half-a-million Italians lived in Switzerland. The majority of them migrated to the German- and French-speaking parts of Switzerland, where most jobs were available.[6] As a result of return migration, their numbers declined to approximately 300,000 by 2001.[7] For a country with seven million inhabitants in total, these numbers are considerable, and Italians still form one of the largest migrant groups in Switzerland.

The majority of Italian migrants were unskilled, landless farmers who migrated from rural areas in the south to industrial Swiss cities. Their settlement process was complicated by economic and political instability, and most migrants dreamed of returning to Italy as soon as they were economically able to do so. During the 1950s and 1960s and under the *Gastarbeiter* (guest worker) scheme, Swiss policies regulating immigration were aimed at the temporary residency of labor migrants. Recruitment of foreign labor was conditional upon work contracts, and for fear that economic growth and labor shortage would only be temporary, immigration was regarded as a cyclical buffer. This system was intended to allow Switzerland to send away surplus laborers when they were not needed in order to provide Swiss nationals full employment.[8]

In the context of these so-called rotation policies, about 70 percent of Italian migrants who came to Switzerland up to the early 1960s were male and unmarried, and about a third of the workforce was rotated each year.[9] One of the most important instruments of Switzerland's immigration policies was the seasonal permit, which allowed for a stay of only nine months a year and prohibited family reunion. Some migrants were granted one-year permits, but they could bring their families to Switzerland only after a certain amount of time. The waiting period was three years until 1964, when it was reduced to eighteen months, and later to fifteen.[10]

After 1964, when new policies facilitated family reunification, more and more women followed their male compatriots. However, female migrants did not only go to Switzerland on family reunification schemes; a substantial number of them were unmarried and joined their brothers and sisters, cousins, and neighbors, some even before 1964.[11]

Separations from spouses and children resulting from restrictive family reunification policies are remembered by Italian migrants even today as difficult and often traumatic. During the 1970s, 45 percent of Italian women in Switzerland lived apart from their children for extended periods of time. In fact, many migrants illegally brought their children to Switzerland. During the 1970s, 10,000 to 15,000 Italian children were illegally living in Switzerland, hidden in migrants' apartments, an issue that has only come to the fore in recent years.[12]

In addition to these restrictive family reunification policies, several anti-immigrant referenda took place during the 1960s and 1970s. Although workers were desperately needed to fill labor shortages, many Swiss perceived Italian migrants as a threat to the integrity of Swiss culture, and in various civil protests and political referenda against immigration, terms such as "excess of foreigners" (*Überfremdung*) and metaphors such as "the boat is full" were used to emphasize that Switzerland could not accept more migrants.[13] An example of such a referendum was the so-called Schwarzenbach referendum against "foreign infiltration" in 1970. It was presented by a populist right-wing party and led by the populist politician James Schwarzenbach. The referendum would have reduced the number of immigrants from 17 to 10 percent of the overall population in Switzerland within a time span of three years.[14] Although it was rejected by the Swiss population, it caused much fear among migrants, and Italians in Switzerland have particularly vivid memories of it. Some of them remember that they made concrete preparations to leave Switzerland should the referendum be accepted. The paradoxical result was a particularly strong attachment to Switzerland among some members of the second generation, who also feared being expelled from the country.

Despite such anti-immigrant political referenda, restrictive immigration policies were eased over time because economic growth continued and, at the same time, fewer Swiss nationals were willing to take the low-paying jobs that foreign workers were doing. Rotation policies and short-term residency permits therefore lost their significance, and increasing attention was paid to immigrant workers who were there to stay.[15] Italian migrants were now granted permanent residency permits, and the Swiss government set up a commission to support the integration of immigrants and their children.[16]

The restrictive state policies during the 1950s and 1960s, and the provisional residency permits that prevented migrants from planning a longer-term future in Switzerland, were paralleled by similarly provisional living conditions. For example, during the first years of their stay in Switzerland and up until the late 1960s, many Italians lived in barracks or communal housing provided by their employers. The barracks were shared by either single men or several families who took turns cooking and taking care of other household tasks. Italians found it very difficult to get their own apartments because of discrimination in the housing market and high rents. But living in communal housing also helped them to save as much money as possible for their return. Many migrants described their living conditions as miserable and humiliating. They felt exploited by their employers (who were often also their landlords) but accepted it because they believed their sacrifices would only be temporary. As they extended their stays in Switzerland, they increased their efforts to find apartments where they could lead more private lives with their families.[17]

This transformation from temporary living to aspirations for more comfortable housing among Italian migrants mirrored both the changes in Swiss state policies regulating migrants' residency status and the changes in Italian migrants' own plans for migration. Confronted with the realities of life in Switzerland and with ongoing economic instability in southern Italy, migrants' plans to earn as much as possible in a short time and go back home slowly transformed into plans to establish a secure existence in both Switzerland and Italy.[18]

The change in state policies and migrants' own changing intentions (from provisional to longer-term settlement) were accompanied by changes in Swiss attitudes toward Italians. While stigmatized from the 1950s to the 1970s as "knife-wielding criminals," seducers of Swiss women, "spaghetti munchers," and lazy slackers, Italians came to be seen by many Swiss as lovely, warm-hearted people and as a model minority.[19] Because their children have been socioeconomically upwardly mobile and have been doing rather well in the labor market, Italians are now presented in museum exhibitions, books, and radio programs as an historical example of migration and its possible outcome, which is generally assessed as positive, despite the many hardships Italians were confronted with.[20] The increasing accommodation of Italians by the Swiss has even been accompanied by a process that could be described as the "Mediterraneazation" of Switzerland, with an increased appreciation for everything associated with the Italian lifestyle (such as good food and fashion).[21] Nevertheless, and despite permanent residency permits and improved working and living conditions, many Italian migrants in Switzerland have continued to dream of returning and have maintained their connections to southern Italy.

The Dream of Returning and the Continual Extension of Provisional Settlement

At the time of migration, most migrants did not have clear plans for how long they would stay in Switzerland and "just went to see what it's like."[22] They saw their migration to Switzerland as provisional and short term, and they therefore continued to maintain strong social networks with relatives and friends in Italy. This was facilitated by the fact that Italy could easily be reached by train, although the uncomfortable train journeys took up to twenty hours and were very expensive.

Although Italian migrants saw themselves as sojourners, they extended their stays year after year, while orienting their lives toward an eventual return. By 1970, return had become a serious issue because of the economic recession. Some migrants lost their jobs and were forced to return to Italy, and others chose to leave Switzerland because of the insecurity of both their work contracts and their residency status.[23] However, of the 522,000 Italians living in Switzerland in 1975, only 60,000 returned to Italy during that year. From then on, the number declined to an average of 15,000 a year during the 1980s, and 11,500 a year during the 1990s.[24] Hence, the majority of migrants, about two-thirds, stayed in Switzerland. Most of them saw a return prior to economic achievement as failure.[25]

Because of the dream of returning and the idea that the stay in Switzerland would be temporary, if longer term, migrants worked as much as they possibly could and lived as modestly as possible, investing all their money in a house in the country of origin. As one of my second-generation Italian interviewees said, "my parents knew nothing else other than work—no pizza in a restaurant, no entertainment."

Despite accumulating savings, migrants found that it continued to be difficult to return because of the precarious job situation in Italy. Thus, only after many years, and often after retiring with a Swiss pension, did some migrants find the return financially viable. However, even if financially possible, with time, other considerations became important. For example, the Swiss health system, which most migrants judge to be better than the Italian system, is a strong incentive to stay in Switzerland, especially as they age. Furthermore, as time passed and as a result of regular visits to the villages of origin, many migrants became aware of how much they had grown used to the efficient Swiss administration and to functioning public services that are still lacking in Italy's south.[26] It is not just the structural conditions that make return difficult. In addition, the changes in perceptions of cultural values and practices among migrants have led to a certain feeling of estrangement in Italy.

However, the most important reason why the majority of Italian migrants have stayed in Switzerland is their children. As their children grew older, Italian migrants had to decide where they would send them to school, and many decided to extend their stays in Switzerland until their children completed their education.[27] Therefore, many postponed their return until their children were grown and economically stable or, as they say, *sistemati*. But once their children were adults, only a few of them were willing to migrate to the villages of origin with their parents.[28] Because many migrants found it difficult to leave their children behind, they decided to extend their stays in Switzerland even longer. Even after the age of retirement, when it is financially easier to return, two-thirds of Italian migrants have decided to stay in Switzerland. Although the original justification for being in Switzerland was work, the reason to stay has now shifted to family ties.[29] This is a rather contradictory outcome of the original goal of migration, which was a better future for the children in Italy. My research confirms Baldassar's observations in the Italian Australian context that a better future for the children or, in other words, the children's socioeconomic improvement can become a barrier to migrants' return to Italy.[30] Many members of the second generation are not prepared to give up their jobs in Switzerland for an insecure professional future in Italy. This places their parents in a dilemma. Especially because of the experience of living apart from children during the early years of migration, to be living away from them again is unimaginable for many. In fact, although the family was very important in southern Italy prior to emigration, the conditions of migration and the wish to return had an important impact on the cultural perceptions of the family among Italian migrants in Switzerland.

The Idealization of the United Family and the Attachment to the Place of Origin

> We celebrate every birthday together and then we are all together at Grandma's place, and we also celebrate Christmas there. . . . The *family* is the most important, you know. . . . To have a family that works, to see each other, it's a pleasure, isn't it?

Luca was born in Switzerland in 1972. His parents had migrated from Sicily in the early 1960s. He grew up in an extended network of kin and was raised by his parents and his grandmother in Switzerland, together with his cousins. This large network of relatives provided him with social stability during his childhood and adolescence, and spending time with his cousins and an uncle of the same age strengthened his identification with co-ethnics. Luca describes his family as "typically Italian" and thereby asserts his Italianness in contrast with the Swiss, whom he describes as individualistic and "colder." Luca's reification of the Italian family exemplifies how among many Italians in Switzerland *la famiglia* is celebrated as the ultimate site of Italian culture, a phenomenon also observed in other contexts, for example among Italians in Britain and in the United States.[31] This reification and idealization of the family has been interpreted as a result of the separation of families in the context of migration because of Swiss state regulations on family reunification. These separations led to a certain "myth of the family" and to the idealization of being united *(essere uniti)* as one of the key elements of identification among Italians in Switzerland.[32] It is experienced with particular intensity during holidays in Italy and is a crucial element of Italian culture in Switzerland, especially for the first generation. Significantly, "being united" has broader connotations than just being together physically. Rather, it implies a sense of standing up for each other no matter what. Migration is viewed as a shared project of the whole family, even though some stayed behind and many lived apart for many years. If anything, long separations strengthened migrants' commitment to family unity and mutual support. Hence, rather than taking the family for granted through constant day-to-day interaction, Italians, like many other migrants with transnational families, construct the idea of a family more deliberately.[33]

Although many migrants have lived in Switzerland for several decades and brought up children there, these ideas of the united family are linked to the wish to live with the family in one place rather than translocally. Since many migrants have been in close contact with relatives in southern Italy over several decades, the place in which the relatives reside is ideally seen as the village of origin. Thus, although migrants have repeatedly extended their stays, they have continued to see their return as a realistic future plan and as the ultimate outcome of their migration. This wish to return to the homeland is based on a strong attachment to the village of origin.

Baldassar has linked this attachment to place among migrants to *campanilismo* in Italy.[34] A common cultural category in both northern and southern Italy, *campanilismo* translates as "parochialism" but is also understood to mean pride in one's hometown. The word stems from the Italian word for "bell tower," a reference to the church as the focal point of the village, and to the local identity of people "who share the same town time and who respond to the same death knells."[35] Although contested, many southern Italian migrants in Switzerland value the attachment to their *paese*[36] and justify their plans of returning to it. Thus, the first generation often wishes for their children to marry someone from the same village of origin, since such a marriage would facilitate their return to their *paese* together with their children and grandchildren. Such expectations—which are more often than not unfulfilled—have led to conflicts in many Italian families in Switzerland.

Closely related to *campanilismo* are the acquisition of land and the building of a house in the village of origin. Not only does owning land and a house, *la casa*, symbolize the dream of returning; it also signifies all the hard work, sacrifice, and economic achievement of the migrant laborer—the achievement of *sistemazione*, a secure economic base. It is both a status symbol and a tangible, lasting object that reinforces the connections to the homeland and transforms the repeatedly postponed dream of returning into a realistic and credible option for the future.[37] Owning property in Italy legitimizes the return as a strategically possible conclusion to the migration plan, and it provides a symbolic site for the (re)united family and an investment that links future generations to the country of origin. As a site that gives meaning to the sacrifices that came with migration, and a place onto which the imagined future of the united family is projected, the house could also be described as a "cultural site" that ties migrants "to homelands in much more concrete ways than through the imagined worlds erected by the creative resources of fantasy."[38]

The continuity of the dream of returning and the desire to live in the homeland, united with the family, has persisted into the present, and it is now expressed on Internet sites that connect the southern Italian village communities with their emigrants. In July 2003, an elderly emigrant wrote the following poem in a chat room on the Web site of his village of origin:

Salve mia cara Salve	Salve my dear Salve
A 18 anni io ti lasciai	I left you at the age of eighteen
ed in Svizzera emigrai.	and emigrated to Switzerland
Poco tempo credevo di stare via	I thought I'd stay away for a short time
per poi tornare nella Salve mia.	in order to return to my Salve.

Ma il tempo si sa è ingannatore	But time always wins,
non ti lascia mai fare quello che hai nel cuore.	it never lets you follow your heart.
In Svizzera una bella famigliola	In Switzerland, a nice family
mi sono formato, mi ritengo fortunato.	I have formed, I am lucky.
47 anni da quel lontano 1956 sono passati	Forty-seven years have passed since this long-gone 1956,
mi ritrovo pensionato, felice nonno	I am retired and a happy granddad
perciò diventa sempre piu difficile un mio ritorno.	and therefore my return gets more and more difficult.
Ma non ti preoccupare, perchè	But don't worry, because whenever I can
tutte le volte che posso, ti vengo a trovare	I come and find you
con un pò di nostalgia	with a bit of nostalgia.
sei sempre nel mio cuore, o Salve mia.	You are always in my heart, oh my Salve.[39]

Holiday Translocalism

Many Italian migrants continue to spend as much time in Italy as possible. Time spent *al paese*, in the village of origin, is perceived as a well-deserved reward for the many years of hard work and sacrifice in Switzerland. At least once a year, mostly in the summer and sometimes also at Christmas, they go to southern Italy to spend time with their relatives in their newly built houses.

Despite the expansion of air travel, most of them continue to do the fifteen- to twenty-hour journey by train or car, partly because it is cheaper, but also because they are generally transporting large quantities of gifts such as chocolate, sausages, and clothes for relatives when going to Italy, and olive oil, pasta, parmesan cheese, coffee, and other Italian foods when returning to Switzerland.

The extent of border crossing between Switzerland and Italy is magnified on the highways and railways that connect the two regions, especially during the summer. For example, the nightly train between Zurich and Lecce (Apulia) is famous for being fully booked every night during summer. Every evening, the same spectacular scenes take place in Lecce and Zurich: Hundreds of people push and shove big suitcases, boxes of Swiss sausages, and empty canisters of olive oil into train compartments when going "down" to Lecce. And when "going up" to Switzerland, they carry heavy canisters of olive oil and boxes of food. Platforms are crowded with people, old and young, who say their farewells and wave as the train departs. And despite the frequency with which people undertake these journeys, the farewell scenes and the scenes taking place inside the trains constitute dramatic performances acted out time and again. Year after year, the family is thereby publicly celebrated as a close-knit unit during these moments of farewell.

Once the train leaves, people unpack their sandwiches, offering them to each other, and on each journey, stories are told of how different and less comfortable the journey used to be some thirty or forty years ago. These are intense fifteen- to twenty-hour journeys during which the destinies and life histories of many migrants are talked about and dealt with time and again.

The journeys as well as the holidays form part of the migrants and their children's everyday lives and have become an integral part of how migrants organize their year, economically and socially. This was summarized best by Annagrazia in talking about her childhood and adolescence. She is a second-generation Italian woman, born in 1973, who lives in Switzerland and continues to go to Italy every year.

> Oh [the holiday] was heaven! From March onward, the holidays were the only thing we talked about: what we would take with us, what we would wear. It was a point of reference also for my parents. When we returned to Switzerland . . . it was a bit like a new start, like the first of January, new objectives, you know . . . and then you worked, and then Christmas came . . . and from January onward, you started saving money again for the summer. Yes, January till February was a bit of a sad time because the summer was still so far away, and then came March and then Easter and you already started preparing.

One of the most positive things about such a lifestyle, according to migrants and their children, is a feeling of being embedded in a big network of relatives while in Italy. This sense of embeddedness, or belonging, is contrasted with a feeling of isolation in Switzerland, where there are not as many relatives and where contacts with them are less regular.[40] In fact, life during the holidays in Italy stands in stark contrast with life in Switzerland. In Apulia, many migrants' houses are always full of relatives and children, and their days are characterized by a constant stream of visitors for lunch, coffee, and aperitifs. In contrast, family life in Switzerland usually unfolds in an apartment in the city and is characterized by long working days and evenings within the nuclear family. The bustling life during the holidays in Italy ("We are always together, the whole family") forms part of the notion of the united family and the fond memories of southern Italy and contributes to the continuing emotional connection to the place of origin.

During the holidays in Italy, much time spent together or "being united" is devoted to eating. Food and cooking are an important part of everyday conversations, especially among women. In fact, the local food, provided by the fertile (home)land, *la terra*, contributes to the nostalgia for the homeland and the romanticization of the past among many Italian migrants. Local food, shared with Italian relatives on holidays in Italy and transported to Switzerland in large olive oil containers and boxes, symbolizes the physically and spiritually nourishing nature of the villages of origin. Sharing food is a sign of reciprocity among family members and between neighbors, and of the importance of being united. Meals together also play a role in the construction of an image of the homeland as a leisurely, sunny place where warmth, spontaneity, and hospitality prevail and things are taken a bit less seriously. Thus, both the family and the food become a symbolic marker of belonging and Italianness in the context of migration. This contrast to the seriousness of life in Switzerland, dominated by work, order, and cleanliness, resembles what Gardner describes as *desh* among Bangladeshi migrants in Britain, meaning the spirituality and the fertility of the homeland in Bangladesh, in contrast to *bidesh*, the economic and political power of the host country.[41]

The contrast between the two places and the realities of the geographic distance separating the emotionally and spiritually nourishing homeland from the host country are particularly apparent at the end of each holiday during the farewells to relatives and friends. Antonietta, who was born in Switzerland, described how she used to feel as a child when she left southern Italy after the long summer holiday: "When I left, I always felt a bit bad. And I remember how, when we were preparing to leave, the relatives came to greet us, and everybody was crying—it seemed like a funeral each time, a tragedy! When we went away, I remember that each time the grandparents cried, that they [the parents] went to greet everybody, *mamma mia,* it really was a tragedy. I will always remember how everybody cried, the parents, and even us." This "tragedy" of saying good-bye left strong impressions of what it means to live apart. In fact, at each visit to the homeland, the struggle of migration, primarily motivated by economic needs, but continually prolonged by the changing life projects of the subsequent generation, comes to the fore.

Despite the difficulties of leaving the homeland behind at the end of the holiday, Italian migrants' everyday experiences of holiday translocalism not only are characterized by a sense of belonging and embeddedness within their families in Italy but are also accompanied by feelings of alienation in Italy.

The Realities of Long-Term Separations

The lively and regular relationships that Italian migrants in Switzerland have maintained with their homeland have had somewhat contradictory effects. The combination of short-term residency permits during the early years of their migration and the migrants' financial investments in the homeland based on the persistent wish to return prevented many of them from settling in Switzerland for good and investing in a better life there. Plans to stay in Switzerland only temporarily have led to a counterreaction among members of the second generation. Today, many second-generation Italians in Switzerland emphasize that they do not want to live in one place and dream of the other, as their parents have done all these years. Rather than investing money and energy in the country of origin, they see their future in Switzerland. They wish to acquire property there, and most of them cannot imagine living in another place. Hence, the families' translocalism and the parents' dream of returning have led to a certain rootedness among members of the second generation in Switzerland.[42] While engaging in border-traversing activities, immigrants and especially their descendants can also develop new local attachments and ties.[43] The new interests and engagements that come with these local attachments often stand in contrast to the translocal involvement of the parents and the original plan of migration. Parallel to their translocal everyday lives during childhood and adolescence, second-generation migrants integrate into different strata and milieus of the host society and, as a consequence, sometimes lose interest in translocal connections.

However, over the course of time and despite the considerable effort that they have put into maintaining relations to the homeland, even their parents begin to find it difficult to relate to the local people who have never left Italy. In the context of forty to fifty years of emigration, with lives characterized by very different work experiences in urban Switzerland, and experiences of diverging cultural values and practices, migrants sometimes struggle to adapt to local southern Italian cultural values and practices, especially in regard to gender relations, corruption, and bureaucracy. For example, women find it difficult to deal with what they experience as high degrees of social control in southern Italian villages, especially after having enjoyed a certain freedom to shape their own lives in Switzerland. Although gender relations in southern Italy have seen changes over the last thirty years, and many women now contribute to the family income through wage labor, emigrant women as well as female returnees complain about what they see as old-fashioned gender relations in their home villages.[44]

An additional factor that contributes to feelings of alienation among both men and women is the experience of being called *Svizzerotto* (a half-joking, half-condescending label for Italians living in Switzerland) by non-migrant relatives and friends. Although used jokingly, the term *Svizzerotto* exemplifies the gap between the life experiences of migrants and non-migrants and the distinction local people make between "us" and "them."

One of my retired informants, a woman from Apulia who commutes regularly, simply said that "emigration has divided us forever." This woman's view of the long-term consequences of emigration shows that for some migrants, the differences that develop when one is away, living in a different place, and having different experiences over a long period of time cannot be bridged easily, even with regular contact. This is experienced in particular by those migrants who do eventually return to their villages of origin. One returnee who went back to Apulia ten years ago told me that he has not been able to reconnect to the local people and that he mainly spends time with other returnees.[45] He also is disappointed with and distressed by this seemingly irreversible and unexpected rupture. Forty to fifty years of emigration and spending more than half of one's life in a different place makes it difficult for migrants to reintegrate socially and culturally into a context in which they have not experienced everyday life for several decades.

The factor of time in this process of alienation shows that the migrants' nostalgia for the homeland is aimed not only at their *place* of origin but also at long-gone *times*. It is a nostalgia for an imagined homeland that does not exist anymore, the image of which has helped many migrants to cope with the difficult conditions they have encountered in Switzerland.

In relation to Italian migrants in Britain, Fortier describes how the country of origin is a subject of longing, while the host county represents the migrants' efforts to belong. While this was also the case among Italians in Switzerland, over the course of time, migrants have had to make efforts to belong in the country of origin, too. The sense of belonging to the communities of origin, taken for granted for so many years, has thus been challenged by both geographical distance and time, and for some migrants, this distance in space and time seems unbridgeable.[46]

Conclusion

Translocalism, based on long-standing attachment to place, has been one of the main characteristics of Italian emigration since the nineteenth century, and although the routes of Italian emigration have changed from the Americas to Australia and then northwestern Europe, the attachment to the place of origin continues to shape Italian émigré identity.[47] I have shown how the relationships of southern Italian labor migrants in Switzerland to their home villages have been, on the one hand, affected by public policies that had a dramatic impact on migrant families' private lives during the early years of their migration and, on the other, by their wish to return to the homeland resulting from strong attachments to the village of origin.

During the early years of migration, short-term residency permits and restrictive policies regarding family reunion led to regular travel back and forth and prolonged separations between spouses, and between parents and children. This state-imposed translocalism and the many separations from children and kin resulted in the idealization of the united family among many Italian migrants. The idealization of family solidarity could thus be interpreted as a counter-position to the state, which forced families to live apart. In fact, in the southern Italian context, so-called familism, the strong reliance on the family and on networks of kin, has been interpreted as resistance against centralized, authoritarian states.[48] In the context of migration, the idealization of the united family could be interpreted as similar cultural resistance to state policies. However, even as policies have allowed family reunion and permanent settlement, migrants have continued to wish to return. After several decades of emigration, and despite the realization that their children would stay in Switzerland, many of them remain attached to their roots in their villages of origin and nurture their nostalgia for the homeland in a variety of ways.

In order to maintain translocal relationships and to keep the dream of returning an actual possibility and real option for the future, migrants resorted to holiday translocalism, spending every summer holiday in Italy. Furthermore, they acquired land and houses in their villages of origin to make the possibility of a future life in Italy more real. Despite this considerable investment of time and financial resources, over the course of time, many migrants have realized how much they have changed because of the many years they have spent in Switzerland. As a result of life experiences very different from those of their non-migrant relatives and friends, they now struggle with local cultural values and practices in southern Italy. Thus, in parallel with the continuation of intimate relationships with relatives in southern Italy, migrants also experience a certain degree of alienation when visiting their homeland.

Members of the second generation, who have reached adulthood and many of whom now have children, are experiencing translocalism very differently from their parents. The regular contact with the *paese* by way of visits formed an integral part of their upbringing and had an important impact on them. However, unlike their parents and despite—or maybe because of—the fact that they grew up in such lively translocal worlds, members of the second generation now wish to put down roots in Switzerland. Rather than investing emotional and financial resources in Italy while living in Switzerland, most of them feel at home in Switzerland, where they grew up, and only a very small minority of second-generation Italians return to live in their parents' villages of origin. At the same time, many of them continue to visit Italy regularly. Thus, translocal intimacies fostered by their parents have taken on a different meaning for members of the second generation, who have developed local attachments in Switzerland.

The second generation's local attachments in Switzerland have, in turn, led to a shift in their parents' emotional engagements. As grandchildren are born, the parents' wish to return to the homeland comes into question, and the desire to be (re)united in the homeland is finally seen as a long-term dream rather than as a realistic option for the future. In fact, the birth of the third generation makes it easier for many migrants to accept that despite all their financial efforts and the maintenance of relationships with family members in the homeland, the original plan to return to the homeland will not be fulfilled. Connections to the homeland may well continue, but home has now been localized by the third generation in Switzerland.

Obligation to People and Place

THE NATIONAL IN CULTURES OF CAREGIVING

Loretta Baldassar

It is not surprising that national awareness comes from outside the community rather than from within. . . . The nostalgic is never a native but a displaced person who mediates between the local and the universal.

—SVETLANA BOYM, *THE FUTURE OF NOSTALGIA*

I have argued elsewhere that the visit home should be understood as an integral part of the migration process.[1] An analysis of people on the move between Italy and Australia over the past century reveals that the first three stages in the classical migration model—arrival (of lone male), family reunion, and settlement—were followed by increased travel and constant and regular contact between kin in both places. This phenomenon of ongoing visits and communication highlights how the migration experience extends beyond settlement. Older constructions of migration as a one-way movement involving separation and removal tended to obscure the reality of continual, albeit at times limited, contact that more recent conceptions of transnationalism and developments in communication and travel technologies have brought to the fore.

In the one hundred years of migration between Italy and Australia, at least two groups of migrants are evident: older labor migrants (both pre– and immediate post–Second World War waves) and recent professionals (arriving since the 1980s).[2] Although each group departed from and arrived in the same places, they left starkly different Italies and settled in very different Australias. An analysis of their visits and transnational communication experiences reveals that although they differ according to historical context, two key themes are a clear constant—obligations to people and to place. In this chapter I examine how these obligations to kin and country are connected and how they manifest in the related emotions of longing and nostalgia. I attempt to explore what these linkages may tell us about the "intimate culture" of nationalism. Is love of family tied to love of country, and is love of home the same as love of nation? The argument I want to develop is not simply that migrants have attachments to Italy as well as to family. Rather, I aim to interrogate the relationship between family and nation through the processes of migration.

The body of fieldwork I draw on is particularly apt, if somewhat unusual—extensive research on transnational caregiving and specifically on how migrants living in Australia manage to care for their aging parents from afar. Data were collected as part of a collaborative study involving over two hundred ethnographic life-history interviews and participant observation conducted between 2000 and 2005.[3] The research was "two ended," involving families living in Perth as well as their kin living in Ireland, Italy, the Netherlands, Singapore, New Zealand, and Iran. The findings document the various practices and processes by which caregiving is provided across distance, including through visits and the use of communication technologies. For the purposes of this chapter, I focus primarily on the approximately twenty-four families (over forty interviews) in the Italian migrant sample. I also draw on ethnographic research conducted over several years in the 1990s consisting of extensive participant observation and in-depth interviews exploring the visit histories of approximately forty families (over eighty interviews) from San Fior, a town in the province of Treviso in the Veneto region, and their kin in Perth and Queensland.

As parents age and begin to lose the ability to live independently, or as their need for support and care increases, kin and social relationships often must be reorganized to accommodate these needs. This particular moment in the family life cycle constitutes, in anthropological terms, a crisis—that is, an event (like birth, marriage, or death) that lays bare the key structures, relationships, and meanings that govern social life. These negotiations highlight the reciprocal obligations of the "intergenerational contract": beliefs and roles governing caregiving between the generations within families. Locating this set of issues within the migration process highlights questions of identity, obligation, and belonging and provides a particularly intimate view on the lived experiences of nationalism.

For Italian migrants, negotiating the aging process of their parents raises a number of key concerns. For many, it brings into question their decision to live so far away, particularly among those who did not have "license to leave"—and who departed against their families' wishes. Without exception, confronting the aging of their parents poses a challenge to notions about obligations to care for parents. In addition, in most cases, parents represent an important link to place. Italian migrants in general feel they have open access to their parents' homes, that they are always welcome there. Hence, while their parents are alive and living in their own homes, migrants generally enjoy a secure sense of belonging in the homeland. As their parents become frail and require care, perhaps losing governance of their households to a child living locally, migrants' sense of connection to place can be threatened. Arguably then, the crisis of aging invites us to tease out how Italian migrant ties to family are linked to ties to country. For example, does the death of parents lead to a diminished sense of belonging to place for migrants?

The ensuing analysis of Italian identities raises the issue of "methodological nationalism," the false assumption that particular cultural traits or processes are "unitary and organically related to, and fixed within, [geographic] territories."[4] The data presented here capture both emic and popularly held perspectives on national, cultural, and ethnic identities. While similar practices and processes were found across the six country group samples in the transnational caregiving study from which the Italian sample is drawn, my focus here is on notions of family and caregiving defined by informants as quintessentially Italian. Consideration is also given to the organizational features of the state and how nation-state borders shape the family and caregiving practices that cross them.[5] These identities are understood as constructed in specific contexts[6] and therefore differ according to the diversity of gender, class, regional, and ethnic background within populations and, importantly, at the time of migration.[7]

Obligations to People: The Trope of Family

The desire to understand migrant connections to homeland in the context of family ties invites a broader discussion of the role of the idea of family in the Italian national imaginary. As mentioned in the introduction to this volume, close families are recognized internationally as characteristic of Italian culture. From Banfield's notion of amoral familism[8] to the *mammismo* of today (see Pojmann's chapter in this volume), Italian families are seen as being very close even beyond the nuclear family, with relationships among extended family members. As Pesman's and Wessendorf's chapters in this volume highlight, a common trope of republican nation building defines families as the cradle of the nation, and (as the chapters in the second part of this volume show) women as their mothers. Notions about close family ties have come to be associated with *italianità* (Italianness) at home and abroad, perhaps most particularly in the migrant imaginary.

In the Australian context, research by Chiro and Smolicz shows that Italo-Australian migrants from both the first and second generations identify close family ties as a "core value" of what it means to be Italian.[9] Similarly, Bertelli has argued that family obligations are the key defining characteristic of Italian Australian families.[10] More recent work by MacKinnon reveals that Italian Australian migrant conceptions of health and well-being are linked to how close family members feel they are.[11] In particular, aging parents' perceptions of well-being seem to be directly tied to how often they see their children, highlighting the importance not just of closeness but of "co-presence," or being together.[12] As noted in several of the chapters in this volume, close family ties are often identified by Italians in Italy (see Pojmann) and Italian migrants abroad as a key characteristic differentiating Italians from other ethnic and national groups, including, for example, the Swiss (see Wessendorf), Germans (see Rieker), and Anglo-Australians (see Miller), who are each described as colder and more individualistic. Similar findings are reported by Zontini among Italians in Britain.[13] In summary, then, we might argue that a particular construction of close family ties defines Italian nationhood. I want to explore the implications of this coupling of family and nation for migrants' connections to place and sense of belonging to Italy.

In diaspora settings like Australia, the notion of close family ties and the practices that are believed to evidence this closeness become important ways of delineating ethnic group boundaries and defining identity and belonging. An important example is the strong sense of obligation to care for aging family members in the home, if not through the provision of accommodation, then through regular visits to provide personal hands-on care. This practice is defined as the "right" way—synonymous with the "Italian" way—of caregiving. This intensive method of family caregiving is predicated on a particular set of gender roles and obligations, particularly in regard to notions of mothering involving self-sacrifice and altruism for the good of the family.

Australia can prove a contradictory site for these notions of family and the gender roles and obligations required to maintain them. On one hand, the prejudice and hostilities experienced from the broader society and, more recently, the politics of multiculturalism can result in a conscientious adherence to notions of traditional Italian models of family in order to preserve ethnic identity. A consequence of this can be the strict control of women, who are charged with maintaining family closeness and identity, through, for example, the time-consuming kin work involved in the organization and preparation of regular family get-togethers.[14]

On the other hand, the broader Australian society offers alternative models of "doing family"[15] and being mothers that support less altruistic conceptions of health and well-being. Miller's chapter in this volume provides a fascinating account of how these contrasting models are played out over three generations of Italian Australian migrant women. What is most interesting about her research is her finding that while younger women are rejecting the self-sacrifice and altruism of their mothers for more individually oriented notions of health and well-being, they continue to define their mothers' ways of family caregiving as quintessentially Italian and are committed to upholding close family ties. Italian migrant children are acutely aware that their parents hope and expect to be cared for by them at home, and this expectation is understood as an Italian family obligation. These values and practices of aged care are contrasted with the use of residential care facilities used by "unfeeling" Australians. De Tona's chapter shows comparable findings for Irish Italian women. My field notes and interview transcripts are full of similar sentiments expressed by Italian migrants; for example, an Italian laborer who migrated in the 1950s shared: "In our culture, children do not abandon their parents. . . . You [Australians] are Anglo-Saxons and we are Latin. We do not abandon them. And I think that the Anglo-Saxons do not have a cult of the family the way we do." Similarly, an Italian professional who migrated in the 1980s stated:

> Because I feel that, you know, they have cared for me, and I should care for them, I feel . . . that's why they lived all their lives, for their children. So, holy cow! If we can't even care for them in the end! I am a bit shocked by the Australian system, because, as you know, I am married into an Australian family . . . and . . . [my husband's grandmother] told me . . . that she doesn't want to go into a nursing home because she feels that her children should care for her, but her children refuse to. And I think that's pretty nasty of them. . . . We have had two grandmothers dying with us, and the Italian philosophy and attitude is that if the relative needs care, you care for them.

While there are more affordable and a larger number of aged care facilities available in Australia than in Italy, there is a great deal of shame associated with their use among Italian migrants. MacKinnon and Baldassar and Pesman report similar findings about how these places are associated with Australian ways of providing aged care, which are defined as distinct from "the Italian way," which is to care for the aged at home.[16] The poor English-language skills of Italian aged migrants and the limited availability of culturally appropriate facilities (Italian-speaking staff, suitable food, and activities) are additional factors contributing to the relative underutilization of aged care facilities by Italian migrants. Studies show that Italian-born elderly in Australia have greater access to children and spouses for care purposes than Australian-born elderly and a greater rate of co-residence with family members, and that they use informal services (mostly provided by kin) more than they do formal service providers.[17]

In Italy, where culture and language are less of an issue, the more limited availability and affordability of aged care facilities has a significant impact on the organization of family caregiving. Blackman, for example, defines Italy as family oriented in the sense that the family is required to provide key services, including aged care.[18] Traditionally, the state intervened only when family members were unable to provide care.[19] Aged care homes were originally only for single people who had no family to care for them. An equally powerful and no doubt interrelated factor is the strongly held belief that it is dishonorable for families to place their kin in these institutions; doing so reflects particularly badly on women. It is this mix of limited services and the stigma surrounding their use that contribute to the growing trend of employing live-in domestic servants to provide aged care within Italian homes. As Pojmann argues in this volume, Italian women pay immigrant women to perform their caregiving duties so that they can adhere to the strict rules governing the role of Italian mothers. This provides Italian women with increased freedom to pursue their own interests without neglecting their duties to their families (including maintaining high standards of housecleaning, and providing home-cooked meals as well as child and aged care in the home), thus ensuring their role as good Italian mothers is not jeopardized. The irony is that the burden of this home care is borne by immigrant workers, who often have to sacrifice the care of their own families as a result.

In both Italy and Australia, then, we see similar models of aged care and "doing family," perhaps resulting from different sets of constraints, but both defined as quintessentially Italian. What I now consider is how these ideas and expectations about Italian caregiving are played out in transnational family contexts. How are these obligations maintained when aging parents are absent and living great distances away? And how do these practices and processes influence migrant connections to homeland? In the migration setting, close family ties and, in particular, hands-on caregiving can only be enacted through visits home and transnational communication. Thus, the trope of family in transnational contexts is closely tied to the trope of nostalgia and longing for homecoming. In this argument, family and nation are again intertwined.

Obligations to Place: The Trope of Nostalgia and Longing

In Boym's discussion of the term "nostalgia," longings for family and for homeland are often intertwined and spoken about as if they are the same. She points out that the term "nostalgia" originated in medicine: "Nostalgia was said to produce 'erroneous representations' that caused the afflicted to lose touch with the present. Longing for their native land became their single-minded obsession."[20] Albert von Haller, the physician who, in his work with soldiers during World War I, first identified this condition, explained that "one of the earliest symptoms is the sensation of hearing the voice of a person that one loves . . . , or to see one's family again in dreams."[21] In these descriptions there is a clear conflation between place and family. These two elements come together in the notions of home and homeland, particularly through the term "homesickness,"[22] as well as words like *patria* or "motherland" and "fatherland"; the patient was said to be possessed by a mania of longing for home.

In my research, longing for homeland, particularly among the older San Fiorese labor migrants, often comprised an interconnected set of sentiments about kin and country. For the more recently arrived and younger professionals, longing for family is considered normal and expected. However, sentiments about missing country are not always evident, at least not overtly. In the following section I discuss the visit histories and contemporary experiences of transnational caregiving of both groups in an effort to examine the nexus between obligations to people and place in the varying contexts of family, community, *paese,* and nation.

Labor Migrant Connections to Kin and Country

In the heyday of Italian labor migration to Australia in the 1950s, distance made return unlikely, if not impossible, and *nostalgia* (the Italian term for homesickness) was a common complaint. It is well documented that Italian labor migrants felt a strong sense of attachment to place *(campanilismo)* and shared a worldview or set of values that oriented their behavior homeward.[23] Delaney points out that "there is an intimate relationship between psychological and physical topography: geography is invested with meaning"; she argues that for peasant migrants (in this case, Turkish), "the small bit of land from which they come is still one of the most salient items in the construction of identity."[24] San Fiorese labor migrants' strong attachments to their hometown are evident in their decision to settle in a hilly district on the outskirts of Perth; as many explained to me, "it looks like San Fior."[25] With the passage of time and the loss of close family, connection to ancestral place for these migrants does not appear to diminish.

In many ways the migration project of the labor migrants can be directly defined in terms of both family and place. To use the San Fioresi as an example, migratory moves represented a family economic strategy developed out of a local peasant-worker tradition of seasonal paid work in nearby neighboring countries (particularly Switzerland). Migration overseas, which grew out of this tradition, was, as Thompson has shown, also meant to be temporary.[26] Able-bodied men and women left behind the young and elderly to seek wage labor abroad in an effort to maintain the family's *sistemazione* and livelihood in the hometown. They departed from their birthplaces with licence to leave from both family and community (although not always nation), because their migration project was characterized by an obligation to send remittances home and eventually to return. Through their very act of migration, labor migrants were meeting their responsibilities to family and community, to kin and hometown. Those who remained behind benefited from remittances and opportunities to travel.

While Italian labor migrants departed from hometowns and provinces with a *campanilismo* (spatial self-identity) defined by this locality, the process of migration to the New World transformed them into Italians with a corresponding sense of national identity. Notwithstanding their strong ties to town, province, and region, they found themselves defined collectively in host country settings as Italians. Hostility and prejudice from the broader community and relegation to low-wage segments of the labor force helped foster inter-regional ties, as did migration requirements of *atti di chiamata* and sponsorship. The resultant high levels of residential and occupational segregation consolidated these connections. Many researchers have examined how, in the context of hostile host country environments, ethnic identity is often carefully monitored and maintained through the invention of traditions supposedly unique to the group or the creation of boundaries that separate insiders from others.[27] As discussed above, the trope of close families has been an important part of Italian migrant community formation, and associated notions of caregiving a way of consolidating a sense of national Italian identity in diaspora.

In a society that values close family and community ties, permanent migration represents, to say the least, an interesting problem. Those migrants who settled permanently abroad transgress traditional obligations, in particular the expectations of closeness and co-presence so important to Italian notions of well-being. A consequence of this transgression is that the migrant often assumes a position of ambiguity in the homeland family, community, and nation, an ambiguity that is often played out in visits home. For many, visits home became a way of compensating for their failure to repatriate, although few could afford to visit as often as they would have liked.

The visit trajectories of the labor migrants began with rare and intermittent journeys, particularly for those who arrived before World War II. In many cases the money and time required to make the journey home were just not available. Arguably, the most common motive for a visit home in these early years was actually attempted repatriation. Reported repatriation rates for Italy vary between about 20 percent in the south and 40 percent in the north.[28] It is impossible to find reliable statistics on failed repatriations, most of which resulted in a return to Australia, as they were nearly always counted as permanent returns rather than temporary visits, and there are no statistics available on repeat migrations.

Those who remained in Australia often did so without actually making a decision; rather, planned repatriations were delayed or aborted, with new attempts intended for the future. Communication by phone was at that time sporadic and often unsatisfying, given the poor connection and prohibitive costs of the calls. Letters were by far the most common way of maintaining contact, although many migrants were less than proficient and not very enthusiastic about writing. Another important way of staying in touch was through the "human telegraph line" provided by townspeople who sent word on each other's behalf, although this news was secondhand and not always reliable. Today these migrants have obtained a level of wealth that enables them to take advantage of the various communication technologies available to stay in touch and many make regular and frequent visits home. Their transnational connections now approximate those of the more recent arrivals.

Recent Professional Migrants: Contextualizing Kin and Country

> She misses her family and friends, not the town. . . . She is missing mainly her family's warmth, not so much the [town]. . . . She is missing the love of her family first and Italy the least, because she is not interested in historical monuments, in fashion, in the life of the rich, as is the way here now.
>
> Mother in Italy reflecting on her migrant daughter

Labor migration represented a family economic strategy aimed at assisting the extended family by raising funds that would secure them a place in the homeland. In direct contrast, the significantly smaller group of recent professionals are more aptly defined as lifestyle migrants, who are motivated not by economic considerations but by a desire to leave the homeland, generally against their families' wishes. Many explain that they migrated in order to "get away" from Italy, although a more detailed analysis of their motives reveals that it is not so much the homeland that they seek to escape as what they describe as the stressful living conditions. While the labor migrants used migration as an avenue to escape poverty and hunger, these younger professionals are seeking a sea change to escape frenetic work patterns, stressful routines, and what many describe as exaggerated consumerism (*troppo benessere)*. This group, particularly the women, rarely have license to leave, as there is no economic incentive to justify their migration. Moving to Australia is difficult for their families to accept because it means the migrants are not living close enough for them to see each other frequently.

In contrast to the labor migrants, the professionals are more likely to eschew attachments to *paese* or specific places, preferring to define themselves as world citizens. Arguably, they have more in common with the cosmopolitan than the migrant.[29] Their primary identifications tend to be to their employment and careers rather than ethnicity or nation. They do not seek out topographies that call to mind their birthplaces, preferring to live close to their place of employment or to take advantage of Perth's geographical features, usually living near beaches. They tend not to identify as members of an immigrant or ethnic community, although the process of migration itself often results in a keen sense of their ethnic and national background and of how these are perceived by the host society. In consequence, much like their older compatriots, many recent professional arrivals consciously articulate beliefs and practices illustrative of their identities as Italian (as opposed to Australian), such as beliefs about close family ties and hands-on aged care. In this way, the notion of the Italian family is central to their constructions of identity and obligation.

The absence or presence of connection to place and even the rejection (or not) of national identity do not necessarily appear to influence the sense of obligation to provide care or the way this sense of obligation and practice of caregiving are defined as Italian. Here we might argue, in agreement with Epstein, that symbolic and affective ethnic and national identity attachments are constituted within intimate culture rather than primarily in the more public realms of state politics.[30] In other words, not feeling a sense of attachment to a homeland does not impede one from sharing particular notions about family and caregiving, and defining these as Italian. Some recent professional arrivals reject any notion of traditional homeland culture as overbearing and backward and tend to embrace life in Australia as liberating and emancipated. While this orientation ensures migrants will not repatriate despite (in some cases continual) parental requests, it does not stop migrants from upholding practices that they define as quintessentially Italian, including observing the cultural obligations of aged care. This said, it is important to recognize that identities and attachments to place change over time. The recent arrivals are in an early phase of their family and migration life cycles, compared to the labor migrants. This phase might be characterized by a diminished homeland focus, particularly if migration constitutes a lifestyle choice. It is possible that with time, the professionals will develop a more conscious set of attachments to homeland places.

Despite the almost opposite conditions of their migration projects, both older labor migrants and recent professional arrivals share notions of what they described as a cultural impetus to visit home. Many defined their desire to visit as a need intrinsically connected to being Italian. Migrants and parents alike spoke of close family relations in Italian society fostering a keenly felt expectation that family members see each other and be together as often as they can. It may well be that the increased opportunities for co-presence provided by more affordable and less time-consuming travel technologies increase the sense of obligation to visit and in turn reinforce the notion of this set of practices as quintessentially Italian.

Visits Today: The Importance of Co-presence

> It is a great pleasure and a great need . . . to go to Italy. Absolutely a need. For me and my family. We all feel very strongly, we are attached to it. For me initially, it was really a matter of survival. I—I really need to—to go at least with that frequency. . . . After my father died, it became quite different, more painful, but I still—I still loved to be there . . . it is still a deep need . . . I feel now very strongly that I really must try to keep the family together. And I feel that the way I can pay back what . . . [my parents] have given me is to . . . keep the family close.
>
> Professional migrant woman

The recent arrivals have always enjoyed highly transnational lives. Visiting the homeland is a constant feature of their lifestyle, as is continual communication. Most of the labor migrants can now afford to sustain similar levels of transnational interaction. The data on the contemporary experience of both labor migrants and recent professionals reveal many similarities and some important differences. The increased access to new technologies fosters and sustains close family ties, not only making transnational communication more easily achievable, but making it a requirement—as there are no excuses for not staying connected.[31]

The importance of seeing and being with family members during visits was voiced by all samples in the transnational caregiving study, not just the Italian one. Seeing and being with kin ensures that their health and well-being can be reliably and comprehensively assessed, something that most interviewees feel cannot be effectively done through the various forms of communication technologies, despite attempts at reading between the lines of letters or interpreting the sound of a person's voice on the phone. For Italians, visits brought reassurance, particularly in the context of the relatively common practice (especially among older Italians in Italy) of concealing information about illness from family members in order not to provoke anxiety.[32]

Across all six country groups, visits to see and be with kin include both parent visits and migrant visits. The most common visits undertaken by parents occur soon after the child's migration and around the birth of grandchildren. These visits help parents come to terms with the child's decision to migrate because they are able to confirm "with their own eyes" that he or she is okay. It also enables them to meet their obligations to care for grandchildren. Italian grandparents often describe their commitment to grandchildren, particularly the role of the *nonna*, as a feature of Italian culture: "I believe in the idea of the *nonna.* She is a very important figure. I have a wonderful relationship with my granddaughter. . . . I spend all my time making up little parcels for her. I send her presents, and she likes it, and you ask her what she is wearing, and she says, "I dress 'Italian-style,' and *Nonna* sends me everything.' . . . I think it is very important for her to get brought up within Italian culture . . . in the sense of some values, the family, in the positive sense, like family values."

Parent visits highlight an important difference between the two samples: While parent visits are common among the recent arrivals, they rarely ever occurred for the labor migrants. The lack of opportunity to receive visits from parents doubtless added to the difficulty of being far away and evoked nostalgia among the labor migrants.

Migrant visits are generally much more frequent than parent visits, and their motivations more varied.[33] Migrant visits become especially important when parents cannot undertake visits themselves or if parents are ailing, especially if disability (e.g., dementia, deafness, paralysis) makes it impossible for them to communicate by phone or through letters or e-mail. For older labor migrants who no longer have parents, connections with siblings often became a focus of the motive for visiting. The visit helps to revive attachments with significant kin and, in the case of grandchildren, form and develop them. Visits ensure that people feel they are maintaining close relationships with significant kin, that they still "know" each other. Visits also often increase and broaden the transnational network of kin and friends.

In the Italian sample, being present and able to do things for parents was particularly important for daughters, who are the main providers of hands-on care in particular. A common feature of Italian migrant daughters' visits motivated by the aged care needs of parents was the provision of respite to siblings who normally provide this care daily and whose own lives are restricted as a result. Visiting migrant siblings can provide a welcome break to the often monotonous but labor-intensive routines of personal (hands-on) caregiving. In so doing, migrant daughters feel they are fulfilling at least some of their often heart-felt obligations to care for their parents. Nursing a dying parent, for example, may go a long way in reassuring a migrant who feels guilty about her absence because of migration, providing a sense of resolution, a squaring up of obligations. These actions consolidate their identities not only as good daughters and sons but also as good Italians, given the way these notions are closely linked in migrant conceptions of roles and identities.

So far I have focused on co-presence with people during visits. But what of co-presence and place? And what of the relationship between family and nation and whether these are linked to a sense of place? Urry claims that "co-present interaction is fundamental to social life," and it seems clear that "intermittent moments of physical proximity to particular peoples, places or events" are important in the migration process.[34] I have elaborated elsewhere how migrants maintain a sense of co-presence and connection to people and family through various types of transnational communication, including physical, virtual, and imagined communication, and communication by proxy.[35] These various forms of connection to people have their parallels in theories of attachments to place and to nation: nation as imagined community, nation-state as territorial entity, and nation building through print culture and technologies.[36] In the remainder of the chapter I reexamine these four constructions of co-presence (physical, virtual, imagined, and by proxy), with a focus on connection to place through the visit experience to further explore the relationship between family and nation in the migration experience.

Family as Place, or the Place of Family

Both older labor migrants and recently migrated professionals maintain a sense of being Italian through their ideas about family and caregiving. Their commitment to practices of aged care, which they define as distinctively Italian, is not dependant on a sense of connection to Italy. This said, there is some evidence to suggest that transnational caregiving practices can reinforce migrants' connections to both family and home country, even when they are fully integrated within the host community.[37] Certainly, notions about appropriate ways of "doing family" and providing aged care involve a sense of obligation about conducting visits home to see and be with family. While recent migrants tend to reject a sense of attachment to place, they often enjoy extensive links and connections to places in Italy through their extended family, work, and friendship networks. It may be that since their connections to place are not in question, they tend to take them for granted more than the labor migrants, who have to consciously seek them out.

There are other types of visits that feature a more overt motivation to reconnect with place. Some labor migrants, in particular, time their visits to coincide with special local festivals that celebrate ties to place, including religious feast days, hometown patron saint days, and migrant festivals. These visits could be defined as secular pilgrimages. Some towns and provinces host an annual *festa dell'emigrante*. This is a ritualized way of reincorporating migrants into community and family life. There are also annual or biennial meetings of provincial and national emigrant associations like the Associazione Nazionale Emigrati ed ex Emigrati in Americhe e Australia and various migrant *associazione nel mondo*. While the heyday of emigration has long been over, these local festivals continue to mark the importance of labor migration in the history of the homelands. Through the program of mass, communal lunch, dancing, and festivities, the migrants' ties to family, community, and locality are reinforced. Particularly striking is the way visiting migrants are celebrated during these occasions. Their old photos adorn the venue and efforts are made to ensure they feel welcome, even if they no longer have many acquaintances among the locals. This public display reinforces the migrants' place in the hometown community.

While these annual migration festivals continue to be held in places that have always had them, it is easy to see that they are of limited relevance to professional migrants, who return often, and for whom the context of migration is quite different. Many feel they are a different type of migrant from the labor migrant, and even a different type of Italian. Theirs is therefore an arguably different experience of nostalgia and raises the question of what happens to the sense of nostalgia in contemporary migration contexts, which are characterized by a high degree of transnational activity. The nostalgia of the labor migrant (like the soldiers whose symptoms gave rise to the very notion) was fueled by an inability to return home and a limited ability to stay in touch. In contrast, regular visits and constant communication have always been relatively easily achievable for recent professional migrants. Here is it interesting to note Boym's argument that contemporary nostalgia is more an ailment of the spirit than of the body, and that it is the preserve no longer of the discipline of medicine but rather of poetry and literature. In this scenario, the ailment is more metaphysical than physical; hence even non-migrants living in their own hometowns can suffer the longings of nostalgia, particularly in the context of rapid social change, which fosters longing for a lost past rather than a lost place.[38] It is in this sense that the "pilgrimage" dimension of the visit can be of relevance to the professional migrant, as a form of homage to place and past. A key dimension of the visit is its physical nature, actually being bodily present in the place so as to experience it fully, with all five senses.

Physical Visits: Pilgrimages

Older migrants, in particular, often spoke of the corporeal need to be physically in place—by breathing or smelling the air of their hometown and touching the earth in order to "regain [their] strength," or seeing and hearing their town's bell tower as if these experiences actually nourish them—a need that can only be met through visits. The return home and immersion in familiar surroundings are often reported as having a capacity to heal.[39] Almost all these migrants have now lost their parents, and there is some evidence to suggest that the places of their origins have come to hold more meaning given the absence of their closest family members. They also often bemoan the scant regard of their extended kin, particularly the younger generations, who often struggle to find the time to see and be with these migrant kin—or even lack interest in doing so. It is possible that connections to place become more important as a result of this decline in attachments to people.

For their part, the professional migrants spoke less vividly about the physicality of the visit. They did speak of a sense of redemption in reconnecting with parents and spending time with them, fulfilling their duties as good (Italian) children. There is also evidence of a sense of renewal of ties to place, particularly in seeing and being in childhood haunts and vistas. Arguably the notion of the visit as secular pilgrimage—a personal quest for spiritual, emotional, and mental well-being—develops over time and is dependent on this.

Some of the needs and motivations for visits, like seeing and being with kin, are manifest and actively sought; others are more latent and less overt. In addition to the conscious consolidation of consociate attachments of kin and family, a more generalized set of connections develops from attachments to place and the accumulation of knowledge about contemporary national events.[40] In this way visits can have an impact on identity formation at many levels, including local, ethnic, national, global, and "diasporic."[41] This is particularly evident in what might be called the tourist visit.

Tourist visits often involve a brief visit to kin as part of a longer itinerary, which includes travel to tourist sites. They are mainly undertaken by individuals who have limited consociate connections with kin and community in Italy. Included in this category are package tours that take groups of travelers to rediscover their origins, for example, Italian regional government tours for second-generation migrants who travel to Italy to visit their ancestral hometowns. There are also tours organized by the various *italiani nel mondo* associations that take Italy-based travelers to visit the countries to which their kin emigrated. The motivation behind these visits is for the visitor to develop a connection to place.

All types of visits, but particularly the physical visit, help travelers develop consociate and contemporary knowledge and attachments, which act as catalysts for transformation. People talk about rediscovering their roots and finding out about their past or reconnecting with it. Where kin connections have been dormant or strained, these visits can provide what Grillo calls an opportunity for "re-transnationalising," where consociate relations are reinstated and reinvigorated.[42] In these ways, the visit may bring about a type of rite of passage through which visitors begin to identify with the places they visit, at both the local and national levels. There is often a corresponding increase in obligation to stay connected, which can result in a greater propensity for nostalgia. The transformation in identity and newly acquired status is evident in, for example, improved language ability, greater local (and national) knowledge and awareness, and, importantly, the acquisition of markers of this new identity. These markers are usually purchased, or received as gifts, and often become prized possessions displayed back home as important markers of "authentic" connections to place, we might say, by proxy.[43]

Visits by Proxy

A sense of place can be achieved indirectly through objects and people whose physical or virtual presence embodies the spirit of the longed-for people or place. Each of the five senses can be utilized to construct this form of presence (the person or object can be touched, heard, seen, etc.); the physical manifestation of this (proxy) presence in the form of, for example, photos and mementos serves as the abstraction of an imagined presence. It is common for migrants to have a photo or painting of their natal towns or houses in a prominent position in their homes. There is no limit to what can serve as a memento for place, but common items include iconic examples of Italian material culture such as traditional handcrafts (bedcovers, crocheted doilies, lace), cookware (pots that hang over open fireplaces, coffeemakers), and even pebbles from homeland courtyards. Interestingly these items signify connections both to family and to place; they are "things from home" or "signs of home." *Bomboniere* (small gifts that act as mementos of an event, commonly a picture frame or vase, always accompanied by a small box or bag of sugared almonds) and bereavement cards are similarly powerful icons of family and place; representing a rite of passage (baptism, wedding, death), they are sent to migrants and are usually displayed in living rooms. They are tangible signs of membership in families, and they often recall nation or place in their materiality.[44]

A common feature of visits is shopping sprees during which visitors purchase markers of family and homeland, including tourist icons and clothing and accessories. These signs and mementos prove the visitor has attained the status of one who has visited, providing migrants with an avenue for maintaining an ethnic identity in the multicultural political climate of the host country. This creation of multiple or hybrid identities affirms ideas about ethnic and national identities being not just a "commodity within corporate multiculturalism" but also a way of "providing some kind of ontological security in a fluctuating world."[45] According to Stewart, "The souvenir may be seen as emblematic of the nostalgia that all narrative reveals—the longing for its place of origin. . . . The souvenir seeks distance (the exotic in time and space), but it does so in order to transform and collapse distance into proximity to, or approximation with, the self. The souvenir therefore contracts the world in order to expand the personal."[46] Stewart examines the ways in which the collection of mementos and souvenirs furthers the process of commodification by which this narrative of the personal operates within contemporary consumer society. Indeed, the role of consumerism and popular culture is important to consider in the broader discussion of cultural intimacies and nationalism. A "national way of life" is largely spread today through popular culture and material consumption (whereas education played that role in the past). Here tourism and nostalgia become entwined.[47]

There is also an argument to be made for attachments to place through community and tourist rituals, which are also a kind of proxy for activities in the homeland. Both recent professional and labor migrants participate in host country celebrations that mark formal Italian national events, including national holiday celebrations. These events often feature cultural activities, including performances by visiting Italian artists. There are a number of local Italian festivals in Australia, some of them touristic, although these arguably have more to do with belonging to multicultural Australia than to Italy. In addition, labor migrants foster Italian provincial and town connections through local clubs and associations that celebrate patron saints' days and other local festivals. Professional migrants are much less likely than labor migrants to participate in these regional and provincial activities. In addition, the Roman Catholic Church—particularly masses conducted in Italian—provides another avenue for the expression of homeland identities. Special national and local feast days and anniversaries (like the birthdays and anniversaries of family and friends) can embody distant places that come to mind on these days, often generating more intense feelings of longing and subsequently ensuring the continued observance of these rituals.

Perhaps the most powerful way co-presence with place by proxy is attained is through the visits of others. For recently arrived professionals, visits from home are relatively more frequent and routine in nature, usually involving parents. Among labor migrants, in contrast, it is still considered very special to host a visitor from Italy. As one second-generation San Fiorese explained, "all stops are taken out to ensure they have a memorable visit." Apart from the mandatory round of sightseeing, visitors are taken to meet other migrants and become a vehicle of attachments to home. This kind of substitute for a sense of place is also created through virtual communication, which often increases before, after, and during a visit, further consolidating the ties formed during the visit.

Virtual Visits

Given the distances in time and geography that separate migrants and their homelands, the most common way to create a sense of place is by virtual connections through various forms of technology. Migrants and their transnational kin often stay in regular and constant contact by telephone, e-mail, SMS, and Skype. In addition to the reciprocal exchange of emotional support and practical advice, common topics of conversation include sports, the weather (including details about the seasonal changes evident in the local environment), current affairs, local and national politics, and other everyday contemporary issues that foster a sense of connection to place and nation. Sharing this information also consolidates relationships between people, particularly if there are joking rivalries between opposing soccer teams or political parties. A certain amount of insider knowledge is required for these conversations to work; hence they foster a kind of cultural intimacy between people.[48] Even getting advice about what to pack for a visit invites a discussion of appropriate dress codes and fashion. Mary Holmes has found that transnational couples create a sense of normal married life by inventing topics of conversation that they can share, like an imaginary pet.[49] Watching the same TV programs and sharing music via the Internet appear to be particularly important to recent migrants, who dedicate time to regular virtual communication with family members, keeping up to date with various everyday events and happenings. The exchange of recipes is a pertinent example of virtual co-presence with place (and people), as it usually features mothers' home cooking, invariably a tie to family and place. It is in these moments of shared virtual co-presence that people may imagine they are in the same place.

Imagined Visits

Imagined co-presence is arguably a dimension of each of the other forms of visits described. Here I am thinking in particular of the importance that many Italian labor migrants and parents of recent arrivals place on thinking about place. The power of imagined community ties has become a well-established social fact.[50] Lee considers whether emotional attachments and imagined connections alone can constitute transnationalism.[51] She cites Wolf, Levitt, and Waters's notion of "emotional transnationalism" and what Batainah calls "transnational identity" as examples of the possibility of such identification occurring without any tangible or direct connections with people or institutions in the homeland.[52]

Comparable processes of imagined transnational identities and belonging are evident in the shared knowledge created through popular culture, including film, TV programs, books, music, sports, newspapers, and Web sites. The well-known Italian journalist for the *Corriere Della Sera* Beppe Severgnini hosts a Web site called Italians (www.corriere.it/italians) that is frequented by Italian migrants around the world. On a recent visit to Australia, Severgnini held dinners that were advertised on his Web site and attracted dozens of Italians fans, including many professional recent migrants. The older generation is more likely to develop imagined community and connection to place through religious, hometown, provincial, and regional migrant newspapers. Many labor migrants, for example, subscribe to *Il Messaggero di Sant'Antonio*, a paper produced by a religious association based in Padua; the local hometown paper; and the relevant *associazione nel mondo* paper and even its Web site. Both cohorts subscribe to satellite TV and watch Italian TV.

Such constructions of a sense of place are arguably all subjective in nature. The more formal means of national belonging are citizenship and voting rights. Since 1992, dual citizenship for Australians and Italians has been available. Hence, most recent arrivals are either Italian citizens or dual citizens. Labor migrants tend to all be Australian citizens who are unable to acquire Italian nationality because of the vagaries of legislation in the past. The advent of the immigrant vote in 2006 has added impetus to the value of Italian citizenship abroad.[53] This said, my research findings suggest, much like McKibben in this volume, that migrants have generally not viewed citizenship as an important indicator of identity. In the transnational caregiving study, citizenship was primarily prized as an asset to the *private* domain and as having to do more with the ease of maintenance of extended family connections than with the public domain of nationalism and patriotism. A passport was considered most valuable when it facilitated travel and allowed travelers to avoid the costly and time-consuming process of obtaining visas. Thus, two passports were always considered better than one, and if people had access to dual citizenship, they usually took advantage of this.

These findings fly in the face of arguments that, for instance, the right to citizenship is based on questions of nationalism, patriotism, and loyalty as well as the common assumption that people who retain their original citizenship cannot have a sense of loyalty to their new country.[54] Interestingly, migrants to Australia who retain their homeland citizenship to facilitate ease of access to their homelands may find they have difficulty getting back into Australia. Here Torpey's argument that passports are important not for leaving but for returning is instructive.[55] One Italian national interviewed told of rushing to her mother's deathbed only to find her reentry into Australia challenged upon her arrival at Perth Airport. What is often overlooked in the usual focus on the public domain of political allegiances and the consequences of such for national unity is the importance of citizenship and nationality in the more private and often significantly more commonplace concerns of transnational family caregiving.

Conclusion: A Sense of Place

One of the challenges of this discussion has been to unpick, where possible, the links among family, place, and nation. "Place" in particular is ambiguous, as it might refer to the hometown, province, region, or nation. Even the sense of family itself can manifest at each of these levels, as well as the migrant family and its place in diaspora. As co-presence plays out as longing not just for family and kin but (directly or indirectly) also for nation and place, the emotions of missing and longing are integral (though not essential) features of the kin work and emotional labor needed to maintain family relationships across borders.

While overt attachments to *paese* (both hometown and country) are less evident for professional migrants when they arrive, they share with the labor migrants an Italian identity and belonging based in values and practices associated with family and caregiving, particularly regarding the provision of hands-on care to the elderly delivered in the home. Further, Italian constructions of caring and well-being are predicated on notions of closeness and co-presence. As a result, in the Italian migration process, there is a strong sense of obligation to be with and see family as often as possible when one is caring for aging parents from afar, in particular through lengthy visits home.

The visit home in the Italian diasporic imaginary is a means of asserting both family identity and solidarity in terms of ethnic and national identity and also fosters connections to place, both local and national, sustaining a collective sense of Italianness. These connections to place are not always covert, but they are always implicit in the way family and national characteristics are conflated. Longings for family and homeland become entwined and the kin work required to maintain contemporary transnational relations by "doing Italian family" often results in affective ties to both kin and country.

In attempting to tease out what is national about nostalgia, I have examined how conceptions of health and well-being and the intimate practices of transnational emotional labor may allow migrants to maintain a sense of Italianness in migrant settings. What does this tell us about the entwining of national and familial emotions of love and caring? The popular and much-cherished stereotype of close Italian families highlights not only the attachment of children and parents but also how a collective national sense of belonging is intrinsically related to family culture. The myths and contradictions of close Italian families often have a deeper resonance and greater resilience in migrants' lives because of the ways stereotypes of Italy—and the role of families and women caregivers in enacting them—figure in the genesis of ethno-national and diasporic identities.

Notes

Home, Family, and the Italian Nation in a Mobile World: The Domestic and the National among Italy's Migrants LORETTA BALDASSAR AND DONNA R. GABACCIA

1. Donna R. Gabaccia, *Italy's Many Diasporas* (London: University College of London Press, 2000); Donna R. Gabaccia and Fraser M. Ottanelli, eds., *Italian Workers of the World: Labor Migration and the Formation of Multiethnic States* (Urbana: University of Illinois Press, 2001); Donna Gabaccia and Franca Iacovetta, eds., *Women, Gender, and Transnational Lives: Italian Workers of the World* (Toronto: University of Toronto Press, 2002); Marie-Claude Blanc-Chaleard, Antonio Bechelloni, Bénédicte Deschamps, Michel Dreyfus, and Eric Vial, *Les Petites Italies dans le monde* (Rennes: Presses Universitaires de Rennes, 2007).

2. We recognize that in calling attention to these associations, we give lower priority to the criminality and violence with which Italianness is also associated in many cultures. For one exploration of these themes, see Fred L. Gardaphé, *From Wiseguys to Wise Men: The Gangster and Italian American Masculinities* (New York: Routledge, 2006).

3. Another pertinent theme of relevance to our discussion is spirituality and religious practices. While this issue is mentioned by some of our contributors, particularly in Part III, it remains relatively underexamined in this volume.

4. In addition to the works cited in note 1, readers can consult Piero Bevilacqua, Andreina De Clementi, and Emilio Franzina, *Storia dell'emigrazione italiana* (Rome: Donzelli, 2001).

5. Benedict Anderson, *Imagined Communities: Reflections on the Origins and Spread of Nationalism* (London: Verso, 1983).

6. Ralph Grillo, ed., *The Family in Question: Immigrant and Ethnic Minorities in Multicultural Europe* (Amsterdam: Amsterdam University Press, 2008); Loretta Baldassar, Cora Vellekoop Baldock, and Raelene Wilding, *Families Caring across Borders: Migration, Ageing and Transnational Caregiving* (Houndsmills, UK: Palgrave Macmillan, 2007); Deborah Bryceson and Ulla Vuorela, eds., *The Transnational Family: New European Frontiers and Global Networks* (Oxford: Berg, 2002).

7. A. L. Epstein, *Ethos and Identity: Three Studies in Ethnicity* (London: Tavistock, 1978), 112.

8. Anthropological debate about the role of emotions in identity formation is perhaps best summarized by A. L. Epstein's critique of the instrumentalist approach; see Abner Cohen, ed., *Urban Ethnicity* (London: Tavistock, 1974). Research on emotions was an early theme in women's history (see, e.g., Carroll Smith-Rosenberg, "The Female World of Love and Ritual: Relations between Women in Nineteenth-Century America," *Signs* 1, no. 1 [1975]: 1–29), but connecting the history of emotion to that of empire building draws on more recent work by anthropologist Ann Laura Stoler, "Tense and Tender Ties: The Politics of Comparison in North American History and (Post) Colonial Studies," *Journal of American History* 88, no. 3 (2001): 829–65, 893–97. See also Kay Milton and Maruška Svašek, eds., *Mixed Emotions: Anthropological Studies of Feeling* (Oxford: Berg, 2005).

9. See especially Jane Schneider, "Of Vigilance and Virgins: Honor, Shame and Access to Resources in Mediterranean Societies," *Ethnology* 10, no. 1 (1971): 1–24.

10. Michael Herzfeld, *Cultural Intimacy: Social Poetics in the Nation-State* (New York: Routledge, 1997); Ghassan Hage, *Against Paranoid Nationalism: Searching for Hope in a Shrinking Society* (Annandale, Va.: Pluto Press, 2002); Anne-Marie Fortier, *Multicultural Horizons: Diversity and the Limits of the Civil Nation* (London: Routledge, 2008); Jennifer Guglielmo and Salvatore Salerno, eds., *Are Italians White? How Race Is Made in America* (New York: Routledge, 2003).

11. See, for example, Eugen Weber, *Peasants into Frenchmen: The Modernization of Rural France, 1870–1914* (London: Chatto and Windus, 1976). We borrow our metaphor of the nation-state's embrace of its citizens and subjects from John Torpey, *The Invention of the Passport: Surveillance, Citizenship and the State* (Cambridge: Cambridge University Press, 2000). We have also learned much from Maurizio Viroli, *For Love of Country: An Essay on Patriotism and Nationalism* (Oxford: Clarendon Press, 1995).

12. We see a multidisciplinary intellectual trajectory stretching from Michelle Zimbalist Rosaldo and Louise Lamphere, eds., *Woman, Culture, and Society* (Stanford, Calif.: Stanford University Press, 1976), through Nira Yuval-Davis and Floya Anthias, *Woman-Nation-State* (New York: St. Martin's Press, 1989); Micaela di Leonardo, ed., *Gender at the Crossroads of Knowledge: Feminist Anthropology in the Postmodern Era* (Berkeley: University of California Press, 1991); and Nira Yuval-Davis, *Gender and Nation* (London: Sage, 1997).

13. Micaela di Leonardo, "The Female World of Cards and Holidays: Women, Families, and the Work of Kinship," *Signs: Journal of Women in Culture and Society* 12, no. 31 (1987): 440–53; Marie de Lepervanche, "The 'Naturalness' of Inequality," in *Ethnicity, Class and Gender in Australia,* ed. Gillian Bottomley and Marie de Lepervanche (Sydney: Allen & Unwin, 1984), 49–71; Gillian Bottomley, Marie de Lepervanche, and Jeannie Martin, eds., *Intersexions: Gender/Class/Culture/Ethnicity* (Sydney: Allen & Unwin, 1991); Anne-Marie Fortier, *Migrant Belongings: Memory, Space, Identity* (Oxford: Berg, 2000).

14. Biko Agozino, ed., *Theoretical and Methodological Issues in Migration Research* (Aldershot, UK: Ashgate, 2000); Giovana Campani, "Women Migrants: From Marginal Actors to Social Actors," in *The Cambridge Survey of World Migration,* ed. Robin Cohen (Cambridge: Cambridge University Press, 1995), 546–50; Mirjana Morokvasic, "Birds of Passage Are Also Women . . . ," *International Migration Review* 18, no. 4 (1984): 886–907.

15. Marie de Lepervanche, "The Family: In the National Interest?" in Bottomley, Lepervanche, and Martin, *Intersexions,* 132–58; Martha Gardner, *The Qualities of a Citizen: Women, Immigration, and Citizenship, 1870–1965* (Princeton, N.J.: Princeton University Press, 2009).

16. Katharine Donato, Donna Gabaccia, Jennifer Holdaway, Martin Manalansan IV, and Patricia R. Pessar, "A Glass Half Full? Gender in Migration Studies," *International Migration Review* 40, no. 1 (2006): 3–26.

17. Bryceson and Vuorela, *The Transnational Family,* 9. See also Louise Ackers, *Shifting Spaces: Women, Citizenship and Migration within the European Union* (Bristol, UK: Policy Press, 1998); Katie Gardner and Ralph Grillo, eds., "Transnational Households and Ritual," special issue, *Global Networks* 2, no. 3 (2002).

18. Gabaccia, *Italy's Many Diasporas.* Gabaccia's careful and largely negative consideration of the issue follows Cohen and suggests extremely different outcomes in different nations around the world. Nevertheless, scholars continue to debate even this limited use of the term. Stefano Luconi, "Italians' Global Migration: A Diaspora?" *Studi Emigrazione* 162 (2006): 467–48; Maddalena Tirabassi, ed., *Itinera: Paradigmi delle migrazioni italiane* (Turin: Edizioni della Fondazione Giovanni Agnelli, 2005).

19. Bernard Deacon and Sharron Schwartz, "Cornish Identities and Migration: A Multi-scalar Approach," *Global Networks* 7, no. 3 (2007): 289–306; Selvaraj Velayutham and Amanda Wise, "Moral Economies of a Translocal Village: Obligation and Shame among South Indian Transnational Migrants," *Global Networks* 5, no. 1 (2005): 27–47. For an historian's thoughts on this issue, see Elliott Barkan, "America in the Hand, Homeland in the Heart: Transnational and Translocal Immigrant Experiences in the American West," *Western Historical Quarterly* 35, no. 3 (2004): 331–54.

20. Safran's definition of diaspora in the first issue of the journal *Diaspora* ("Modern diasporas are ethnic minority groups of migrant origins residing and acting in host countries but maintaining strong sentimental and material links with their countries of origin—their homelands") clearly is reminiscent of the classic definition of transnationalism ("a social process in which migrants establish social fields that cross geographic, cultural, and political borders") given by Glick-Schiller, Basch, and Blanc-Szanton. William Safran, "Diasporas in Modern Societies: Myths of Homeland and Return," *Diasporas* 1, no. 1 (1991): 3; Nina Glick Schiller, Linda Basch, and Cristina Blanc-Szanton, *Towards a Transnational Perspective on Migration: Race, Class, Ethnicity, and Nationalism Reconsidered* (New York: New York Academy of Sciences, 1992), ix.

21. For example, the role of long-distance nationalism; see Zlatko Skrbiš, *Long-Distance Nationalism: Diasporas, Homelands and Identities* (Aldershot, UK: Ashgate, 1999).

22. As Ralph Grillo points out, diaspora studies have tended to be more overtly concerned with the politics of national identity and migration, that is, with the experiences of racism, prejudice, and marginalization that often characterize host country settlement (personal communication, April 3, 2008).

23. Khalid Koser, *New African Diasporas* (New York: Routledge, 2003).

24. Robin Cohen, *Global Diasporas: An Introduction* (Seattle: University of Washington Press, 1997).

25. Pnina Werbner, "Theorising Complex Diasporas: Purity and Hybridity in the South Asian Public Sphere in Britain," *Journal of Ethnic and Migration Studies* 30, no. 5 (2004): 895–911.

26. Roger Waldinger and David Fitzgerald, "Transnationalism in Question," *American Journal of Sociology* 109, no. 5 (2004): 1177–95.

27. Schiller, Basch, and Blanc-Szanton, *Towards a Transnational Perspective on Migration,* ix.

28. Katie Gardner and Ralph Grillo, "Transnational Households and Ritual: An Overview," *Global Networks* 2, no. 3 (2002): 179–90. See also Donna Gabaccia, "When the Migrants Are Men: Italy's Women and Transnationalism as a Working-Class Way of Life," in *Women, Gender and Labour Migration: Global and Historical Perspectives,* ed. Pamela Sharpe (New York: Routledge, 2001), 190–208.

29. See, for example, Pnina Werbner, "Diasporic Political Imaginaries: A Sphere of Freedom or a Sphere of Illusions?" *Communal/Plural* 6, no. 1 (1998): 11–31; Pnina Werbner, *Imagined Diasporas among Manchester*

Muslims: The Public Performance of Pakistani Transnational Identity Politics, World Anthropology Series (Santa Fe, N.M.: SAR Press, 2002); Michel S. Laguerre, "Homeland Political Crisis, the Virtual Diasporic Public Sphere, and Diasporic Politics," *Journal of Latin American Anthropology* 10, no. 1 (2005): 206–25; Arjun Appadurai, *Modernity at Large: Cultural Dimensions of Globalization* (Minneapolis: University of Minnesota Press, 1996), 21–22; and Nancy Fraser, "Transnationalizing the Public Sphere," http://www.republicart.net/disc/publicum/fraser01_en.htm (accessed 27 March 2007). We considered using the concept of a diasporic private sphere in earlier iterations of our collective project but ultimately found it too constraining. Equally provocative is the notion of "diasporic intimacies," which Svetlana Boym defines as "not limited to the private sphere" but incorporating "collective frameworks of memory" that are "haunted by images of home and homeland." Svetlana Boym, "On Diasporic Intimacy: Ilya Kabakov's Installations and Immigrant Homes," *Critical Inquiry* 24, no. 2 (1998): 500. Also of relevance is Anne-Marie Fortier's notion of "ethnic intimacies." Anne-Marie Fortier, "Community, Belonging and Intimate Ethnicity," *Modern Italy* 11, no. 1 (2006): 63–77.

30. Ulrich Beck and Natan Sznaider, eds., "Cosmopolitan Sociology," special issue, *British Journal of Sociology* 57, no. 1 (2006). These ideas have stirred historians too; see Derek Heater, *World Citizenship and Government: Cosmopolitan Ideas in the History of Western Political Thought* (New York: St. Martin's Press, 1996).

31. Donna Gabaccia, "Honour and Shame in a Mobile World" (unpublished manuscript, University of Pittsburgh, 2003).

32. Bruno P. Wanrooij, *Storia del pudore: La questione sessuale in Italia, 1860–1940* (Venice: Marsilio Editori, 1990); George L. Mosse, *Nationalism and Sexuality: Middle-Class Morality and Sexual Norms in Modern Europe* (Madison: University of Wisconsin Press, 1985).

33. Maura O'Connor, *The Romance of Italy and the English Political Imagination* (New York: St Martin's Press, 1998).

34. An idea most often explored in the North American context; see Jay Fliegelman, *Prodigals and Pilgrims: The American Revolution against Patriarchal Authority* (London: Cambridge University Press, 1982).

35. Linda K. Kerber, "The Republican Mother: Women and the Enlightenment—an American Perspective," in *Toward an Intellectual History of Women: Essays* (Chapel Hill: University of North Carolina Press, 1997), 43.

36. Appadurai, *Modernity at Large.*

37. Robert Aldrich, *The Seduction of the Mediterranean* (London: Routledge, 1993).

38. Giorgio Bertellini, "Duce/Divo: Masculinity, Racial Identity, and Politics among Italian Americans in 1920s New York City," *Journal of Urban History* 31, no. 5 (2005): 685–726.

39. Michael Rocke, *Forbidden Friendships: Homosexuality and Male Culture in Renaissance Florence,* Studies in the History of Sexuality (New York: Oxford University Press, 1996).

40. Maureen J. Giovannini, "Woman: A Dominant Symbol within the Cultural System of a Sicilian Town," *Man,* n.s., 16 (1981): 408–26.

41. Victor Turner, *The Ritual Process: Structure and Anti-structure* (London: Routledge & K. Paul, 1969).

42. C. Wright Mills, *The Sociological Imagination* (New York: Oxford University Press, 1959).

43. Grillo, *The Family in Question.*

44. Baldassar, Baldock, and Wilding, *Families Caring across Borders.*

45. Herbert Gans, "Symbolic Ethnicity: The Future of Ethnic Groups and Cultures in America," in *Theories of Ethnicity: A Classical Reader,* ed. Werner Sollers (New York: New York University Press, 1996), 425–59.

46. Nicola Yeates, "Global Care Chains: Critical Reflections and Lines of Enquiry," *International Feminist Journal of Politics* 6, no. 3 (2004): 369–91; Nicola Yeates, "A Global Political Economy of Care," *Social Policy and Society* 4, no. 2 (2005): 227–34.

47. An *autocoscienza,* or consciousness-raising feminist group.

48. Bryceson and Vuorela, *The Transnational Family,* 10.

49. Peter Loizos, "Are Refugees Social Capitalists?" in *Social Capital: Critical Perspectives,* ed. Stephen Baron, John Field, and Tom Schuller (Oxford: Oxford University Press, 2000), 124–41.

50. Baldassar, Baldock, and Wilding, *Families Caring across Borders.*

51. Ruba Sahli, *Gender in Transnationalism: Home, Longing and Belonging among Moroccan Migrant Women* (London: Routledge, 2003).

52. Alfredo Niceforo, *L'Italia barbara contemporanea* (Palermo: Remo Sandron Editore, 1898), 247.

53. On the impact of Italian racial theorizing on the immigration restriction movement in the United States, see Peter D'Agostino, "Craniums, Criminals, and the 'Cursed Race': Italian Anthropology in American Racial Thought, 1861–1924," *Comparative Studies in Society and History* 44, no. 2 (2002): 319–43.

The Marriage of Giorgina Craufurd and Aurelio Saffi: Mazzinian Nationalism and the Italian Home ROS PESMAN

1. Donna R. Gabaccia, "Honour and Shame in a Mobile World" (unpublished manuscript, University of Pittsburgh, 2003). See also her "Class, Exile, and Nationalism at Home and Abroad: The Italian Risorgimento," in *Italian Workers of the World: Labor Migration and the Formation of Multiethnic States*, ed. Donna R. Gabaccia and Fraser M. Ottanelli (Urbana: University of Illinois Press, 2001), 21–40. Italian scholars of the Risorgimento have begun to pay increasing attention to the private lives of the patriots. See, for example, Marina D'Amelia, *La mamma* (Bologna: Il Mulino, 2005); Angela Russo, *"Nel desiderio delle tue care nuove": Scritture private e relazioni di genere nell'Ottocento risorgimentale* (Milan: Franco Angeli, 2006); Ilaria Porciani, ed., *Famiglia e nazione nel lungo Ottocento italiano: Modelli, strategie, reti di relazioni* (Rome: Vielli, 2006); Marta Bonsanti, "Amore familiare, amore romantico e amore di patria," in *Storia d'Italia, Annali*, vol. 22, *Il Risorgimento*, ed. Alberto Mario Banti and Paul Ginsborg (Turin: G. Einaudi, 2007), 127–52; Luisa Levi D'Ancona, "Padri e figli nel Risorgimento," in Banti and Ginsborg, *Il Risorgimento*, 153–79. See now also Marta Bonsanti, "Public Life and Private Relations in the Risorgimento (1848–1860)," (PhD thesis, Birkbeck College, University of London, 2008).

2. On Mazzini's teaching, see Gaetano Salvemini, *Il pensiero religioso politico sociale di Giuseppe Mazzini* (Messina: A. Trimarchi, 1905); Simon Levis Sullam, "'Dio e il Popolo': La rivoluzione religiosa di Giuseppe Mazzini," in Banti and Ginsborg, *Il Risorgimento*, 401–22. For bibliographical introductions in English to writing on Mazzini and his thought, see Denis Mack Smith, *Mazzini* (New Haven, Conn.: Yale University Press, 1994), 232–35; Roland Sarti, *Mazzini: A Life for the Religion of Politics* (Westport, Conn.: Praeger, 1997), 233–38.

3. Joseph Mazzini, *The Duties of Man*, in *The Duties of Man and Other Essays* (London: J. M. Dent, 1910), 58.

4. Mazzini quoted in Sarti, *Mazzini*, 31.

5. Mazzini, *The Duties of Man*, 60.

6. Because it is seen as containing both conservative and radical elements (the radical becoming more evident in the later part of his life), Mazzini's writing on women has presented problems for scholars, especially those interested in his contribution to women's emancipation. On Mazzini's teaching on women's roles, see Franca Pieroni Bortolotti, *Alle origini del movimento femminile in Italia, 1848–1892* (Turin: G. Einaudi, 1963); Judith Howard, "The Woman Question in Italy, 1861–1880" (PhD thesis, University of Connecticut, 1977); Maria Pia Roggero, "La donna e la sua emancipazione nel pensiero italiano dai 'Lumi' a Mazzini," *Il Risorgimento* 2 (1983): 149–64; Laura E. Nym Mayhall, "The Rhetorics of Slavery and Citizenship: Suffragist Discourse and Canonical Texts in Britain, 1880–1914," *Gender & History* 13, no. 3 (2001): 481–97; Ilaria Porciani, "Famiglia e nazione nel lungo Ottocento," *Passato e Presente* 57 (2002): 9–39; Liviana Gazzetta, *Giorgina Saffi: Contributo alla storia del mazzinianesimo femminile* (Milan: Franco Angeli, 2003); Simonetta Soldani, review of Gazzetta, *Giorgina Saffi*, in *Passato e Presente* 22, no. 2 (2004): 187–90; Sonia Amarena, *Donne mazziniane, donne repubblicane* (Imola: Santerno Edizioni, 2005).

7. For Mazzini's later views on women's political rights, see his letter to Elena Ballilo, 4 Oct. 1867, in *Edizione nazionale degli scritti editi e inediti di Giuseppe Mazzini* (Imola: Paolo Galeati, 1906–1943), 82:230.

8. Mazzini, *The Duties of Man*, 122.

9. Mazzini to Caroline Stansfeld, 6 June 1870, in *Edizione nazionale*, 89:130. See also Mazzini to Clementia Taylor, 16 April 1868, in *Edizione nazionale*, 87:44–45, and 12 Dec. 1868, in *Edizione nazionale*, 87:219–23; to Emilie Ashurst Venturi, 2 May 1870, in *Edizione nazionale*, 89:152–57; and to William Shaen, 28 Sept. 1870, in *Edizione nazionale*, 90:42–43.

10. Mazzini to Emilie Ashurst Venturi, 2 May 1870, in *Edizione nazionale*, 89:157.

11. "Lo stile è l'uomo, così le sue dottrine erano lui." Aurelio Saffi, "Proemio al volume IX degli scritti editi e inediti di Giuseppe Mazzini," in *Ricordi e scritti* (Forlì: Municipio di Forlì, 1893–1912; Bologna: Edizioni Analisi, 1992), 4:20. Citations are to the 1992 reprint.

12. Maura O'Connor, *The Romance of Italy and the English Political Imagination* (New York: St. Martin's Press, 1998). All biographies of Mazzini discuss his British sojourn and supporters. See also Harry W. Rudman, *Italian Nationalism and English Letters* (London: Allen & Unwin, 1940); Emilia Morelli, *L'Inghilterra di Mazzini* (Rome: Istituto per la storia del Risorgimento, 1965); Franco Della Peruta, *Mazzini e i rivoluzionari italiani* (Milan: Feltrinelli, 1974); William Roberts, *Prophet in Exile: Joseph Mazzini in England, 1837–1868* (New York: Peter Lang, 1989); Maurizio Isabella, "Italian Exiles and British Politics before and after 1848," in *Exiles from*

European Revolutions: Refugees in Mid-Victorian England, ed. Sabine Freitag (New York: Berghahn Books, 2003), 59–87.

13. Paul Ginsborg, "Il mito del Risorgimento nel mondo britannico," *Il Risorgimento* 48 (1995): 396. On this network, see Eugenio Biagini, *Liberty, Retrenchment and Reform: Popular Liberalism in the Age of Gladstone, 1860–1880* (Cambridge: Cambridge University Press, 1992); Margot Finn, *After Chartism: Class and Nation in English Radical Politics, 1848–1874* (Cambridge: Cambridge University Press, 1993); Kathryn Gleadle, *The Early Feminists: Radical Unitarians and the Emergence of the Women's Rights Movement, 1831–1851* (New York: St. Martin's Press, 1995).

14. [Emilie Ashurst Venturi], *Joseph Mazzini: A Memoir by E.A.V.* (London: H. S. King, 1875), 2; Emilie Ashurst to Amelia Venturi, Nov. 1866, in Domenco Montini, *Scene e figure del Risorgimento veneto (1848–1862)* (Città di Castello: Casa editrice S. Lapi, 1913), 243.

15. Biagini, *Liberty, Retrenchment and Reform*, 41–49.

16. Ros Pesman, "Mazzinian Discipleship: Sara Nathan and Jessie White," *Spunti e Ricerche* 21 (2007): 37–38; Emilie Ashurst Venturi to Amelia Venturi, 29 Jan. 1868 and 12 Dec. 1872, in Montini, *Scene e figure*, 245, 255.

17. For Mazzini's loving friendships with the women in his British network, see Ros Pesman, "Mazzini in esilio e le inglesi," in Porciani, *Famiglia e nazione*, 56–82. On love in the attraction of outsiders to the Risorgimento struggles, see Marjan Schwegman, "In Love with Garibaldi: Romancing the Italian Risorgimento," *European History Review* 12, no. 2 (2005): 383–401.

18. Sarti, *Mazzini*, 10–12.

19. I am currently working on the marriages of Italian exiles to foreign women, a subject first opened up by Giorgio Spini in his "Immagini dell'Inghilterra nel Risorgimento italiano," *Rassegna Storica Toscana* 33, no. 1 (1987): 21–30.

20. On Aurelio Saffi, see G. Quagliotti, *Aurelio Saffi: Contributo alla storia del mazzinianesimo* (Rome: Ed. Italiane, 1944); Roberto Balzani, *Aurelio Saffi e la crisi della sinistra romantica (1882–1887)* (Rome: Edizioni dell'Anteneo, 1988); Giovanni Spadolini, introduction to Saffi, *Ricordi e scritti*, 1: n.p.

21. Clara M. Lovett, *The Democratic Movement in Italy, 1830–1876* (Cambridge, Mass.: Harvard University Press, 1982), 77–78; Bonsanti, "Amore familiare," 135–36.

22. Saffi, "Cenni biografici e storici," in *Ricordi e scritti*, 4:5.

23. Ibid., 4:19.

24. On Saffi and Mazzinianism as religion, see Saffi, "Cenni sulle dottine religiose e morali, politiche e sociale di G. Mazzini," in *Ricordi e scritti*, 10:152–202; Balzani, *Aurelio Saffi*, 15–21.

25. Saffi, "Per suffragio universale: Lettera al Comizio di Milano," 1880, in *Ricordi e scritti*, 11:226.

26. See, for example, Saffi, "A Giuseppe Petroni in occasione delle nozze di sua figlia Erminia nel settembre 1871," in *Ricordi e scritti*, 10:107–9.

27. Balzani, *Aurelio Saffi*, 17.

28. On the life of Giorgina Craufurd, see Fanny Manis, "Giorgina Saffi: Nell'anniversario della sua morte," *Rivista d'Italia* 15, no. 8 (1912): 327–41; Maria Pia Roggero, "Giorgina Janet Craufurd Saffi," *Archivio trimestrale* no. 4 (1980), 693–706; Laura Mariani, "L'emancipazione femminile in Italia: Giacinta Pezzani, Giorgina Saffi, Gualberta Beccari," *Rivista di storia contemporanea* 1, no. 1 (1990): 3–31; Luisa Giorgi, "Giorgina Craufurd, 1827–1911: Una donna inglese nel Risorgimento italiano" (thesis, University of Florence, 2000–2001); and Livia Gazzetta's recent excellent biography, *Giorgina Saffi*.

29. Mazzini to Maria Drago Mazzini, 7 April 1837 and 12 Nov. 1837, in *Edizione nazionale*, 14:352, 15:281

30. Manis, "Giorgina Saffi," 330.

31. The poem concludes:

> *Then tell me not 'tis my Fatherland*
> *This Northern land so cold*
> *My heart is in the warm southern land*
> *E'en now as 'twas of old.*

"Nina's Lament," Biblioteca Comunale dell'Archiginnasio di Bologna, Fondo Saffi (hereafter cited as BABFS), Carte Craufurd, b90, Quaderno 9. (The Saffi papers are being reclassified.) Aurelio Saffi to Virginia [Saffi], 7 March 1857, copy, BABFS, b20, 1, 5/16.

32. Manis, "Giorgina Saffi," 328.

33. Giorgina Saffi to Margherita Albana Mignaty, 1 Feb. 1882, Biblioteca Nazionale Firenze, Carte varie, 201/133.

34. Giorgina Saffi, diary 1, 19.2.1852, in Giorgi, "Giorgina Craufurd," 39.

35. Giorgina Saffi to Aurelio Saffi, 12 April 1872 in Giorgi, "Giorgina Craufurd," 8.

36. Giorgina Saffi to Margherita Albana Mignaty, 12 Aug. 1883, Biblioteca Nazionale Firenze, Carte varie, 201/140.

37. Giorgina Saffi, "La Vita è Dovere," Gazzetta, *Giorgina Saffi*, Appendice Documentaria,165–66.

38. The tensions among the women are evident in Mazzini's correspondence. See, for example, Mazzini to Caroline Stansfeld, 10 Oct. 1860, *Edizione nazionale*, 70:152; to Emilie Ashurst, 25 Dec. 1857, in *Edizione nazionale*, 60:213. On the rivalry to translate Mazzini's works, see, for example, Mazzini to Sophia Craufurd, 9 July 1861, in *Edizione nazionale*, 71:300; to Jessie White Mario, 3 Aug. 1862, in *Edizione nazionale*, 73:39, and 24 Dec. 1862, in *Edizione nazionale*, 73:229; and to Matilda Biggs, 28 Nov. 1862, in *Edizione nazionale*, 73:290, and 16 Jan. 1863, in *Edizione nazionale*, 73:338, and 23 Jan., 1863, in *Edizione nazionale*, 73:355.

39. Mazzini to Emilie Ashurst, 25 Dec. 1857, in *Edizione nazionale*, 60:213; Gazzetta, *Giorgina Saffi*, 117–20.

40. Giorgina Saffi to Aurelio Saffi, Naples, 28 Aug., 29 Aug., 3 Sept., and 5 Sept. 1870, BABFS, b10, 12, Lettere familiari 1870, 22/31, 23/48, 24/52, 25/56. In her letter of 3 September, she wrote that all their friends there and elsewhere would prefer that she, rather than "the poor old lady," who would be far more of a vexation and anxiety than comfort to Mazzini, should attend to him. "The poor old lady" is a reference to Emilie Ashurst Venturi.

41. Giorgio Asproni, *Diario politico*, 6 vols., ed. B. Anneda, C. Sole, and T. Orrù (Milan: Giuffre Editore, 1980), 6:289–91. Emilie Ashurst Venturi expressed her anger at being kept away from Mazzini's deathbed in a letter to her sister-in-law, Amelia Venturi, 12 Dec. 1872, in Montini, *Scene e figure*, 255. See also Sergio Luzzatto, *La mummia della repubblica: Storia di Mazzini imbalsamato, 1872–1946* (Milan: Rizzoli, 2001), 43, 67–69.

42. Catherine Craufurd to Margherita Albana Mignaty, 28 May 1854, Biblioteca Nazionale Firenze, Carte varie, 194/203.

43. Giorgi, "Giorgina Craufurd," 205.

44. Aurelio Saffi to Giorgina Craufurd, 3 [Jan.] 1852, copy, BABFS, b19, 3, f.23.

45. Aurelio Saffi to Giorgina Craufurd, 12 Sept. 1856, copy, BABFS, b19, 3, f.12v. On the Saffi marriage as a private and political commitment profoundly imbued with the Mazzinian creed, see also Bonsanti, "Amore familiare," 145–49.

46. Giorgina Saffi to Aurelio Saffi, 10 Feb. 1862, copy, BABFS, b19, lettere 1862–1863, 5, f.20.

47. Aurelio Saffi to "caro P" [Mazzini], 14 July 1854, copy, BABFS, b20, 1, 4/15. Much the same sentiments were expressed by Aurelio in a letter to Catherine Craufurd, 14 July 1854, copy, BABFS, b19, ff. 108–9.

48. Aurelio wrote constantly, reassuring Giorgina that "tu non corri pericolo d'infidelità nè che nei fatti nè anco nei pensieri." Aurelio Saffi to Giorgina Craufurd Saffi, 7 Jan. 1861, copy, BABFS b10, 3, 1/1.

49. "Rimase non poco mortificato quando io gli [Bruzzeli] direi che io lo aveva creduto autore involontario della storia del nostro divorzio." Giorgina Craufurd Saffi to Aurelio Saffi, 19 Feb. 1865, copy, BABFS, b10, 7, 9/16.

50. Giorgina Saffi to Aurelio Saffi, 19 [Jan.] 1862, copy, BABFS, b19, 1862–1863, 1, f.16.

51. Giorgina Saffi to Aurelio Saffi, 14 [Jan.] 1862, copy, BABFS, b19, 1862–1863, 1, f.10.

52. Giorgina Saffi to Aurelio Saffi, 12 Feb. 1862, copy, BABFS, b19, 1862–1863, 1, f.24.

53. Aurelio Saffi to [Giorgina Saffi], 9 Nov. 1861, 10 Dec. 1861, and 17 Jan. 1862, in Saffi, "Frammenti di lettere," in *Ricordi e scritti*, 7:244–45, 268, 291.

54. Aurelio Saffi to [Giorgina Saffi], 10 Dec. 1861, in *Ricordi e scritti*, 7:269.

55. Aurelio Saffi to [Giorgina Saffi], 18 Dec. 1862, in *Ricordi e scritti*, 7:352.

56. See for example, Aurelio Saffi to [Giorgina Saffi], 20 Aug. 1859 and 17 Jan. 1862, in *Ricordi e scritti*, 5:175, 7:291.

57. Aurelio Saffi, "Dimissione dal Parlamento," in *Ricordi e scritti*, 7:437–38.

58. Balzani, *Aurelio Saffi*, 42.

59. Public statement of appreciation issued by Giorgina after Aurelio's death, 21 April 1890, in Manis, "Giorgina Saffi," 333.

60. Asproni, Naples, June 1861 and July 1862, in *Diario politico*, 3:96.

61. *MDCCCLVII–MDCCXLI*, compiled by R. Sperati (Bologna: Stag. Tip. Zamorani e Albertazzi, 1891), 94.

62. Aurelio Saffi to Giorgina Craufurd Saffi, 31 Dec. 1862, copy, BABFS, b19, lettere 1861–1862, 7, f.10.

63. Mariani, "L'emancipazione femminile," 10.

64. Giorgina Saffi to Aurelio Saffi, 2 Aug. 1865, copy, BABFS, b10, 7, 22/53.

65. For her brother, see ibid.; for her sons, see Gazzetta, *Giorgina Saffi*, 87–90.

66. Giorgina Saffi to Felice Dagnino, 9 June 1875, Biblioteca Comunale, Forlì, Fondo Dagnino. Seven years later, on the anniversary of Mazzini's death, she wrote to Dagnino that they would be with him in spirit, asking him to leave a flower on "quella amata tomba." 8 March 1882, Biblioteca Comunale, Forlì, Fondo Dagnino. On the cult of Mazzini's commemoration of the days of his birth and death, see Franco della Peruta, *Realtà e mito nell'Italia dell'Ottocento* (Milan: Franco Angeli, 1996), 89; Pietro Finelli, "'È divenuto un Dio,' Sanità, patria e rivoluzione nel 'culto di Mazzini' (1872–1905)," in Banti and Ginsborg, *Il Risorgimento*, 665–95.

67. Giorgina Saffi to Jessie White Mario, 24 Aug., 1885, Museo Centrale del Risorgimento, Rome, Archivio Jessie White Mario, 430, F0000–28.

68. G. Mazzatinti, ed., *Lettere di Mazzini ad Aurelio Saffi e alla famiglia Craufurd (1850–1872)* (Rome: Società Editrice Dante Alighieri, 1905); Gazzetta, *Giorgina Saffi*, 118–19.

69. On Mazzinianism after 1860 and on associations, see Associazione Mazziniana Italiana–Ravenna, *L'Azione dei mazziniani in Romagna nei primi decenni dopo l'unità* (Ravenna: Edizioni del Girasole, 1973); Giovanni Spadolini, *I Repubblicani dopo l'Unità (1871–1980)* (Florence: Le Monnier, 1960); Maurizio Ridolfi, *Il partito della Repubblica: I repubblicani in Romagna e le origini del Pri nell'italia liberale, 1872–1895* (Milan: Franco Angeli, 1989); Maurizio Ridolfi, *Il circolo virtuoso: Sociabilità democratica, associazionismo e rappresentanza politica nell'Ottocento* (Florence: Centro Editoriale Toscana, 1990). On Saffi's political activities, see Balzani, *Aurelio Saffi*, 40–51.

70. Aurelio Saffi to [Giorgina Saffi], 16 Dec. 1861, in Saffi, "Frammenti di lettere," in *Ricordi e scritti*, 7:280.

71. Aurelio Saffi to [Giorgina Saffi], 23 July 1862, in Saffi, "Frammenti di lettere," in *Ricordi e scritti*, 7:197; Giorgina Saffi, "Alla Signora Anna Cicognani, Direttrice della Società Operaia Femminile di Forlì," Biblioteca Comunale, Forlì, Archivio Piancastelli, Carte Romagna, 424 23/b.

72. Giorgina Saffi to E. de Amicis, 11 Dec. 1880, in Gazzetta, *Giorgina Saffi*, 92.

73. Giuseppe Mazzini to Giorgina Saffi, 11 Aug. 1861, in *Edizione nazionale*, 71:343. A year later, he wrote to her: "Vi stimo sempre e v'amo come sorella; che so che rimanete sempre fedele alla nostra fede e all'affetto." Mazzini to Giorgina Saffi, 13 Nov. 1862, in *Edizione nazionale*, 73:188.

74. Gazzetta, *Giorgina Saffi*, 40.

75. Giorgina Craufurd Saffi to Aurelio Saffi, 7 Jan. 1863, copy, BABFS, b19, lettere 1862–1863, 8, f2. On women and associations, see Franca Strocchi, "Le prime esperienze di associazionismo femminile repubblicano a Forlì," *Bollettino del Museo del Risorgimento* 29–30 (1984–1985): 193–200; Maurizio Ridolfi, "L'apprendistato alla cittadinanza: Donne e sociabilità popolare nell'Italia liberale," *Meridiana: Rivista di storia e scienze sociali* 22–23 (1995): 67–95; Gazzetta, *Giorgina Saffi*, 53–69.

76. Sophia Craufurd to Miss Dick Lauder, 15 Nov. 1862, BABFS, Carte Craufurd, b91, 56/154.

77. Giorgina Saffi, "Alla Società Operaia Femminile di Mutuo Soccorso di Forlì," Biblioteca Comunale, Forlì, Archivio Piancastelli, Carte Romagna, 424 23/a.

78. Giorgina Saffi to Società Artigiana Femminile di Forlì, London, 1 Jan. 1865, and *Il Democratico*, 15 Feb. 1865, in A. Mambelli, *Aurelio Saffi e i suoi congiunti: Memorie storiche* (Forlì: Rotary Club di Forlì, 1961), 73.

79. Giorgina Saffi to Luigi Minuti, 31 May 1880, in Mambelli, *Aurelio Saffi*, 83.

80. On the campaign in Italy, see Rina Macrelli, *L'indegna schiavitù: Anna Maria Mozzoni e la lotta contro la prostituzione di Stato* (Rome: Editori Rinuniti, 1980); Mary Gibson, *Prostitution and the State in Italy, 1860–1915* (New Brunswick, N.J.: Rutgers University Press, 1986); Gazzetta, *Giorgina Saffi*, 99–113; Bruno P. F. Wanrooij, "Josephine Butler and Regulated Prostitution in Italy," *Women's History Review* 17, no. 2 (2008): 153–71; and Marjan Schwegman, "Amazons in Italy: Josephine Butler and the Transformation of Italian Female Militancy," *Women's History Review* 17, no. 2 (2008): 173–78.

81. For a list of Giorgina Saffi's writings on prostitution, see Macrelli, *L'indegna schiavitù*, 256–57. For the texts of a number of them, see Gazzetta, *Giorgina Saffi*, Appendice Documentaria, 153–75.

82. Giorgina Saffi to Luigi Minuti, 31 May 1880, in Mambelli, *Aurelio Saffi*, 83.

83. Aurelio Saffi, "Discorso inaugurale al Congresso della Federazione Britannica e Continentale," in *Ricordi e scritti*, 12:53–64.

84. Aurelio Saffi, "Lettera al Signor Giacomo Stuart," in *Ricordi e scritti*, 34.

85. Gabaccia, "Honour and Shame in a Mobile World."

86. See Franca Pieroni Bortolotti's introduction to Macrelli, *L'indegna schiavitù*, xxv–xviii.

The Atlantic Valentino: The "Inimitable Lover" as Racialized and Gendered Italian GIORGIO BERTELLINI

I wish to thank Donna Gabaccia and Loretta Baldassar for editorial hospitality and cogent critical feedback, Silvio Alovisio and Raffaele De Berti for sharing Italian materials on Valentino, Gaylyn Studlar for sharing her knowledge on the subject and her MoMA photographs, and Jacqueline Reich for her invaluable insights. Unless otherwise noted, all translations are my own. I dedicate this essay to Martino Marazzi.

1. Charles Musser, "A Cornucopia of Images: Comparison and Judgment across Theater, Film and the Visual Arts during the Late Nineteenth Century," in *Moving Pictures: American Art and Early Film, 1880–1910,* ed. Nancy Mowll Mathews with Charles Musser (Manchester, Vt.: Hudson Hills Press, 2005), 33ff.

2. Peter Brooks, *The Melodramatic Imagination: Balzac, Henry James, Melodrama, and the Mode of Excess* (New Haven, Conn.: Yale University Press, 1976).

3. Musser, "A Cornucopia of Images."

4. Howard Greenfeld, *Caruso* (New York: Putnam's Sons, 1983), 109 (unreferenced quote).

5. Such imagery was not only American but of cosmopolitan latitude, as it developed from the aesthetic normalization of Italy—even before it became a politically unified nation—as the sacred shrine of artistic culture and humanist civilization. On Americans on the Grand Tour, see Paul R. Baker, *The Fortunate Pilgrims: Americans in Italy, 1800–1860* (Cambridge, Mass.: Harvard University Press, 1964), and Beth Lynn Lueck, *American Writers and the Picturesque Tour: The Search for National Identity, 1790–1860* (New York: Garland, 1997).

6. Richard H. Brodhead, "Strangers on a Train: The Double Dream of Italy in the American Gilded Age," *Modernism/Modernity* 1, no. 2 (1994): 1–19.

7. On the racial discourse on the south during the fascist regime, see Aaron Gillette, *Racial Theories in Fascist Italy* (London: Routledge, 2002), chap. 3.

8. In October 1922, a little more than a year after *The Four Horsemen of the Apocalypse* hit America's movie theaters and launched Valentino's career in the spring of 1921, Mussolini forcefully and publicly marched on Rome with the Blackshirts to claim full power.

9. I have compared the two Italian male icons in Bertellini, "Duce/Divo: Masculinity, Racial Identity, and Politics among Italian-Americans in 1920s New York City," *Journal of Urban History* 31, no. 5 (2005): 685–726.

10. Biographies of the Italian *divo* tend at times to be rather celebratory and even sensationalist. One eloquent exception is Emily W. Leider, *Dark Lover: The Life and Death of Rudolph Valentino* (New York: Farrar, Straus and Giroux, 2003).

11. In several of his earlier roles, he appeared as a dancer and an American. In a few instances, he played foreigners and Italians. He was an aristocratic Italian gigolo in *A Married Virgin* (1918), a Bowery gangster in *Virtuous Sinner* (1919), a prince in *Passion's Playground* (1920), a rich Milanese benefactor in *Once to Every Woman* (1920), and a Brazilian writer in *Stolen Moments* (1920).

12. Titles include *The Black Hand* (1906), *In Little Italy* (1909), *The Detectives of the Italian Bureau* (1911), and *The Padrone's Ward* (1913). For a discussion, see Bertellini, "Black Hands and White Hearts: Italian Immigrants as 'Urban Racial Types' in Early American Film Culture," *Urban History* 31, no. 3 (2004): 374–98.

13. Beban's film career began in 1915 with the hits *The Italian* and *The Alien,* also known as *The Sign of the Rose,* and continued until his untimely accidental death in 1926. For a profile of his career, see Bertellini, "George Beban: Character of the Urban Picturesque," in *Star Decades: The 1910s,* ed. Jennifer Bean (New Brunswick, N.J.: Rutgers University Press, forthcoming).

14. Thus a direct comparison between Beban and Valentino is a faulty one. While the former could only *play* Italians on-screen, the latter was unmistakably recognized as belonging, on- and offscreen, to a different race.

15. "Biracialism" emerged within the new race-consciousness of the mid-1910s in the works of such authors as Madison Grant, Lothrop Stoddard (who coined the term), W. E. B. Du Bois, and Marcus Garvey. Cf. Matthew Pratt Guterl, *The Color of Race in America, 1900–1940* (Cambridge, Mass.: Harvard University Press, 2001), 6 and 12ff. Guterl has argued that the success of Griffith's film "southernized" the American racial discourse. Jacobson places this focus on biracialism in the 1920s.

16. Franz Boas, *Changes in Bodily Form of Descendants of Immigrants* (New York: Columbia University Press, 1912), 5.

17. Michael Rogin, *Blackface, White Noise: Jewish Immigrants in the Hollywood Melting Pot* (Berkeley: University of California Press, 1998), particularly chaps. 4 and 5.

18. Richard deCordova defines this discourse as the "marked expansion of the type of knowledge that could be produced about the player." Richard deCordova, *Picture Personalities: The Emergence of the Star System in America* (1990; Urbana: University of Illinois Press, 2001), 98.

19. On early and silent film stardom in Hollywood, see deCordova, *Picture Personalities;* Gaylyn Studlar, *This Mad Masquerade: Stardom and Masculinity in the Jazz Age* (New York: Columbia University Press, 1996); and Diane Negra, *Off-White Hollywood: American Culture and Ethnic Female Stardom* (New York: Routledge, 2001).

20. "Kipling and Valentino," *New York Times*, 28 Aug. 1926, quoted in Samantha Barbas, *Movie Crazy: Fans, Stars, and the Cult of Celebrity* (London: Palgrave, 2001), 171 (emphasis added).

21. Significant and eloquent samples of such adulatory terms and expressions, further exaggerated by Valentino's untimely death, are in the memorial literature. See, for instance, Charles Mank Jr., ed., *What the Fans Think of Rudy Valentino: A Memorial Book* (Staunton, Ill.: Charles Mank Jr., 1929).

22. Ben-Allah Newman, *Rudolph Valentino: His Romantic Life and Death* (Hollywood, Calif.: Ben-Allah, 1926), 32.

23. Mank, *What the Fans Think*, 9 and passim.

24. Newman, *Rudolph Valentino*, 16–17 (emphasis added). Further playing the Horatio Alger card against the lesser accomplishments of Italian immigrants, Newman notes that Valentino "accomplished everything that man seeks in this life, that is possible of attainment. . . . No man from Europe has done what has been done by his sleek-haired young man from ancient Italy" (16).

25. "Like Rome, the capital of his country, which received its death blow following the reign of Romulus Augustus—a name combining the founder of the city and the founder of the Empire—so did death come to Valentino following the making of 'The Son of the Sheik.' It seems peculiarly proper to the course of his life that the word 'Sheik' should be in the title of the final picture of his roster of life work." Newman, *Rudolph Valentino*, 46–47.

26. Newman, *Rudolph Valentino*, 47, 54, and 56.

27. Ibid., 70.

28. Beulah Livingstone, *Remember Valentino: Reminiscences of the World's Greatest Lover* (New York: Strand Press, 1938), 2, 3–4 (emphasis added).

29. As Miriam Hansen writes, "The figure of the male as erotic object undeniably sets into play fetishistic and voyeuristic mechanisms, accompanied . . . by a feminization of the actor's persona." Cf. Hansen, *Babel and Babylon: Spectatorship in American Silent Film* (Cambridge, Mass.: Harvard University Press, 1991), 252.

30. Gaylyn Studlar has been the most perceptive about the connection between Valentino's fame and the exotic and orientalist dance culture (or "madness") of the 1910s. See Studlar, "Optical Intoxication: Rudolph Valentino and the Dance Madness," in *This Mad Masquerade*, 150–98.

31. "I hate Valentino! All men hate Valentino." Dick Dorgan, "A Song of Hate," *Photoplay* 22, no. 1 (1922): 26.

32. In the early 1910s, the renowned American sociologist Edward Alsworth Ross popularized and expanded these theories in North America. See his "Italians in America" and "Racial Consequences of Immigration," *Century Magazine* 87 (July 1914): 444–45 and 619.

33. "None of the Italian people is as shallow, unstable, and restless as the Neapolitan one, which has the inconsistency typical of femininity. We could almost say that it's a female people." Alfredo Niceforo, *L'Italia barbara contemporanea* (Milan-Palermo: Sandron, 1898), 247.

34. On the notion of types in American political, literary, and racial culture, see Susan Harris Smith and Melanie Dawson, eds., *The American 1890s: A Cultural Reader* (Durham, N.C.: Duke University Press, 2000), 75–141. For the notion of character, I am indebted to the brilliant study by Cathy Boeckmann, *A Question of Character: Scientific Racism and the Genres of American Fiction, 1892–1912* (Tuscaloosa: University of Alabama Press, 2000).

35. Apart from anthropology, sociology, and eugenics, urban crowds and racial characters were a favorite subject of mainstream (and sensationalist) journalism; reformers' writings; the pioneering social photography of Jacob Riis and Lewis Hine; the new "realist" literature of William Dean Howells, Theodore Dreiser, and Henry James; and the so-called tenement melodramas of Abraham Cahan, Fanny Hurst, and Israel Zangwill, as well as countless vaudeville sketches. Laura Browder, *Slippery Characters: Ethnic Impersonators and American Identities* (Chapel Hill: University of New Carolina Press, 2000).

36. Newman, *Rudolph Valentino*, 82–83.

37. Ibid., 89. Directed by Clarence G. Badger, *it* was adapted from Elinor Glyn's *Cosmopolitan* article of the same title, and turned the same year into a book. Glyn had scripted Valentino's *Beyond the Rocks* (1922).

38. "Valentino was [Love's] embodiment. [Love] was his personality, his being, his life." Glyn, *it* (New York: Macaulay, 1927), 84–85.

39. Since an ethnography of film reception is impossible, I will read here critics' written reports on Valentino's popularity against the grain of the nation's discourses on film art, Italian identity, and race.

40. A notable exception was Carmen Boni, an actress whose measured, minimalistic, and even androgynous style made her most radically different from the *dive dannunziane*. On this point, see Francesco Pitassio, *Ombre silenziose* (Paisan di Prato: Campanotto Editore, 2002), 198ff.

41. Sebastiano Arturo Luciani, *Verso una nuova arte: Il cinematografo* (Rome: Ausonia, 1920), 56ff.

42. Giacomo Debenedetti and Alberto Consiglio, "Dive, maschere e miti del cinema," *Cinema,* 10 Sept. 1936, reprinted in Giacomo Debenedetti, *Al cinema*, ed. Lino Micciché (Venice: Marsilio, 1983), 157–58.

43. On the ideological competition among different models of virility in Italian culture, before and during the fascist regime, see the outstanding work of Barbara Spackman, *Fascist Virilities: Rhetoric, Ideology, and Social Fantasy in Italy* (Minneapolis: University of Minnesota Press, 1996).

44. These actors remained secondary stars when compared to the objects of their affections.

45. Further review of release dates is necessary. *The Four Horsemen* was released in Italy in the late summer of 1923. One review published in 1923 mentions that Italian audiences had already appreciated him in *Camille* (*La signora dalle camelie,* 1921), which, however, was officially released only in the fall 1923 (and re-released in 1925). See Mak in *La Rivista Cineamatografica,* 10 Sept. 1923, and Ro.Ma in *La Rivista Cineamatografica,* 31 March 1925. In 1924, Pier Giovanni Merciai wrote that *The Four Horsemen* had been a huge success: It was shown without interruption for thirty-eight consecutive days. Cf. *La Rivista Cinematografica,* 25 March 1924.

46. Beginning in 1924, the popular illustrated weekly *Cine-Cinema* embraced Hollywood film culture by reporting on (and fictionalizing) celebrities' private lives. Soon dailies, weeklies, and illustrated film magazines (*Le Grandi Films, Cinemalia,* and *Cine Romanzo*) followed suit by offering special supplements devoted to a particular film star. See Raffaele De Berti and Marina Rossi, "Cinema e stampa popolare," in *Un secolo di cinema a Milano,* ed. De Berti (Milan: Il Castoro, 1996), 230ff.

47. For the following references to Italian film periodicals, I am indebted to Vittorio Martinelli's "Filmografia," in *Valentino: Lo schermo della passione,* ed. Paola Cristalli (Ancona: Transeuropa, 1996), 135–56, and his *L'eterna invasione: Il cinema americano degli anni Venti e la critica italiana* (Gemona: La Cineteca del Friuli, 2002).

48. Aurelio Spada, *L'Impero,* 11 Dec. 1923.

49. Pier Giovanni Merciai, *La Rivista Cinematografica,* 25 March 1924.

50. Arrò, *L'Epoca,* 15 June 1924.

51. Since 1911, while he was still a socialist, Mussolini had engaged in combating these allegations. Cf. Benito Mussolini, "Il Trentino veduto da un socialista," in *Opera omnia di Benito Mussolini,* vol. 16 (1951; Florence: La Fenice, 1964), 154. For general discussion of Italian racial culture in this period, see Aaron Gillette, *Racial Theories in Fascist Italy* (London: Routledge, 2002), chaps. 1 and 2.

52. Until the public learned of Valentino's death, in fact, a number of pro-fascist publications explicitly condemned him as a "traitor" and "opportunist" ready to abandon his heritage for money. "If the artist is great, without a doubt, the man has shown a first-class spinelessness. By renouncing his Italian citizenship, he has lost several of his merits. He is not the faraway immigrant that we love for the faith that animated him and for the results that he achieved. He is now the denier of the homeland [*Patria*]; as such he deserves repudiation and loathe." This quote is from a fictionalized biography that appeared in a fascist periodical, quoted but unfortunately not referenced by Sergio Trinchero and Sergio Russo, *Rodolfo Valentino* (Ivrea: Priuli & Verlucca Editori, 1975), 7.

53. By January 1925, a number of Valentino's popular films had regularly been shown in Italy: *The Four Horsemen of the Apocalypse, The Sheik,* and *Blood and Sand* (*Sangue e arena*) were reviewed in August 1923, June 1924, and January 1925, respectively. Cf. Martinelli, *L'eterna invasione,* 482–83, 515, 519. After Valentino publicly announced his decision to acquire American citizenship, Mussolini officially banned his films. Yet after Valentino's tragic and sudden death, not only did the duce allow for their re-release as a result of popular demand, but he also enabled nationalistic appropriations. In 1926, the year of Valentino's death, fascist sympathizer Mario Camerini directed *Maciste contro lo sceicco* (*Maciste against the Sheik*), featuring Mussolini's cinematic alter ego, strongman Maciste, who had starred in a series of action films since 1915, pitted against an Arab sheik—a clear reference to Valentino's 1921 character. For discussions of masculinity in Maciste films, I am indebted to Jacqueline Reich's work and research on the topic.

54. Pier Giovanni Merciai, *La Rivista Cinematografica,* 30 Sept. 1926; Mascamort, *La Rivista Cinematografica,* 10 May 1927.

55. Ablas, *Lo Schermo,* 25 Sept. 1926.

56. Mariani Dell'Anguillara, "In memoria di Rodolfo Valentino," *Cinematografo,* 21 Aug. 1927, 10, quoted in Pitassio, *Ombre silenziose,* 221.

57. Walter Benjamin, "The Work of Art in the Age of Mechanical Reproduction," in *Illuminations: Essays and Reflections,* ed. Hannah Arendt, and trans. Harry Zohn (New York: Schocken Books, 1968), 242.

"George the Queer Danced the Hula": Mike Stabile, American Soldier in Hawaii CAROL A. STABILE

I am grateful to Mark Unger, Allen Larson, and James R. Stabile for their help with this essay. A Women's Studies Program Faculty Research Grant from the University of Pittsburgh funded some of the research for this project. Without Donna Gabaccia's insistence that I write about Mike's diary, I probably would not have undertaken this project in the first place, and I am fortunate to have had her support, guidance, and friendship.

1. Mike Stabile's unpublished diary is in possession of the author's brother. Entries were made retroactively while Mike was undergoing Ranger training in 1944, and no entries were made for a few days after he was wounded, but other than that, an entry exists for every single day of his time in the army.

2. Ben Bradlee, "A Return," *New Yorker,* 2 Oct. 2006, 55.

3. Caroline Steedman, *Landscape for a Good Woman* (New Brunswick, N.J.: Rutgers University Press, 1987), 5.

4. See Robert C. Schmitt, *Hawaii in the Movies, 1898–1959* (Honolulu: Hawaii Historical Society, 1988).

5. Beth Bailey and David Farber, *The First Strange Place: The Alchemy of Race and Sex in World War II Hawaii* (New York: Free Press. 1992), 22, 23.

6. Mike used "Jeep" throughout the diary as an affectionate reference to other soldiers. In one of the popular culture references that permeate the diary, "Jeep" refers to "Eugene the Jeep," a resourceful and uncharacteristically cute creature that was introduced into E. C. Segar's *Popeye* cartoon strip on 16 March 1936.

7. Mike had surprisingly positive comments to make about army chow, likely because years of Depression-era privation made abundant army fare more than simply palatable. "The food is swell," he wrote on 5 April 1941. "The food is delicious and we all make short work of it," he noted on 17 July 1941. Indeed, except for when his unit was in combat on the islands of Saipan and Okinawa, Mike has remarkably few complaints about army food.

8. It may be that Mike got circumcised as a preventative against venereal diseases, as the U.S. Army was at the time promoting adult male circumcision. See David Gollaher, *Circumcision: A History of the World's Most Controversial Surgery* (New York: Basic Books, 2001).

9. Interview with the author, 14 Jan. 2005.

10. Allan Bérubé, *Coming out under Fire* (New York: Free Press, 2001), 59.

11. Thomas A. Guglielmo, *White on Arrival: Italians, Race, Color, and Power in Chicago, 1890–1945* (New York: Oxford University Press, 2003), 8.

12. The 369th Coast Artillery Regiment, better known as the Harlem Hellfighters, arrived in Hawaii in 1942.

13. Bailey and Farber, *The First Strange Place,* 133.

14. There were very few black women in Hawaii until after the war. Mike mentioned encountering a black woman only once: "Met a black babe and had things fixed up for some banging. Joe and Jasek unconsciously screwed this up" (5 July 1942).

15. There are some more reflective moments in the diary, where Mike made distinctions between the Japanese military and ordinary people. Onboard a ship making its way to attack Saipan, Mike wrote, "Sometimes I wonder why the Japanese ever started a war. They can never hope to win. It is the simple plain people who suffer because of their mistakes" (11 June 1944). Later, talking about soldiers taking "souvenirs" from dead bodies, he wrote, "They killed the two Japs and then took a few souvenirs from them. I could see blood on their fingers and wondered who are the more savage—we or the Japs?" (16 July 1944).

16. Throughout the diary, the word "gook" is frequently enclosed in quotations in Mike's handwritten entries. It is difficult to discern whether this reflected any ambivalence about its usage.

17. Cynthia Enloe, *Maneuvers: The International Politics of Militarizing Women's Lives* (Berkeley: University of California Press, 1999).

18. Bailey and Farber, *The First Strange Place,* 95.

19. Eve Kosofsky Sedgwick, *Between Men: English Literature and Male Homosocial Desire* (New York: Columbia University Press, 1985); Eve Kosofsky Sedgwick, *Epistemology of the Closet* (Berkeley: University of

California Press, 1992); John D'Emilio and Estelle Freedman, *Intimate Matters: A History of Sexuality in America,* 2nd ed. (Chicago: University of Chicago Press, 1997); Bérubé, *Coming out under Fire.*

20. Bérubé, *Coming out under Fire,* 36.

21. Ibid.

22. Bérubé, *Coming out under Fire;* George Chauncey, *Gay New York: Gender, Urban Culture, and the Making of the Gay Male World, 1890–1940* (New York: Basic Books, 1993).

23. Bérubé, *Coming out under Fire,* 36.

24. George would later gain notoriety for a hoax he perpetrated on the white developers who swarmed to Hawaii in the postwar years.

25. Chauncey, *Gay New York,* 73.

26. Ibid., 74.

27. Steven S. Cohan, *Masked Men: Masculinity and Movies in the Fifties* (Bloomington: Indiana University Press, 1997), 86.

28. Bérubé, *Coming out under Fire,* 191.

29. Ibid., 41.

30. Cohan, *Masked Men,* 86.

31. This is not to say that homophobia was absent from Mike's writings: "Saw Joe Pie and he tried to promote again. These queers are a bitch" (31 May 1943). In another entry, he recorded having met "an old queer" in Waipahu "who used his hands on the boys and I told him to beat it, or I'd have to lower the boom on him" (7 June 1943).

32. D'Emilio and Freedman, *Intimate Matters,* 35.

Domesticating the Diaspora: Remembering the Life of Katie DeRorre

CAROLINE WALDRON MERITHEW

1. Gerry Allard, "Dedication, Catherine DeRorre," Collinsville Historical Museum, Illinois.

2. Martha Hodes, "The Mercurial Nature and Abiding Power of Race," *American Historical Review* 108, no. 1 (2003): 85–86.

3. This challenge might be part of what Merry Wiesner-Hanks calls the "new new social history." See Merry Wiesner-Hanks, "World History and the History of Women, Gender, and Sexuality," *Journal of World History* 18, no. 1 (2007): 66

4. Earl Lewis, "To Turn on a Pivot: Writing African Americans into a History of Overlapping Diasporas," *American Historical Review* 100, no. 3 (1995): 783.

5. On defining and using the word "transnationalism," see Matthew Frye Jacobson, "More 'Trans-' Less 'National,'" *Journal of American Ethnic History* 25, no. 4 (2006): 74–84; Donna R. Gabaccia and Franca Iacovetta, eds., *Women, Gender, and Transnational Lives: Italian Workers of the World* (Toronto: University of Toronto Press, 2002); David Thelen, "The Nation and Beyond: Transnational Perspectives on United States History," *Journal of American History* 86, no. 3 (1999): 965–75; Marcel van der Linden, "Transnationalizing American Labor History," *Journal of American History* 86, no. 3 (1999): 1078–92; Peggy Levitt and Mary C. Waters, eds., *The Changing Face of Home: The Transnational Lives of the Second Generation* (New York: Russell Sage Foundation, 2002).

6. The historical exceptions to this claim are Carol Lynn McKibben, *Beyond Cannery Row: Sicilian Women, Immigration, and Community in Monterey, California, 1915–99* (Urbana: University of Illinois Press, 2006), and Thomas Guglielmo, *White on Arrival: Italians, Race, Color, and Power in Chicago, 1890–1945* (Oxford: Oxford University Press, 2003). For early psychological analysis of the second generation, see Irvin L. Child, *Italian or American? The Second Generation in Conflict* (New Haven, Conn.: Yale University Press, 1943).

7. Despite the gap, some try to make comparisons between the new immigrants and the fourth wave. Nancy Foner, for example, recently stated, "Among earlier European immigrants, transnationalism had a fairly short life . . . [and] fell off sharply after the first generation." Nancy Foner, "Second-Generation Transnationalism, Then and Now," in Levitt and Waters, *The Changing Face of Home,* 243. My findings suggest something different.

8. "Al leggere quelle memorie mi pareva di tornare ai tempi in cui il socialismo in Italia era nella sua fase rosea, l'epoca dei Prampolini e dei Massarenti. Essi credvan di conquistare il mondo con la bonita," and "Le lapidi dei primi cristiani nelle catacombe di Roma." Giuseppe Prezzolini, "Diario di New York, " *Il Borghese,* 20 July 1961, 454–55. For Prezzolini's connection to Italian fascism, see Gaetano Salvemini, *Italian Fascist Activities in the United States* (New York: Center for Migration Studies, 1977), 169–70, and Philip V.

Cannistraro, *Blackshirts in Little Italy: Italian Americans and Fascism, 1919–1929* (West Lafayette, Ind.: Bordighera Press, 1999), 115. There are many references to Katie's left-wing or "militant" stance. See, for example, letters of 18 Jan. 1935 and 25 Oct. 1937, Agnes Burns Wieck Collection, Walter P. Reuther Library, Wayne State University, Detroit (hereafter ABW Collection).

9. "Obituaries and Eulogies of Mrs. Katie DeRorre," *Collinsville Herald*, 11 January 1960, Folder "DeRorre—Katie," Box 1, Gerry Allard Papers, Illinois State Historical Library, Springfield (hereafter GA Papers).

10. Jack Battuello, "A Biography of Katie DeRorre," Folder 2–30, Box 2, ABW Collection.

11. Maddelena Marinari, "Toward a New Era: World War II and the Fight against Immigration Restriction" (paper presented at the Organization of American Historians Annual Meeting, Minneapolis, 2007).

12. Much of Katie's early family history comes from an oral history done with Babe in 1975 by Barbara Herndon and Nick Cherniavsky. It is in the Oral History Collection, University of Illinois, Springfield Archives. I also did an interview with Babe at her home in July 2005 with follow-up written correspondence. That material is in my possession. Babe's oral history states that Katie immigrated in 1900, but the census gives the year as 1904. U.S. Bureau of the Census, *Fifteenth Census of the United States: 1930*, DuQuoin City, Perry County, Illinois, Ward 3, Enumeration Pages, accessed via Heritage Quest; *Collinsville Herald*, 11 Jan. 1960, Folder "DeRorre—Katie," Box 1, GA Papers.

13. Donna R. Gabaccia, "When the Migrants Are Men: Italy's Women and Transnationalism as a Working-Class Way of Life," in *American Dreaming, Global Realities: Rethinking U.S. Immigration History*, ed. Donna R. Gabaccia and Vicki Ruiz (Urbana: University of Illinois Press, 2006), 192–94.

14. Daniel Jensen Prosser, *Coal Towns in Egypt: Portrait of an Illinois Mining Region, 1890–1930* (PhD diss., Northwestern University, 1973), 26–62.

15. *DuQuoin Evening Call*, 15 May 1915.

16. Mans interview, Oral History Collection.

17. *DuQuoin Evening Call*, 15 May 1915. Thanks to Ali Kinsella for finding the marriage certificate and baptismal records at Sacred Heart.

18. U.S. Bureau of the Census, *Fifteenth Census*.

19. Sacred Heart Catholic Church baptismal records. Felix, Antoinette, and Babe were baptized by Rev. C. J. Eschmann (the same priest who married the DeRorres) in October 1917, November 1919, and January 1921, respectively.

20. Interview with Julie Gruber, 1 June 2007, Collinsville, Illinois.

21. Mans interview, Oral History Collection.

22. *Progressive Miner*, 21 April 1933, 3.

23. Babe's oral history hints that her brother might have helped with the household chores as well.

24. Mans interview, Oral History Collection.

25. Interview with Julie Gruber, 1 June 2007.

26. See, for example, 19 Nov. 1935 and 8 March 1936, DeRorre Correspondence, ABW Collection.

27. Annelise Orleck, *Common Sense and a Little Fire: Women and Working-Class Politics in the United States, 1900–1965* (Chapel Hill: University of North Carolina Press, 1995), 6.

28. *Progressive Miner*, 17 March 1933, 2

29. *Progressive Miner*, 5 May 1933, 1.

30. Ibid., 3.

31. DeRorre to Clarence Hathaway, 17 Aug. 1936, DeRorre Correspondence, ABW Collection.

32. DeRorre, "In the Wake of the Flood," *Woman Today*, April 1937, 15.

33. Allard, "Dedication, Catherine DeRorre."

34. *East St. Louis Journal*, 22 Oct. 1933, Folder 1–32, Box 1, ABW Collection.

35. Mary Voyzey to Wieck, 18 Aug. 1935, and Celine Burrell to Wieck, 3 Sept. 1935, "Misc Letters," Folder 2–34, Box 2, ABW Collection.

36. Undated letter, DeRorre Correspondence, ABW Collection.

37. 25 Oct. 1937, DeRorre Correspondence, ABW Collection.

38. 9 May 1938, DeRorre Correspondence, ABW Collection.

39. 9 Nov. 1935 and 8 March 1936, DeRorre Correspondence, ABW Collection.

40. 9 May 1938, DeRorre Correspondence, ABW Collection.

41. DeRorre to Agnes Wieck and Family, 22 Oct. 1934, ABW Collection.

42. "Correspondence and News Clippings, 1951, 1953–1956," Folder "DeRorre—Katie," Box 1, GA Papers.

43. "Obituaries and Eulogies of Mrs. Katie DeRorre," *Collinsville Herald*, 11 Jan. 1960, Folder "DeRorre—Katie," Box 1, GA Papers.

44. DeRorre to Wieck, around March 1937, Folder 2–23, Box 2, ABW Collection.

45. DeRorre Correspondence, 22 Nov. 1933, and 15 July 1936, ABW Collection.

46. Mans interview, Oral History Collection. Katie also mentions dressing differently to avoid recognition. See her letter to Agnes Wieck, 7 May 1933, ABW Collection.

47. Bylaws of Alpina Dogali Independent Auxiliary, 1 April 1927, Local Collection, Collinsville Historical Museum, Illinois.

48. Executive Board Meeting, 12 June 1956, and Resolution to the Officers and Delegations of the P.M.W.A. convention held 16 October 1957 , both in Box 1, Record Series J9/5/24, Coal Mining in Illinois Project, University of Illinois, Springfield Archives.

49. Prezzolini, "Diario di New York, " *Il Borghesse,* 20 July 1961, 454–55.

50. Allard, "Dedication, Catherine DeRorre."

51. Sister Katie Day Scrapbook, private collection of Catherine Mans, Springfield, Illinois. This scrapbook includes cards, letters, photographs, and undated newspaper clippings.

52. Undated article in ibid.

53. John Bodnar, "Remembering the Immigrant Experience in American Culture," *Journal of American Ethnic History* 15, no. 1 (1995): 3–27.

54. Representative Melvin Price, 84th Cong., 2nd sess., *Congressional Record,* appendix, 102 (21 May 1956): A4581, quoted in the *St. Louis Post-Dispatch,* 4 June 1956.

55. An *East St. Louis Journal* article of 19 July 1956 notes that people referred to Katie as the Good Samaritan for thirty years. In my research, the term appears first in the 1950s. The *Journal* article is also filled with factual inaccuracies—including an erroneous report that Katie was born in the United States.

56. Folder 2–30, Box 2, ABW Collection.

57. Sister Katie Day Scrapbook.

58. Ibid.

59. Ibid.

60. Emily S. Rosenberg, "Consuming Women: Images of Americanization in the 'American Century,'" *Diplomatic History* 23, no. 4 (1999): 479.

61. 84th Cong., 2nd sess., *Congressional Record,* appendix, 102 (21 May 1956): A4581. Zeidler's remarks are quoted in the *St. Louis Post-Dispatch,* 4 June 1956.

62. Sister Katie Day Scrapbook.

63. Ibid.

64. Elaine Tyler May, *Homeward Bound: American Families in the Cold War Era* (New York: Basic Books, 1988), 10.

65. Newspaper clipping from the *Collinsville Herald,* 6 June 1956, in Sister Katie Day Scrapbook.

66. Chiou-Ling Yeh, "'In the Traditions of China and in the Freedom of America': The Making of San Francisco's Chinese New Year Festivals," *American Quarterly* 56, no. 2 (2004): 398.

67. *East St. Louis Journal,* 19 July 1956.

68. Ibid.

69. Ibid.

70. Ibid.

71. David R. Roediger, *Working toward Whiteness: How America's Immigrants Became White: The Strange Journey from Ellis Island to the Suburbs* (New York: Basic Books, 2005), 177–87.

72. The petition for membership in the Alpina Dogali Independent Auxiliary included a document that stated, "I am of Caucasian race," which petitioners were required to sign. Collinsville Historical Museum, Illinois.

73. Sister Katie Day Scrapbook.

74. DeRorre Correspondence , Folder 2–23, Box 2, ABW Collection.

75. Sister Katie Day Scrapbook.

76. *Progressive Miner,* 21 April 1933, 3. See also *Progressive Miner,* 20 Jan. 1933, 1.

77. Folder 2–30, Box 2, ABW Collection.

78. Letter of 9 May 1938, DeRorre Correspondence, ABW Collection.

79. *East St. Louis Journal,* 19 July 1956.

80. Sister Katie Day Scrapbook.

81. Agnes Burns Wieck's son David Thoreau Wieck mentions Katie in the biography he wrote of his mother, *Woman from Spillertown: A Memoir of Agnes Burns Wieck* (Carbondale: University of Southern Illinois Press, 1992). David Wieck understood Katie's importance. In the 2005 interview with me, Babe said that David

had pushed her to write a biographical piece on her mother. Like her mom, Babe is shy about being in the public eye.

82. *Progressive Miner*, 9 June 1933, 1.

Calculating Babies: Changing Accounts of Fertility Decisions among Italians in Melbourne, Australia PAVLA MILLER

1. The interviews were conducted in Italian and English as part of a 2000 ARC project titled "Fertility Rates, Gender Regimes and Ethnicity in Australia." I thank Angela DiPasquale for her capable assistance with interviews and translations. All names have been changed to protect participants' privacy.

2. Pavla Miller, "Tradition, Modernity and Italian Babies," *Histoire Sociale / Social History* 35, no. 69 (2002): 195–214.

3. See, for example, Peter McDonald, "Gender Equity in Theories of Fertility," *Population and Development Review* 26, no. 3 (2000): 427–39; Pavla Miller, "Demography and Gender Regimes: The Case of Italians and Ethnic Traditions," *Journal of Population Research* 21, no. 2 (2004): 199–222.

4. Marcel Mauss, *The Gift: Forms and Functions of Exchange in Archaic Societies* (London: Cohen & West, 1966); Alan D. Shrift, *The Logic of the Gift: Toward An Ethic of Generosity* (New York: Routledge, 1997).

5. For examples of theoretical interest in altruism and gifts, see Linda L. Layne, ed., *Transformative Motherhood: On Giving and Getting in a Consumer Culture* (New York: New York University Press, 1999).

6. Siew-Ean Khoo, Peter McDonald, and Dimi Giorgas, *Second Generation Australians* (Canberra: Australian Centre for Population Research and the Department of Immigration and Multicultural and Indigenous Affairs, AGPS, 2002), 9.

7. Massimo Livi Bacci and Marco Breschi, "Italian Fertility: An Historical Account," *Journal of Family History* 15, no. 4 (1990): 385–408.

8. Janet McCalman, *Sex and Suffering: Women's Health and a Woman's Hospital: The Royal Women's Hospital, 1856–1996* (Melbourne: Melbourne University Press, 1998), 307.

9. Jane C. Schneider and Peter T. Schneider, *Festival of the Poor* (Tucson: University of Arizona Press, 1996).

10. *Marcia in dietro*, or reverse gear, is the colloquial expression for coitus interruptus.

11. Today, Australia has one of the largest—and still growing—nongovernment school sectors among OECD countries, and Italians tend to be overrepresented among their clients. Richard Teese and John Polesel, *Undemocratic Schooling* (Melbourne: Melbourne University Press, 2003).

12. Khoo, McDonald, and Giorgas, *Second Generation Australians*, 78, table 5.1.

13. Ibid., 117, table 6.12; 67, table 4.20.

14. This colloquial expression refers to the practice of wrapping small and fragile items in cotton wool so they will not break.

15. Tonina Gucciardo and Oriella Romanin, *"Someone's Mother, Someone's Wife": The Italo-Australian Woman's Identity and Roles* (North Fitzroy, Vic.: Catholic Intercultural Resource Centre, 1988), 4.

16. This section focuses on women. It would be fascinating to consider a parallel transition in men's lives, but I do not have sufficient material to do so.

17. Historians too stress that the mythical time when all the elderly were lovingly and respectfully cared for in the bosom of their families never existed, whether in Italy or in other parts of the world.

18. Gucciardo and Romanin, *"Someone's Mother, Someone's Wife."* The issues raised by the authors cut across complex English-language feminist debates about ethnocentrism and the differently patriarchal domination of women in various "ethnic cultures." In Italy, too, there have been extensive feminist debates about the persona of the self-sacrificing mother. For two representative texts, see Luisa Passerini, "The Interpretation of Democracy in the Italian Women's Movement of the 1970s and 1980s," *Women's Studies International Forum* 17, no. 2–3 (1994): 235–39, and Jan Pettman, *Living in the Margins: Racism, Sexism and Feminism in Australia* (North Sydney: Allen & Unwin, 1992).

19. Gucciardo and Romanin, *"Someone's Mother, Someone's Wife,"* 41.

20. Valerie MacKinnon and Antonella Nelli, *Now We Are in Paradise, Everything Is Missing* (Footscray: Department of Nursing, Victoria University of Technology, 1996); Loretta Baldassar and Ros Pesman, *From Paesani to Global Italians: Veneto Migrants in Australia* (Crawley: University of Western Australia Press, 2005), chap. 5; Loretta Baldassar, "Transnational Families and Aged Care: The Mobility of Care and the Migrancy of Ageing," *Journal of Ethnic and Migration Studies* 33, no. 2 (2007): 275–97; Loretta Baldassar, "Transnational Families and the Provision of Moral and Emotional Support: The Relationship between Truth and Distance,"

Identities 14, no. 4 (2007): 385–409. In Italy, many families utilize live-in servants to assist with elder care. In Australia, with its highly restrictive immigration intake, this option is too expensive to be widely used.

21. MacKinnon and Nelli found that older Italians' perceptions about their health and well-being were associated with how close they felt to their children. Those who had little or no family help agonized over the lack of support, understanding, and comfort that they were experiencing. Even where children did help, the respondents wished for a still closer relationship. MacKinnon and Nelli, *Now We Are in Paradise*, 74.

Mothering Contradictory Diasporas: Negotiation of Traditional Motherhood Roles among Italian Migrant Women in Ireland CARLA DE TONA

1. Marta Boneschi, *Santa Pazienza: La storia delle donne italiane dal dopoguerra a oggi* (Milan: Mondadori, 1998), 40.

2. Donna R. Gabaccia, *Italy's Many Diasporas* (London: UCL Press, 2000); Donna R. Gabaccia and Franca Iacovetta, eds., *Women, Gender, and Transnational Lives: Italian Workers of the World* (Toronto: University of Toronto Press, 2002); Roslyn Pesman, "Voices of Their Own: Italian Women in Australia," in *The Italian Diaspora: Migration across the Globe*, ed. George Pozzetta and Bruno Ramirez (Toronto: Multicultural Society of Ontario, 1992), 155–71; Ros Pesman, "Italian Women and Work in Post–Second World War Australia: Representation and Experience," in Gabaccia and Iacovetta, *Women, Gender, and Transnational Lives*, 386–409; Ellie Vasta, "Cultural and Social Change: Italian-Australian Women and the Second Generation," in *The Columbus People: Perspectives in Italian Immigration to the Americas and Australia*, ed. Lydio Tomasi, Piero Gastaldo, and Thomas Row (New York: Center for Migration Studies, 1994), 406–26; Micaela di Leonardo, "The Female World of Cards and Holidays: Women, Families and the Work of Kinship," in *Gender in Cross-Cultural Perspective*, ed. Caroline Brettell and Carolyn Sargent (London: Prentice-Hall International, 2001), 340–56; Tracey Reynolds and Elisabetta Zontini, *A Comparative Study of Care and Provision across Caribbean and Italian Transnational Families*, Families and Social Capital ESRC Research Group Working Paper No. 16 (London: London South Bank University, 2006); Anne-Marie Fortier, *Migrant Belongings: Memory, Space, Identity* (Oxford: Berg, 2000); Loretta Baldassar, *Visits Home: Migration Experiences between Italy and Australia* (Melbourne: Melbourne University Press, 2001); Loretta Baldassar, Raelene Wilding, and Cora Baldock, "Long-Distance Care-Giving: Transnational Families and the Provision of Aged Care," in *Family Caregiving for Older Disabled People*, ed. Isabella Paoletti (New York: Nova Science, 2007), 201–27; Maddalena Tirabassi, "Bourgeois Men, Peasant Women: Rethinking Domestic Work and Morality in Italy," in Gabaccia and Iacovetta, *Women, Gender, and Transnational Lives*, 106–29; Loretta Baldassar, "Marias and Marriage: Ethnicity, Gender and Sexuality among Italo-Australian Youth in Perth," *Australian and New Zealand Journal of Sociology* 35, no. 1 (1999): 359–80; Franca Iacovetta, *Such Hardworking People: Italian Immigrants in Postwar Toronto* (Toronto: University of Toronto Press, 1993).

3. Sheila Ernst, "Mothers and Daughters within a Changing World," in *Mothering Ambivalence*, ed. Wendy Hollway and Brid Featherstone (London: Routledge, 1997), 80.

4. Sarah Earle and Gayle Letherby, eds., *Gender, Identity and Reproduction: Social Perspectives* (Basingstoke, UK: Palgrave Macmillan, 2003), 3.

5. Shari L. Thurer, *The Myths of Motherhood: How Culture Reinvents the Good Mother* (Boston: Houghton Mifflin, 1994).

6. Ibid., xvi–xvii.

7. Aminata Forna, *Mother of All Myths: How Society Moulds and Constrains Mothers* (London: HarperCollins, 1998), 260.

8. While women are socialized to want more than "a diaper in one hand and a dust rag in the other," they are expected at the same time "to subordinate their personal objectives" by a motherhood ideology that insists that unless they do so, "they will damage their children for life." Thurer, *Myths of Motherhood*, xxiv.

9. Marina D'Amelia, *La storia della maternità* (Rome: Laterza, 1997); Giovanna Fiume, *Madri: Storia di un ruolo sociale* (Venice: Marsilio, 1995); Boneschi, *Santa Pazienza*.

10. Fiume, *Madri*. Notably, in Italy the consolidation of specialist fields of knowledge of maternity has been under the continuous and powerful influence of the Catholic Church. The debates on the 2004 referendum on in vitro fertilization, and in 2006 on the 194 Law (the abortion law) and on RU-486 (the abortion pill) have shown how strong the role of the state and the Catholic Church still is in making decisions for women regarding their sexuality and their reproductive capacity. "Scontro sulla pillola RU486—Storace: 'A sinistra c'è confusione,'" *La Repubblica*, 13 Nov. 2005; "Spaventano donne e medici ma non stravolgeranno

la 194," *La Repubblica,* 22 Nov. 2005; "Le donne tornano in piazza per la 194 a Milano sfilano in duecentomila," *La Repubblica,* 14 Jan. 2006.

11. Floya Anthias and Nira Yuval-Davis, *Woman, Nation, State* (Basingstoke, UK: Macmillan, 1989); Nira Yuval-Davis, *Gender and Nation* (London: Sage, 1997).

12. Marina D'Amelia, *La mamma* (Bologna: Il Mulino, 2005), 331.

13. See Wendy Pojmann's "Mothering across Boundaries" in this volume.

14. Paolo Jedlowski, *Sorie comuni: La narrazione nella vita quotidiana* (Milan: Mondadori, 2000).

15. Boneschi, *Santa Pazienza,* 40.

16. bell hooks, *Talking Back: Thinking Feminist, Thinking Black* (London: Sheba, 1989), 21.

17. Anthias and Yuval-Davis, *Woman, Nation, State,* 11.

18. Boneschi, *Santa Pazienza.*

19. hooks, *Talking Back,* 20.

20. Ibid., 21.

21. Ernst, "Mothers and Daughters within a Changing World."

22. Gabaccia and Iacovetta, *Women, Gender, and Transnational Lives;* Caroline Waldron Merithew, "Anarchist Motherhood: Towards the Making of Revolutionary Proletariat in Illinois Coal Towns," in Gabaccia and Iacovetta, *Women, Gender, and Transnational Lives,* 218; Ellie Vasta, "Immigrant Women and the Politics of Resistance," *Australian Feminist Studies* 18 (1993): 5–23; Baldassar, "Marias and Marriage"; Kathie Friedman-Kasaba, *Memories of Migration: Gender, Ethnicity, and Work in the Lives of Jewish and Italian Women in New York, 1870–1924* (Albany: State University of New York Press, 1996), 112–15.

23. Baldassar, "Marias and Marriage"; Baldassar, Wilding, and Baldock, "Long-Distance Care-Giving"; Gina Buijs, *Migrant Women: Crossing Boundaries and Changing Identities* (Oxford: Berg, 1993).

24. As an Italian migrant woman researching Italian migrant women, I must also position myself within this research project. My attempt to unshackle the complexities of migrant motherhood is linked to my own positionality as an Italian woman living in Ireland for nine years, acutely aware of the cultural and ontological implications of experiencing migration. The extremely powerful tie that I have with my mother, who lives in Italy (and who is my most important source of love, care, and support), provided the interpretative guidance for this analysis. The model of motherhood she transmitted to me helped me interpret the stories of motherhood as they emerged from my interviews. It is beyond the scope of this paper to look in depth into the methodological implications of my positionality, but this is a position I want to acknowledge, because it is as a woman implicated in an Italian motherhood model that I want to deconstruct (and perhaps provocatively question) the many assumptions about motherhood.

25. Brian Reynolds, *Casalattico and the Italian Community in Ireland* (Dublin: UCD Foundation for Italian Studies, 1993).

26. Central Statistics Office Ireland, *Census 2002,* vol. 4, *Usual Residence, Migration, Birthplaces and Nationalities,* http://www.cso.ie/census/Vol4.htm (accessed 4 June 2006).

27. Gabaccia, *Italy's Many Diasporas.*

28. Newer migrants connected to these chain migrations continue to arrive in Ireland and to be mostly occupied in the catering food industry, even though, together with fish-and-chips shops, new Italian restaurants and food outlets have now been opened. See Carla De Tona, "'I Remember When Years Ago in Italy': Nine Italian Women in Dublin Tell the Diaspora," *Women's Studies International Forum* 27, no. 4 (2004): 315–34; Carla De Tona, "'When Letters and Contraceptives Don't Stop at the Customs': Kin Work, Networks, and Cultural Capital of Italian Migrant Women in Ireland," *Irish Journal of Anthropology* 9, no. 3 (2007): 64–74.

29. Carla De Tona, "*Gente di Passaggio*: Liminality and Representation of Italianness in Ireland," in *Facing the Other: Interdisciplinary Studies on Race, Gender and Social Justice in Ireland,* ed. Borbála Faragó and Moynagh Sullivan (Newcastle, UK: Cambridge Scholars, 2006), 93–107.

30. Seungsook Moon, "Immigration and Mothering: Case Studies from Two Generations of Korean Immigrant Women," *Gender and Society* 17, no. 6 (2003): 856.

31. De Tona, "I Remember When Years Ago in Italy."

32. Julie Bettie, *Women without Class: Girls, Race and Identity* (Berkeley: University of California Press, 2003).

33. Boneschi, *Santa Pazienza,* 130.

34. Trinh T. Minh-ha, "Other Than Myself/My Other Self," in *Travellers' Tales: Narratives of Home and Displacement,* ed. George Robertson et al. (London: Routledge, 1994), 8–25.

35. De Tona, "I Remember When Years Ago in Italy" and "When Letters and Contraceptives Don't Stop."

36. Adrienne Rich, *Blood, Bread and Poetry: Selected Prose, 1979–1985* (London: Norton, 1986).

37. Baldassar, Wilding, and Baldock, "Long-Distance Care-Giving."

38. Floya Anthias and Gabriella Lazaridis, *Gender and Migration in Southern Europe: Women on the Move* (New York: Berg, 2000), 38.

39. In 1935 the Irish Criminal Law (Amendment Act 1935, Section 17) prohibited the sale and importation of contraceptives in Ireland. The law was amended in 1979, but only in 1985 was the legislation changed to permit the sale of condoms without prescription to those age eighteen and over. See Evelyn Mahon, "Contraception," in *The Blackwell Companion to Modern Irish Culture*, ed. William J. McCormack (Oxford: Blackwell, 1999), 137.

40. Anthias and Lazaridis, *Gender and Migration*, 38.

Love Crossing Borders: Changing Patterns of Courtship and Gender Relations among Italian Migrants in Germany YVONNE RIEKER

1. Pseudonyms are used in this chapter. Quotations from the interviews were translated by Yvonne Rieker. Interviewees often switched languages during the interview, with some parts spoken in Italian, and some in German. From 1998 to 2002 I worked on a research project concerning Italian migration to the Federal Republic of Germany. Data for this project were drawn from two primary sources: archival documents and a collection of thirty oral history interviews with Italian immigrants living for at least two decades in Germany. The analysis of the interviews focused on the following issues: reasons for and traditions of migration, changes in gender relations during the migration process, acculturation as a process determined and activated by migrants rather than as a simple reaction to social circumstances, changes in working conditions and children's education as well as the terms of social and political participation, and the immigrants' own assessments of the migration project in the course of their lives. The study was published under the title *"Ein Stück Heimat findet man ja immer": Die italienische Einwanderung in die Bundesrepublik* (Essen: Klartext Verlag, 2003).

2. The male interviewees usually came to Germany as young labor migrants. They found work at the national railway company or in construction, mining, or the metallurgical industry. In the course of their migrations, some managed to establish a small enterprise, usually a pizzeria or an ice cream parlor. Female interviewees often came as young wives from the same village of origin as their husbands. Most of them work part time in low-paying jobs.

3. Rita's uneasiness talking about the difficulties of her marriage, and especially sexual matters, is not uncommon among southern Italian women of her age. See Victoria A. Goddard, *Gender, Family and Work in Naples* (Oxford: Berg, 1996), 151. See also Miller in this volume.

4. Ann Cornelisen, *Frauen im Schatten: Leben in einem süditalienischen Dorf* (Frankfurt am Main: Fischer Taschenbuch, 1978); David D. Gilmore, ed., *Honor and Shame and the Unity of the Mediterranean* (Washington, D.C.: American Anthropological Association, 1987); David D. Gilmore, *Manhood in the Making: Cultural Concepts of Masculinity* (New Haven, Conn.: Yale University Press, 1990).

5. About the mother-son relationship in Italy in the 1990s, see Paul Ginsborg, *Italy and Its Discontents: Family, Civil Society, State* (New York: Palgrave Macmillan, 2003), 79.

6. "Sozialdienst für Italiener, Betreuung italienischer Arbeitnehmer. Korrespondenz und Berichte. 1955–1959," folder 1, Archiv des Deutschen Caritasverbandes, Freiburg.

7. Fortunata Piselli, *Parentela ed emigrazione: Mutamenti e continuità in una comunità calabrese* (Turin: G. Einaudi, 1981).

8. Paul Ginsborg, *A History of Contemporary Italy: Society and Politics, 1943–1988* (London: Penguin Books, 1990), 121–209.

9. Concerning the migration of Italian women to postwar Germany, see also Rieker, *"Ein Stück Heimat,"* 102–4.

10. Ginsborg, *Italy and Its Discontents*, 68–100, 121–26.

11. Edward Shorter, *The Making of the Modern Family* (London: Collins, 1976).

12. See Antonio Di Carlo and Serena Di Carlo, eds., *I luoghi dell'identita: Dinamiche culturale nell'esperienza di emigrazione* (Milan: Franco Angeli, 1986), 28–43; Christian Giordano, "Zwischen Mirabella und Sindelfingen," *Schweizerische Zeitschrift für Soziologie* 2 (1984): 437–65.

13. "Chianti am Rhein," *Die Zeit*, 4 April 1957.

14. Ginsborg, *A History of Contemporary Italy*, 212–44.

15. See also Carmine Abate and Meike Behrmann, *I Germanesi: Storia e vita di una communità calabrese e dei suoi emigrante* (Cosenza: Pellegrini, 1986).

16. See Bertellini in this volume.

17. Markus Schaefer and Dietrich Thränhardt, "Inklusion und Exklusion: Die Italiener in Deutschland," in *Jahrbuch Migration–Yearbook Migration, 1997/98,* vol. 6, *Einwanderung und Einbürgerung in Deutschland,* ed. Dietrich Thränhardt (Münster: LIT Verlag, 1998), 149–78.

18. Goddard, *Gender, Family and Work,* 146.

19. This is an often remarked-on contrast to some groups of Turkish immigrants. The percentage of young Turkish immigrants with close German friends is significantly lower than that of Italian immigrants with close German friends, and a higher percentage of Turkish parents than Italian parents rejects the idea of their child having a German partner. Mona Granato, *Bildungs- und Lebenssituation junger Italiener* (Berlin: Bundesinstitut für Berufsbildung, 1994), 57–64; Arthur Fischer, Yvonne Fritzsche, and Werner Fuchs-Heinritz, *Jugend 2000,* vol. 13, *Shell Jugendstudie* (Opladen: Westdeutscher Verlag, 2000).

20. William R. Jankowiak, ed., *Romantic Passion: A Universal Experience?* (New York: Columbia University Press, 1995).

21. W. von der Vogelweide, *Frau Welt, ich hab von dir getrunken* (Berlin: Aufbau Taschenbuch Verlag, 1998).

22. Norbert Elias, *Über den Prozeß der Zivilisation: Soziogenetische und psychogenetische Untersuchungen,* vol. 2, *Wandlungen der Gesellschaft: Entwurf zu einer Theorie der Zivilisation* (Frankfurt am Main: Suhrkamp Verlag, 1979), 88–122.

23. The role of women in this context is contested in scholarly research. Georges Duby describes courtly love as a game celebrating male values. Georges Duby, *Die Frau ohne Stimme: Liebe und Ehe im Mittelalter* (Berlin: Wagenbach Verlag, 1989). Andrea Esmyol, in her research on women as concubines and lovers in the early Middle Ages, stresses that sexual desire as well as the right of disposal of one's partner was practiced by men alone. Andrea Esmyol, *Geliebte oder Ehefrau? Konkubinen im frühen Mittelalter* (Cologne: Böhlau Verlag, 2002).

24. Reinhart Koselleck, "'Erfahrungsraum' und 'Erwartungshorizont'—zwei historische Kategorien," in *Vergangene Zukunft: Zur Semantik geschichtlicher Zeiten* (Frankfurt am Main: Suhrkamp Verlag, 1979), 349–75.

25. The German *Brockhaus Dictionary* of 1820 introduced the notion of *Liebesehe,* or marriage for love. Reinhart Koselleck, "Sozialgeschichte und Begriffsgeschichte," in *Sozialgeschichte in Deutschland: Entwicklungen und Perspektiven im internationalen Zusammenhang,* vol. 1, *Die Sozialgeschichte innerhalb der Geschichtswissenschaft,* ed. Wolfgang Schieder und Volker Sellin (Göttingen: Vandenhoeck und Ruprecht, 1986), 89–110.

26. William J. Goode, *Soziologie der Familie* (Munich: Juventa Verlag, 1967), 65–87.

27. See, for example, the story of Dorothea Schlegel in Carola Stern, *"Ich möchte mir Flügel wünschen": Das Leben der Dorothea Schlegel* (Reinbek bei Hamburg: Rowohlt Verlag, 1990).

28. Uwe Frevert, *Frauen-Geschichte Zwischen Bürgerlicher Verbesserung und Neuer Weiblichkeit* (Frankfurt am Main: Suhrkamp Verlag, 1992), 15–145; Owen Hufton, *Frauenleben: Eine europäeische Geschichte, 1500–1800* (Frankfurt am Main: Suhrkamp Verlag, 1998), 93–245; Phillipe Ariès and Georges Duby, eds., *Geschichte des privaten Lebens,* vol. 4, *Von der Revolution zum großen Krieg* (Frankfurt am Main: Suhrkamp Verlag, 1992), 95–200.

29. Ginsborg, *History of Contemporary Italy,* 121–40, 210–53.

30. Charlotte Gower Chapman, *Milocca: A Sicilian Village* (Cambridge, Mass.: Schenkman, 1971), 36–49. Chapman states that men sang self-composed love songs on their way to work in the fields, yet traditional gender roles remained unquestioned and changes seemed inconceivable.

31. Ginsborg, *Italy and Its Discontents,* 76.

32. Goddard, *Gender, Family and Work,* 146–48.

33. For a theoretical approach to transnational identities, see Avtar Brah, *Cartographies of Diaspora: Contesting Identities* (London: Routledge, 1996), 178–210.

34. Niklas Luhmann, *Liebe als Passion: Zur Codierung von Intimität* (Frankfurt am Main: Suhrkamp Verlag, 1982).

35. Norbert Elias, *Watteaus Pilgerfahrt zur Insel der Liebe* (Frankfurt am Main: Insel Verlag, 2000).

Mothering across Boundaries: Immigrant Domestic Workers and Gender Roles in Italy WENDY POJMANN

1. "Mammismo," BBC Radio Woman's Hour, 28 March 2003, available at http://www.bbc.co.uk/radio4/womanshour/2003_12_fri_03.shtml (accessed 3 June 2004).

2. *Corriere della Sera*, 16 May and 29 Oct. 2004.

3. Helma Lutz, "At Your Service, Madam! The Globalization of Domestic Service," *Feminist Review* 70 (2002): 89–104; Rhacel Salazar Parreñas, *Servants of Globalization: Women, Migration, and Domestic Work* (Stanford, Calif.: Stanford University Press, 2001); Bridget Anderson, *Doing the Dirty Work? The Global Politics of Domestic Labour* (London: Zed Books, 2000).

4. Lutz, "At Your Service, Madam!" 98.

5. Nicola Yeates, "Global Care Chains: Critical Reflections and Lines of Enquiry," *International Feminist Journal of Politics* 6, no. 3 (2004): 369–91; Nicola Yeates, "A Global Political Economy of Care," *Social Policy and Society* 4, no. 2 (2005): 227–34.

6. Deborah Bryceson and Ulla Vuorela, eds., *The Transnational Family: New European Frontiers and Global Networks* (Oxford: Berg, 2002), 10.

7. Victoria De Grazia, *How Fascism Ruled Women: Italy, 1922–1945* (Berkeley: University of California Press, 1992); Lucia Re, "Fascist Theories of 'Woman' and the Construction of Gender," in *Mothers of Invention: Women, Italian Fascism, and Culture,* ed. Robin Pickering-Iazzi (Minneapolis: University of Minnesota Press, 1995), 76–99.

8. Luisa Tasca, "The Average Housewife in Post–World War II Italy," *Journal of Women's History* 16, no. 2 (2004): 92–115.

9. Kristin Ross, *Fast Cars, Clean Bodies: Decolonization and the Reordering of French Culture* (Cambridge, Mass.: MIT Press, 1996).

10. Tasca, "The Average Housewife," 110.

11. Wendy Pojmann, "Emancipation or Liberation? Women's Associations and the Italian Movement," *Historian* 67, no. 1 (2005): 73–96.

12. Paola Bono and Sandra Kemp, eds., *Italian Feminist Thought: A Reader* (Cambridge, Mass: Blackwell, 1991), 260.

13. Teresa De Lauretis, ed., *Sexual Difference: A Theory of Social-Symbolic Practice* (Bloomington: Indiana University Press, 1987).

14. Virginia Picchietti, *Relational Spaces: Daughterhood, Motherhood, and Sisterhood in Dacia Maraini's Writings and Films* (Madison, N.J.: Farleigh Dickinson University Press, 2002), 102.

15. *Autocoscienza* is a form of consciousness-raising used by many feminist groups.

16. Jacqueline Andall, *Gender, Migration and Domestic Service: The Politics of Black Women in Italy* (Aldershot, UK: Ashgate, 2000); Victoria Chell, "Female Migrants in Italy: Coping in a Country of New Immigration," in *Gender and Migration in Southern Europe: Women on the Move,* ed. Floya Anthias and Gabriella Lazaridis (New York: Berg, 2000), 103–24.

17. Chell, "Female Migrants in Italy," 108.

18. Jacqueline Andall, "Catholic and State Constructions of Domestic Workers: The Case of Cape Verdean Women in Rome in the 1970s," in *The New Migration in Europe: Social Constructions and Social Realities,* ed. Khalid Koser and Helma Lutz (London: Macmillan, 1998), 124–42.

19. Charito Basa and Rosalud Jing de la Rosa, *Me, Us, and Them: Realities and Illusions of Filipina Domestic Workers* (Rome: Ograro, 2004), 39.

20. Ibid.

21. Ibid., 40.

22. Andall, *Gender, Migration and Domestic Service*; Amelia Crisantino, *Ho trovato l'Occidente: Storie di donne immigrate a Palermo* (Palermo: La Luna, 1992).

23. Isabella Peretti, paper pressented at "L'assistenza familiare svolta dalle immigrate straniere," Migranti e Native/i: Reti di esperienze, reti di accoglienze, Università degli studi "Roma Tre," 28 June 2005.

24. Basa and de la Rosa, *Me, Us, and Them,* 38.

25. Rhacel Salazar Parreñas, "Mothering from a Distance: Emotions, Gender, and Intergenerational Relations in Filipino Transnational Families," *Feminist Studies* 27, no. 2 (2001): 361–90; Parreñas, *Servants of Globalization,* 122.

26. Translations from Italian sources are mine. Punto di Partenza, "Donne di nazionalità e culture diverse si confrontano sui diritti: Un resoconto del seminario di giugno in preparazione delle prossime tappe previste per settembre ed ottobre a Firenze," 2002, available at http://www.ecn.org/reds/donne/italia/italia0902PUNTOINC.html (accessed Aug. 2007).

27. Caritas, *Dossier immigrazione* (Rome: Antarem, 2002).

28. Ribka Sebathu, *Il cittadino che non c'è: L'immigrazione nei media italiani* (Rome: Edup, 2004).

29. Caritas, *Le donne nel contesto dell'immigrazione in Italia: Aspetti socio-statistici* (Rome: Carocci, 2002).

30. Punto di Partenza, "Donne di nazionalità e culture diverse."

31. Rosa Mendes, "Comments," Seminario con le donne dei/nei movimenti, 21–22 Sept. 2002, Empoli, Italy.

32. Punto di Partenza, "Donne di nazionalità e culture diverse."

33. Sara Ongaro, "Comments," Seminario con le donne dei/nei movimenti," 21–22 Sept. 2002, Empoli, Italy.

34. Wendy Pojmann, *Immigrant Women and Feminism in Italy* (Aldershot, UK: Ashgate, 2006).

35. Punto di Partenza, "Donne di nazionalità e culture diverse."

36. Ibid.

37. Graziella Favaro and Mara Tognetti Bordogna, *Donne dal mondo: Strategie migratorie al femminile* (Milan: Guerini e Associati, 1991).

38. Parreñas, "Mothering from a Distance," and Cecelia Tacoli, "International Migration and the Restructuring of Gender Asymmetries: Continuity and Change among Filipino Labor Migrants in Rome," *International Migration Review* 33, no. 3 (1999): 658–71.

39. No.Di. Associazione i nostri diritti, paper presented at "L'assistenza familiare svolta dalle immigrate straniere," Migranti e Native/i: Reti di esperienze, reti di accoglienze. Università degli studi "Roma Tre," 28 June 2005.

Between Public and Private: The Transnational Community of Sicilians in Monterey, California CAROL LYNN McKIBBEN

1. Interview with Elizabeth Grammatico, 25 Aug. 2004.

2. James R. McGoodwin, *Crisis in the World's Fisheries: People, Problems, Policies* (Stanford, Calif.: Stanford University Press, 1990); Maria Binkley, *Set Adrift: Fishing Families* (Toronto: University of Toronto Press, 2002); Caroline B. Brettell, *We Have Already Cried Many Tears: The Stories of Three Portuguese Migrant Women* (Prospect Heights, Ill.: Waveland Press, 1995); Russell Bourne, *View from Front Street: Travels through New England's Historic Fishing Communities* (New York: W. W. Norton, 1989); Sally Cooper Cole, *Women of the Praia* (Princeton, N.J.: Princeton University Press,1991); Antonio Carlos Sant'Ana Diegues, ed., *Tradition and Social Change in the Coastal Communities of Brazil: A Reader of Maritime Anthropology* (São Paulo: University of São Paulo Press, 1992); Carol Ellis, *Fisher Folk: Two Communities on Chesapeake Bay* (Lexington: University Press of Kentucky, 1986); Richard Feinberg, ed., *Seafaring in Contemporary Pacific Islands: Studies in Continuity and Change* (DeKalb: Northern Illinois University Press, 1995); Edvard Hviding, *Guardians of Marovo Lagoon: Practice, Place, and Politics in Maritime Melanesia* (Honolulu: University of Hawaii Press, 1996); John Charles Kennedy, *People of the Bays and Headlands: Anthropological History and the Fate of Communities in the Unknown Labrador* (Toronto: University of Toronto Press, 1995); Jane Nadel-Klein and Dona Lee Davis, eds., *To Work and to Weep: Women in Fishing Economies,* Social and Economic Papers 18 (Essex, UK: Institute of Social & Economic Research, University of Essex, 1988); David C. Mauk, *The Colony That Rose from the Sea: Norwegian Maritime Migration and Community in Brooklyn, 1850–1910* (Champaign: University of Illinois Press, 1998); James Miller, *Salt in the Blood: Scotland's Fishing Communities Past and Present* (Edinburgh, UK: Canongate, 1995); Estellie M. Smith, ed., *Those Who Live from the Sea: A Study in Maritime Anthropology* (St. Paul, Minn.: West, 1977); Alexander Spoehr, ed., *Maritime Adaptations: Essays on Contemporary Fishing Communities* (Pittsburgh: University of Pittsburgh Press, 1980); *Women in Fishing Communities: Guidelines, a Special Target Group of Development Projects* (Washington, D.C.: Food & Agriculture Organization of the United States, 1993); David A. Taylor, *Documenting Maritime Folk Life: An Introductory Guide,* Publications of the American Folk Life Center (Washington, D.C.: Government Printing Office, 1994); Cynthia Neri Zayas, *The Ethnographies of Two Japanese Maritime Communities: Gyoson, Nihon* (Quezon City, Philippines: Third World Studies Center, 1999).

3. Dino Cinel, *From Italy to San Francisco: The Immigrant Experience* (Stanford, Calif.: Stanford University Press, 1982), 221.

4. For a recent analysis of this phenomenon in Mexican immigrant communities, see Tomás R. Jiménez, *Replenished Ethnicity: Mexican Americans, Immigration, and Identity* (Berkeley: University of California Press, 2010).

5. I use the word "translocal" as defined by Elliott Barkan: "Immigrant experiences actually span a full spectrum of newcomer responses—from disengagement from one's society of origin at one end to extensive, transnational engagement in homeland affairs at the other. In between these two contrasting alternatives lies 'translocalism'—an array of moderate actions more indicative of how I find most immigrants responding to

issues, norms, values, and events linking the two arenas." Elliott Barkan, "America in the Hand, Homeland in the Heart: Transnational and Translocal Immigrant Experiences in the American West," *Western Historical Quarterly* 35, no. 3 (2004): 331.

6. I interviewed the Sardina, Mineo, Aliotti, Arancio, Peroni, Asaro, Torrente, Catalano, Bonnano, and Aiello families between January and March 2004.

7. Oral histories, Monterey Fishermen's Historical Association, Monterey History and Art Association, Monterey, Calif., 1995.

8. Robert B. Johnston, *Old Monterey County: A Pictorial History* (Monterey, Calif.: Monterey Savings and Loan Association, 1970), 96.

9. Monterey County Tax Assessment, 1914, Records (hard copy), Office of the County Clerk, 168 West Alisal, First Floor, Salinas, Calif.

10. U.S. Bureau of the Census, Federal Manuscript Census, Monterey County, 1920.

11. Ibid.

12. U.S. Bureau of the Census, California, Monterey County, 1930 Population Schedule, Microfilm Publication T626, Roll 179, *Sixteenth Census of the United States, 1940, Population*, vol. 2, *Characteristics of the Population* (Washington, D.C.: Government Printing Office, 1942–1943); Earl H. Rosenberg, "A History of the Fishing and Canning Industries in Monterey, California" (master's thesis, University of Nevada, 1961); John Walton, "Cannery Row: Class, Community, and the Social Construction of History," in *Reworking Class*, ed. John R. Hall (Ithaca, N.Y.: Cornell University Press, 1997), 243–83.

13. Monterey County Tax Assessor Records, 1940–1961, Office of the County Clerk, 168 West Alisal, First Floor, Salinas, Calif.

14. Interview with Fred Cohn, deputy city manager, Monterey, and Kay Russo, director of community services, Monterey.

15. Jim Conway, *Monterey: Presidio, Pueblo, and Port* (Charleston, S.C.: Arcadia, 2003), 103.

16. William L. Scofield, "Sardine Fishing Methods at Monterey, California," *Fish Bulletin* 19 (1929): 17.

17. Monterey Planning Department, "Master Plan of the City of Monterey" (unpublished document, 1939), 17, Monterey Public Library, California Room, Monterey, Calif.

18. Walton, "Cannery Row."

19. Martha Norkunas, *The Politics of Public Memory: Tourism, History, and Ethnicity in Monterey, California* (Albany: State University of New York Press, 1993).

20. James R. McGoodwin, *Crisis in the World's Fisheries: People, Problems, and Policies* (Stanford, Calif.: Stanford University Press, 1990).

21. Linda Reeder, "When the Men Left Sutera: Sicilian Women and Mass Migration, 1880–1920," in *Women, Gender, and Transnational Lives: Italian Workers of the World*, ed. Donna R. Gabaccia and Franca Iocovetta (Toronto: University of Toronto Press, 2002), 45–67.

22. Interview with Theresa Sollazzo, 9 Feb. 1996.

23. Interview with Anita Ferrante, 16 May 2003.

24. Interview with Peter Cutino, 12 Aug. 2004.

25. Interview with Anna Sardina, 10 March 2005.

26. Interview with Nancy Mangiapane, 19 Aug. 1991.

27. Interview with Rose Marie Cutino Topper, 6 Jan. 1994.

28. Interview with Jack and Janet Russo, 26 Aug. 2004.

29. Interview with Jack and Janet Russo, 26 Aug., 2004.

30. Interview with Anita Ferrante, 10 Sept. 2005.

31. Interview with JoAnn Mineo, 10 March 10 2005

32. Interview with Anita Ferrante, 5 Sept. 1995.

33. Interview with Mary Brucia Darling, 16 Nov. 1997.

34. Interview with Albert Mangiapane, 5 May 1998.

35. Interview with Peter Cutino, 14 May 1998.

36. Gloria Ricci Lothrop, "A Shadow on the Land: The Impact of Fascism on Los Angeles Italians," in *Fulfilling the Promise of California: An Anthology of Essays on the Italian American Experience in California*, ed. Lothrop (Spokane, Wash.: California Italian American Task Force and Arthur H. Clark, 2000), 206.

37. Interview with Peter Cutino, 14 May 1998.

38. Interview with Rose Aiello Cutino, 16 April 1998.

39. Sandy Lydon, *The Japanese in the Monterey Bay Region: A Brief History* (Santa Cruz, Calif.: Capitola, 1997), 70.

40. U.S. Congress, House, *Report of the Select Committee Investigating National Defense Migration*, 77th Cong., 2nd sess., H.R. 1911 (19 March 1942): 2.

41. Interview with Joe Favazza, 12 Feb. 1997.

42. *Monterey County Herald*, 17 Feb. 1942, 1.

43. Interview with Rosalie Ferrante, 17 May 1998.

44. Interview with JoAnn Mineo, 8 March, 2005.

45. See John Steinbeck, *The Log from the Sea of Cortez* (New York: 1941), 24–25, quoted in Walton, "Cannery Row," 266.

46. Interview Vitina Peroni and Vitina Spadaro, 21 March 1998.

47. Interview Vitina Peroni, 21 March 1998.

48. Interview with Josephine Aranciò, 8 March 1995.

49. Special desserts made for the *festa*.

50. Interview with Anna Sardina, 10 March 2005.

51. Interview with JoAnn Mineo, 8 March 2005.

52. Interview with Anita Ferrante, 2 April 1997.

53. Interview with Maria Tringali, 9 Sept. 1994.

54. Anonymous source, 15 June 1998, Marettimo, Sicily.

55. Anonymous source, 8 June 1998, San Vito Lo Capo, Sicily.

56. Interview with Pat Spadaro, 10 March 1997.

57. Interview with Marielena Spadaro, 16 Sept., 1996.

58. Interview with Rose Ann Aliotti, 7 July 1997.

59. Betty Boyd Caroli, Robert F. Harney, and Lydio F. Tomasi, eds., *The Italian Immigrant Woman in North America* (Toronto: Multicultural History Society of Ontario, 1978); Miriam Cohen, *Workshop to Office: Two Generations of Italian Women in New York City, 1900–1950* (Ithaca, N.Y.: Cornell University Press, 1992); Micaela Di Leonardo, *The Varieties of Ethnic Experience: Kinship, Class, and Gender among California Italian-Americans* (Ithaca, N.Y.: Cornell University Press, 1984); Donna R. Gabaccia, *From Sicily to Elizabeth Street: Housing and Social Change among Italian Immigrants* (Albany: State University of New York Press, 1984); Donna R. Gabaccia, *From the Other Side: Women, Gender, and Immigrant Life in the U.S., 1820–1990* (Bloomington: Indiana University Press, 1994); Virginia Yans-McLaughlin, *Family and Community: Italian Immigrants in Buffalo, 1880–1930* (Ithaca, N.Y.: Cornell University Press, 1977).

60. See Douglas S. Massey, *Return to Aztlan: The Social Processes of International Migration from Western Mexico* (Berkeley: University of California Press, 1987); Saskia Sassen, *Losing Control? Sovereignty in an Age of Globalization* (New York: Columbia University Press, 1996); Alejandro Portes and Ruben Rumbaut, *Immigrant America: A Portrait* (Berkeley: University of California Press, 1996); Shirley Geok-Lin Lim, Larry E. Smith, and Wimal Dissanayake, eds., *Transnational Asia Pacific: Gender, Culture, and the Public Sphere* (Urbana: University of Illinois Press, 1999); Nancy Foner, *New Immigrants in New York* (New York: Columbia University Press, 2001); Pierrette Hondagneu-Sotelo, ed., *Gender and U.S. Immigration: Contemporary Trends* (Berkeley: University of California Press, 2003).

State-Imposed Translocalism and the Dream of Returning: Italian Migrants in Switzerland SUSANNE WESSENDORF

1. Loretta Baldassar, *Visits Home: Migration Experiences between Italy and Australia* (Melbourne: Melbourne University Press, 2001); Donna R. Gabaccia, *Italy's Many Diasporas* (London: UCL Press, 2000).

2. Carmine Abate and Meike Behrmann, *I Germanesi: Storia e vita di una communità calabrese e dei suoi emigranti* (Cosenza: Pellegrini, 1986); Christian Giordano, "Zwischen Mirabella und Sindelfingen: Zur Verflechtung von Uniformierungs- und Differenzierungsrozessen bei Migrationsphänomonen," *Schweizerische Zeitschrift für Soziologie* 10 (1984): 437–63; Marianne Pletscher, "Die umgekehrte Emigration: Rückkehr in die Heimat," in *Basta! Fremdarbeiter in den 80er Jahren: Ein Lesebuch*, ed. Adriano Gloor (Zurich: Limmat, 1980), 161–208.

3. Anne-Marie Fortier, *Migrant Belongings: Memory, Space, Identity* (Oxford: Berg, 2000); Claudia Martini, *Italienische Migranten in Deutschland: Transnationale Diskurse* (Berlin: Reimer Verlag, 2001); Elisabetta Zontini, "Continuity and Change in Transnational Italian Families: The Caring Practices of Second-Generation Women," *Journal of Ethnic and Migration Studies* 33, no. 7 (2007): 1103–19; Loretta Baldassar, "Transnational Families and Aged Care: The Mobility of Care and the Migrancy of Ageing," *Journal of Ethnic and Migration Studies* 33, no. 2 (2007): 275–97.

4. Others define translocal relations as those that occur between regions within a nation-state. See, for example, Loretta Baldassar, Cora Vellekoop Baldock, and Raelene Wilding, *Families Caring across Borders: Migration, Ageing and Transnational Caregiving* (Houndsmill, UK: Palgrave Macmillan, 2007), 3.

5. The material presented here draws on qualitative ethnographic research carried out in the German part of Switzerland and in southern Italy (Apulia) over the course of fifteen months in 2004 and 2005. Along with participant observation, fifty-eight life-history interviews were undertaken with first- and second-generation Italian migrants. Although the main focus of the research was the second generation, it also included interviews and participant observation of first-generation migrants and returnees.

6. Switzerland is divided into four linguistic areas. Seventy-five percent of the Swiss population speak German, 20 percent French, 4 percent Italian, and 1 percent Romansh. Hans Mahnig and Andreas Wimmer, "Integration without Immigrant Policy: The Case of Switzerland," in *The Integration of Immigrants in European Societies: National Differences and Trends of Convergence*, ed. F. Heckmann and D. Schnapper (Stuttgart: Lucius & Lucius, 2003), 135–64.

7. Josef M. Niederberger, "Die Integrationspolitik der Schweiz nach dem zweiten Weltkrieg," in *Das Jahrhundert der Italiener in der Schweiz*, ed. Ernst Halter (Zurich: Offizin, 2003), 93–107.

8. Lucio Boscardin, *Die italienische Einwanderung in die Schweiz mit besonderer Berücksichtigung der Jahre 1946–1959* (Zurich: Polygr, 1962); Rudolf Braun, *Soziokulturelle Probleme italienischer Migranten in der Schweiz* (Erlenbach-Zurich: Eugen Rentsch, 1970).

9. Heinz Nigg, ed., *Da und fort: Leben in zwei Welten. Interviews, Berichte und Dokumente zur Immigration und Binnenwanderung in der Schweiz* (Zurich: Limmat, 1990).

10. Werner Haug, *". . . und es kamen Menschen": Ausländerpolitik und Fremdarbeit in der Schweiz, 1914–1980* (Basel: Z-Verlag, 1980).

11. Katharina Ley, *Frauen in der Emigration* (Frauenfeld: Huber, 1979).

12. Giovanna Meyer-Sabino, *Un sud oltre i confini l'emigrazione calabrese in Svizzera: Cenni storici, testimonianze, prospettive* (Zurich: Edizioni dell'Avvenire dei Lavoratori, 2000); Meyer Sabino, "Süditalien: Agrarfrage und Emigration," in Halter, *Das Jahrhundert der Italiener*, 13–22.

13. Braun, *Soziokulturelle Probleme*; Jörg Stolz, "Einstellungen zu Ausländern und Ausländerinnen 1969 und 1995: Eine Replikationsstudie," in *Das Fremde in der Schweiz: Ergebnisse soziologischer Forschung*, ed. Hans-Joachim Hoffmann-Nowotny (Zurich: Seismo, 2001), 33–73.

14. Niederberger, "Die Integrationspolitik der Schweiz."

15. Braun, *Soziokulturelle Probleme*; Haug, *". . . und es kamen Menschen."*

16. Importantly, Switzerland's citizenship policies exclude migrants and their children from political participation, and migrants and their children can only apply for citizenship after living in Switzerland for twelve years. Pascal Steiner and Hans-Rudolf Wicker, eds., *Paradoxien im Bürgerrecht: Sozialwissenschaftliche Studien zur Einbürgerungspraxis in Schweizer Gemeinden* (Zurich: Seismo, 2004); A. Juhasz and E. Mey, *Die zweite Generation: Etablierte oder Aussenseiter? Biographien von Jugendlichen ausländischer Herkunft* (Wiesbaden: Westdeutscher Verlag, 2003); Hans-Rudolf Wicker, "Einleitung: Migration, Migrationspolitik und Migrationsforschung," in *Migration und die Schweiz: Ergebnisse des Nationalen Forschungsprogramms "Migration und interkulturelle Beziehungen,"* ed. Hans-Rudolf Wicker, Rosita Fibbi, and Werner Haug (Zurich: Seismo, 2003), 12–62.

17. Braun, *Soziokulturelle Probleme*; Alexander J. Seiler, *Siamo Italiani: Die Italiener* (Zurich: EVZ, 1965).

18. Ley, *Frauen in der Emigration.*

19. Stolz, "Einstellungen zu Ausländern und Ausländerinnen."

20. Dieter Bachmann, *Il lungo addio: Una storia fotografica sull'emigrazione italiana in Svizzera dopo la guerra / Der lange Abschied: 138 Fotografien zur italienischen Emigration in die Schweiz nach 1945* (Zurich: Limmat Verlag, 2003); Francesca Cangemi and Daniel von Aarburg, eds., *Eigentlich wollten wir nicht lange bleiben. Si pensava di restare poco. 12 Geschichten aus der Emigration. 12 storie d'emigrazione* (Zurich: Frenetic, 2004); Halter, *Das Jahrhundert der Italiener.* For examples of such exhibitions, see http://www.da-und-fort.ch, http://www.italiazurigo.ch, and http://www.dolcelingua.ch.

21. Daniel Blickenstorfer, "Locker wie Latinos. Essen und Feiern, Erotik und Freude: Mediterranes Lebensgefühl erobert die Schweiz," *Facts* 31 (Dec. 2002), http://www.secondo.net/pages/presse_2002.htm; Susanne Wessendorf, "Italian Families in Switzerland: Sites of Belonging or Golden Cages?" in *The Family in Question: Immigrant and Ethnic Minorities in Multicultural Europe*, ed. Ralph Grillo (Amsterdam: Amsterdam University Press, 2008), 205–24.

22. Braun, *Soziokulturelle Probleme*, 79.

23. Axel Schulte, *Produktive Rückkehr? Rückwanderung, Beschäftigungsproblematik und Kooperativen in einer abhängigen entwickelten Region: Das Beispiel Süditalien* (Berlin: Express Ed, 1986).

24. E-mail from Swiss Federal Office of Statistics.

25. Mauro Grassi, *Die Arbeitsemigration im italienischen Süden und die gesellschaftliche Problematik der Reintegration* (Berlin: Universität Berlin, 1980).

26. Claudio Bolzman, Rosita Fibbi, and Marie Vial, "Où habiter après la retraite? Les logiques de décision des migrants face aux risques de pauvreté," in *Povertà, migrazione, razzismo: Il lavoro sociale ed educativo in Europa*, ed. V. Bolognari and K. Kühne (Bergamo: Edizioni Junior, 1997), 95–114.

27. Braun, *Soziokulturelle Probleme*; Cord Pagenstecher, "Die 'Illusion' der Rückkehr: Zur Mentalitätsgeschichte von 'Gastarbeit' und Einwanderung," *Soziale Welt* 47, no. 2 (1996): 149–79.

28. Susanne Wessendorf, "'Roots-Migrants': Transnationalism and 'Return' among Second-Generation Italians in Switzerland," *Journal of Ethnic and Migration Studies* 33, no. 7 (2007): 1083–102.

29. Bolzman, Fibbi, and Vial, "Où habiter après la retraite?"

30. Loretta Baldassar, "Home and Away: Migration, the Return Visit and 'Transnational' Identity," in *Home, Displacement, Belonging*, ed. Ien Ang and Michael Symonds (Kingswood: Research Centre in Intercommunal Studies, University of Western Sydney, Nepean, 1997), 70–94.

31. Fortier, *Migrant Belongings;* Patricia Boscia-Mulè, *Authentic Ethnicities: The Interaction of Ideology, Gender Power, and Class in the Italian-American Experience* (Westport, Conn.: Greenwood Press, 1999). But see Wessendorf, "Italian Families in Switzerland," on contested notions of the family and the experience of the family as a "golden cage" among second-generation Italians in Switzerland.

32. Cristina Allemann-Ghionda and Giovanna Meyer Sabino, *Donne italiane in Svizzera* (Basel: Fondazione Ecap, 1992).

33. Deborah Bryceson and Ulla Vuorela, "Transnational Families in the Twenty-first Century," in *The Transnational Family: New European Frontiers and Global Networks*, ed. Bryceson and Vuorela (Oxford: Berg, 2002), 3–30.

34. Baldassar, *Visits Home*, "Home and Away."

35. Baldassar, "Home and Away," 75–76.

36. The Italian word *paese* means "country," "village," and "home." Italian migrants usually use the word *paese* to refer to their village communities.

37. Elke Korte, "Die Rückkehrorientierung im Eingliederungsprozess von Migrantenfamilien," in *Generation und Identiät*, ed. Hartmut Esser and Jurgen Friedrichs (Opladen: Westdeutscher Verlag, 1990), 207–59; Leonardo La Rosa, "'La Casa'—der Opferreiche Traum vom Eigenen Haus," in Halter, *Das Jahrhundert der Italiener*, 293–300.

38. Karen Fog Olwig and Kirsten Hastrup, *Siting Culture: The Shifting Anthropological Object* (London: Routledge, 1997), 35.

39. SalveWeb, "I messaggi dei Salvesi," http://www.salveweb.it/posta/posta2003l.htm (accessed Jan. 2004).

40. Importantly, not all members of the second generation enjoyed these holidays. Some experienced the visits of relatives as a strain and experienced social pressures during their stay in the village. See Susanne Wessendorf, "Italian Families in Switzerland."

41. Katy Gardner, "Desh-Bidesh: Sylethi Images of Home and Away," *Man* 28, no. 1 (1993): 1–15.

42. However, a small minority of members of the second generation decide to relocate to their parents' villages of origin. Wessendorf, "Roots-Migrants."

43. Ewa T. Morawska, "Immigrant Transnationalism and Assimilation: A Variety of Combinations and the Analytic Strategy It Suggests," in *Toward Assimilation and Citizenship: Immigrants in Liberal Nation-States*, ed. Christian Joppke and Ewa T. Morawska (Basingstoke, UK: Palgrave Macmillan, 2003), 133–76.

44. Victoria Goddard, *Gender, Family and Work in Naples* (Oxford: Berg, 1996); Luisa Passerini, "Gender Relations," in *Italian Cultural Studies: An Introduction*, ed. David Forgacs (Oxford: Oxford University Press, 1996), 144–59. King and Zontini speak of an "imperfect transition to gender equality" in southern Italy, where, since the 1970s, women have increasingly taken up education and professional careers while at the same time being expected by their husbands and partners to do most of the domestic tasks such as cooking, cleaning, and caring for children and elderly parents. Russell King and Elisabetta Zontini, "The Role of Gender in the South European Immigration Model," *Papers* 60 (2000): 43. See also Pojmann in this volume.

45. The formation of returnee communities in the context of long-term labor emigration and return has also been reported in other contexts, for example, in the Caribbean. See George Gmelch, *Double Passage: The Lives of Caribbean Migrants Abroad and Back Home* (Ann Arbor: University of Michigan Press, 1993); Elizabeth Thomas-Hope, "Transnational Livelihoods and Identities in Return Migration to the Caribbean: The Case of Skilled Returnees to Jamaica," in *Work and Migration: Life and Livelihoods in a Globalizing World*, ed. Nina Nyberg Sorensen and Karen Fog Olwig (London: Routledge, 2002), 187–201.

46. Fortier, *Migrant Belongings.*

47. Francesco Cerase, "Expectations and Reality: A Case Study of Return Migration from the United States to Southern Italy," *International Migration Review* 8, no. 2 (1974): 245–62; Gabaccia, *Italy's Many Diasporas;* Baldassar, *Visits Home.*

48. John A. Davis, *Land and Family in Pisticci* (Edinburgh, UK: Constable, 1973); Jane Schneider, "Of Vigilance and Virgins: Honor, Shame and Access to Resources in Mediterranean Societies," *Ethnology* 10, no. 1 (1971): 1–24; Sydel F. Silverman, "Agricultural Organization, Social Structure and Values in Italy: Amoral Familism Reconsidered," *American Anthropologist* 70, no. 1 (1968): 1–20.

Obligation to People and Place: The National in Cultures of Caregiving LORETTA BALDASSAR

1. Loretta Baldassar, *Visits Home: Migration Experiences between Italy and Australia* (Melbourne: Melbourne University Press, 2001).

2. For a comparison of these two groups of migrants, see Loretta Baldassar, "Transnational Families and Aged Care: The Mobility of Care and the Migrancy of Ageing," *Journal of Ethnic and Migration Studies* 33, no. 2 (2007): 275–97.

3. Loretta Baldassar, Cora Vellekoop Baldock, and Raelene Wilding, *Families Caring across Borders: Migration, Ageing and Transnational Caregiving* (New York: Palgrave Macmillan, 2007).

4. Andreas Wimmer and Nina Glick Schiller, "Methodological Nationalism and Beyond: Nation-State Building, Migration and the Social Sciences," *Global Networks* 2, no. 4 (2002): 305.

5. Cristina Szanton Blanc, Linda Basch, and Nina Glick Schiller, "Transnationalism, Nation-States and Culture," *Current Anthropology* 36, no. 4 (1995): 685.

6. Thomas H. Eriksen, "The Cultural Contexts of Ethnic Differences," *Man,* n.s., 26 (1991): 127–44.

7. Peggye Dilworth-Anderson, Ishan Canty Williams, and Brent E. Gibson, "Issues of Race, Ethnicity, and Culture in Care-Giving Research: A 20-Year Review (1980–2000)," *Gerontologist* 42, no. 3 (2002): 237–72.

8. Edward C. Banfield, *The Moral Basis of a Backward Society* (New York: Free Press, 1958).

9. Giancarlo Chiro and Jerzy Jaroslaw Smolicz, "Italian Family Values and Ethnic Identity in Australian Schools," *Educational Practice and Theory* 24, no. 2 (2002): 37–51.

10. Lidio Bertelli, "Italian Families," in *Ethnic Family Values in Australia,* ed. Des Storer (Sydney: Prentice Hall, 1985), 33–73.

11. Valerie J. MacKinnon, "Language Difficulties and Health Consequences for Older Italian-Australians in Ascot Vale," *Australian Journal of Primary Health* 4, no. 4 (1998): 31–43.

12. Loretta Baldassar, "Missing Kin and Longing to Be Together: Emotions and the Construction of Co-presence in Transnational Relationships," Journal of Intercultural Studies 29, no. 3 (2008): 247–66.

13. Elisabetta Zontini, "Continuity and Change in Transnational Italian Families: The Caring Practices of Second-Generation Women," *Journal of Ethnic and Migration Studies* 33, no. 7 (2007): 1103–19.

14. Micaela di Leonardo, "The Female World of Cards and Holidays: Women, Families, and the Work of Kinship," *Signs* 12, no. 3 (1987): 440–53.

15. Bandana Purkayastha describes the set of practices associated with family identity as a particular way of "doing family." Bandana Purkayastha, *Negotiating Ethnicity: Second-Generation South Asian Americans Traverse a Transnational World* (New Brunswick, N.J.: Rutgers University Press, 2005).

16. MacKinnon, "Language Difficulties"; Loretta Baldassar and Ros Pesman, *From Paesani to Global Italians: Veneto Migrants in Australia* (Crawley: University of Western Australia Press, 2005).

17. Christine Benham and Diane Gibson, *Independence in Aging: The Social and Financial Circumstances of Older Overseas-Born Australians* (Canberra: Department of Immigration and Multicultural Affairs, with the Australian Institute of Health and Welfare, 2000), 73. Findings from the Australian Bureau of Statistics report on older people in Australia indicate that immigrants from non-English-speaking countries are almost twice as likely (33.5 percent) as immigrants from English-speaking countries (18.8 percent) or the Australian born (17.2 percent) to see, on a daily basis, an adult son or daughter living independently. They are also twice as likely to live with a son or daughter. John McCallum, "The Mosaic of Ethnicity and Health in Later Life," in *The Health of Immigrant Australia: A Social Perspective,* ed. Janice Reid and Peggy Trompf (Sydney: Harcourt Brace Jovanovich, 1990), xi–xvii, 328.

18. Tim Blackman, "Defining Responsibility for Care: Approaches to the Care of Older People in Six European Countries," *International Journal of Social Welfare* 9, no. 3 (2002): 181–90.

19. Loretta Baldassar, "Debating Culture across Distance: Transnational Families and the Obligation to Care," in *The Family in Question: Immigrant and Ethnic Minorities in Multicultural Europe,* ed. Ralph Grillo

(Amsterdam: Amsterdam University Press, 2008), 269–91; Baldassar, Baldock, and Wilding, *Families Caring across Borders.*

20. Boym, *The Future of Nostalgia* (New York: Basic Books, 2001), 3.

21. Haller quoted in ibid.

22. For the purposes of this chapter, "homesickness" is synonymous with "nostalgia," which derives from the Greek *nostos*, "to return home."

23. See, for example, S. L. Baily, "The Village Outward Approach to the Study of Social Networks: A Case Study of the Agnonesi Diaspora Abroad, 1885–1989," *Studi Emigrazione* 29 (1989): 43–67.

24. Carol Delaney, "The Hajj: Sacred and Secular," *American Ethnologist* 17, no. 3 (1990): 517, 522.

25. Baldassar, *Visits Home.*

26. Stephanie Lindsay Thompson, *Australia through Italian Eyes: A Study of Settlers Returning from Australia to Italy* (Melbourne: Oxford University Press, 1980).

27. W. Sollors, *The Invention of Ethnicity* (New York: Oxford University Press, 1989); Fredrick Barth, *Ethnic Groups and Boundaries: The Social Organization of Culture Difference* (Boston: Little, Brown, 1969).

28. Thompson, *Australia through Italian Eyes.*

29. Stuart Hall, "Political Belonging in a World of Multiple Identities," in *Cosmopolitanism: Theory, Context, Practice,* ed. Steven Vertovec and Robin Cohen (Oxford: Oxford University Press, 2002), 25–31; Zlatko Skrbiš, Gavin P. Kendall, and Ian Woodward, "Locating Cosmopolitanism: Between Humanist Ideal and Grounded Social Category," *Theory, Culture and Society* 21, no. 6 (2004): 115–36.

30. A. L. Epstein, *Ethos and Identity: Three Studies in Ethnicity* (Chicago: Aldine, 1978).

31. Raelene Wilding, "Virtual Intimacies: Family Communications across Transnational Borders," *Global Networks* 6, no. 2 (2006): 125–42.

32. L. Baldassar, "Transnational Families and the Provision of Moral and Emotional Support: The Relationship between Truth and Distance," *Identities* 14, no. 4 (2007): 385–409.

33. For a discussion of different types of visits, including routine, crisis, special, and duty and ritual visits, see Baldassar, Baldock, and Wilding, *Families Caring across Borders.*

34. John Urry, "Social Networks, Travel and Talk," *British Journal of Sociology* 54, no. 2 (2003): 164.

35. Baldassar, "Missing Kin."

36. Benedict Anderson, *Imagined Communities: Reflections on the Origin and Spread of Nationalism* (London: Verso, 1983).

37. For parents and other homeland-based kin, these intersections across borders underpin continued transnational relationships and may even result in attachments to the migrant's place of residence.

38. Boym, *The Future of Nostalgia.*

39. See, for example, Val Colic-Peisker, *Split Lives: Croatian Australian Stories* (Fremantle, Australia: Fremantle Arts Press, 2004).

40. My distinction between "consociate" and "contemporary" is based on Schutz's use of these terms. Alfred Schutz, *The Phenomenology of the Social World* (Evanston, Ill.: Northwestern University Press, 1967). Consociates share co-presence; contemporaries share time. The people you know are your consociates; the people you only know about are your contemporaries.

41. For a definition and discussion of diaspora, see Robin Cohen, *Global Diasporas: An Introduction* (Seattle: University of Washington Press, 1997). For the Italian diaspora, see Donna R. Gabaccia, *Italy's Many Diasporas* (London: UCL Press, 2000).

42. Ralph Grillo, "Betwixt and Between: Trajectories and Projects of Transmigration," *Journal of Ethnic and Migration Studies* 33, no. 4 (2007): 199–217.

43. The immersion during the return home provides migrants with reaffirmation of their Italianness, yet it also commonly leads to a realization that they no longer fit in, and an increased awareness of their Italo-Australian identities.

44. Herbert J. Gans, "Symbolic Ethnicity and Symbolic Religiosity: Towards a Comparison of Ethnoreligious Acculturation," *Ethnic and Racial Studies* 17, no. 4 (1994): 573–92.

45. Anne-Marie Fortier, "Community, Belonging, and the Effervescence of Ethnicity" (unpublished manuscript, Lancaster University, 2003); Anne-Marie Fortier, "Italian Diasporas Share the Neighborhood," paper delivered at the Europeans Seminar, Institute of Advanced Studies, University of Western Australia, July 2003; Anthony Giddens, *Modernity and Self-Identity: Self and Society in the Late Modern Age* (Cambridge: Polity Press, 1991).

46. Susan Stewart, *On Longing: Narratives of the Miniature, the Gigantic, the Souvenir, the Collection* (Durham, N.C.: Duke University Press, 1992).

47. Zlatko Skrbiš, "From Migrants to Pilgrim Tourists: Diasporic Imagining and Visits to Medjugorje," *Journal of Ethnic and Migration Studies* 33, no. 2 (2007): 313–29.

48. Michael Herzfeld, *Cultural Intimacy: Social Poetics in the Nation-State* (New York: Routledge, 1997).

49. Mary Holmes, "Love Lives at a Distance: Distance Relationship over the Lifecourse," *Sociological Research Online* 11, no. 3 (2006), http://www.socresonline.org.uk/11/3/holmes.html (accessed 3 April 2010).

50. Anderson, *Imagined Communities.*

51. Helen Lee, ed., *Ties to the Homeland: Second Generation Transnationalism* (Cambridge: Cambridge Scholars, 2008).

52. Diane Wolf, Peggy Levitt, and Mary C. Waters, eds., *The Changing Face of Home: The Transnational Lives of the Second Generation* (New York: Russell Sage Foundation, 2002); Hania Batainah, "Issues of Belonging: Exploring Arab-Australian Transnational Identities," in Lee, *Ties to the Homeland,* 151–67.

53. Bruno Mascitelli and Simone Battiston, *The Italian Expatriate Vote in Australia: Democratic Right, Democratic Wrong, or Political Opportunism?* (Ballan, Australia: Connor Court, 2008).

54. Will Kymlicka, *Multicultural Citizenship: A Liberal Theory of Minority Rights* (Oxford: Oxford University Press, 1995); Stephen Castles, "Multicultural Citizenship: The Australian Experience," in *Citizenship and Exclusion,* ed. Veit-Michael Bader (London: Macmillan, 1997), 113–36; Rainer Bauböck, *Transnational Citizenship: Membership and Rights in Migration* (Aldershot, UK: Hants, 1994); Laksiri Jayasuriya, "Rethinking Australian Multiculturalism: Towards a New Paradigm," *Australian Quarterly* 62, no. 1 (1990): 30–63.

55. John Torpey, *The Invention of the Passport: Surveillance, Citizenship and the State* (Cambridge: Cambridge University Press, 2000).

Contributors

Loretta Baldassar is a professor in the Department of Anthropology and Sociology at the University of Western Australia and director of the Monash University Centre in Prato, Italy. She has published widely on migration studies and transnational family relations, including co-edited special issues of the *Journal of Intercultural Studies* (2007), the *Journal of Ethnic and Migration Studies* (2007), and the *Journal of Modern Italy* (2006). Her books include *Visits Home: Migration Experiences between Italy and Australia* (Melbourne University Press, 2001); *From Paesani to Global Italians: Veneto Migrants in Australia* (University of Western Australia Press, 2005), co-written with Ros Pesman; and *Families Caring across Borders: Migration, Aging, and Transnational Caregiving* (Palgrave Macmillan, 2007), with Cora Baldock and Raelene Wilding. Her next publication is a co-edited special issue of the journal *Recherches sociologiques et anthropologiques* titled "Transnational Care Dynamics: Between Emotions and Rationality."

Giorgio Bertellini is associate professor in screen arts and cultures and romance languages and literatures at the University of Michigan. Editor and co-editor of *The Cinema of Italy* (Wallflower, 2004, 2007), *Early Cinema and the "National"* (John Libbey, 2008), and *Silent Italian Cinema: A Reader* (John Libbey, forthcoming), he has published numerous essays on questions of film form and geographic, racial, and national identity in Italian and silent cinema. He is the author of *Emir Kusturica* (Castoro, 1996, 2010) and *Italy in Early American Cinema: Race, Landscape, and the Picturesque* (Indiana University Press, 2009).

Carla De Tona is a postdoctoral research associate in the School of Social Sciences at the University of Manchester, UK, working on school choice and the impact of race, ethnicity, and class. She was a postdoctoral fellow at Trinity College Dublin, Ireland (2007–9), where she worked on migrant women's networks and organizations in Ireland. In 2007, she completed a PhD on Italian migrant women in Ireland ("Diaspora, Gender and Narrative Journeys: Italian Migrant Women in Ireland") in the Sociology Department at Trinity College Dublin. Her research interests include gender and migration, diaspora, memories and narratives, and qualitative research methodologies.

Donna R. Gabaccia is Rudolph J. Vecoli Chair in Immigration History and director of the Immigration History Research Center at the University of Minnesota. She is the author of many books and articles on immigrant life in the United States and Italian migration around the world, including *From the Other Side: Women, Gender, and Immigrant Life in the U.S., 1820–1990* (Indiana University Press, 1994) and *Italy's Many Diasporas* (UCL Press, 2000). *American Dreaming, Global Realities: Rethinking U.S. Immigration History* (University of Illinois Press, 2006) was co-edited with Vicki Ruiz. Her next book is tentatively titled *Foreign Relations: An International History of American Immigration.*

Carol Lynn McKibben is the author of *Beyond Cannery Row: Sicilian Women, Immigration, and Community in Monterey, California, 1915–1999* (University of Illinois Press, 2006). She taught history and policy studies at the Monterey Institute of International Studies from 1992 to 2001 and is the director of the Seaside History Project. She is the author of *Seaside* (Arcadia Press, 2009) and is completing work on the narrative history of Seaside, titled *Race, the Military, and* *the Shaping of a Minority-Majority City, Seaside, California, 1890–2006.* She currently teaches courses in public history and California history at Stanford University.

Caroline Waldron Merithew is associate professor of history at the University of Dayton. She served as a research associate at the Five Colleges Women's Studies Research Center at Mount Holyoke in 2010. Among her publications are "Lynch-Law Must Go!" in the *Journal of American Ethnic History* (2000); "Anarchist Motherhood," in *Women, Gender, and Transnational Lives* (University of Toronto Press, 2002); "Making the Italian Other," in *Are Italians White?* (Routledge, 2003); and "'We Were Not Ladies': Gender Class, and a Women's Auxiliary's Battle for Mining Unionism," in the *Journal of Women's History* (2006), which was awarded the Anita S. Goodstein Junior Scholar Prize in Women's History. Her chapter in this volume is part of a larger book project about memory, forgetting, and the domestic sphere in the working-class diaspora during the twentieth century.

Pavla Miller is professor of historical sociology at RMIT University in Melbourne, Australia. Her publications include *Long Division: State Schooling in South Australian Society* (Wakefield, 1986) and *Transformations of Patriarchy in the West, 1500–1900* (Indiana University Press, 1998). She has also published on demographic explanations of low fertility, masters and servants legislation, and children and work. Pavla Miller is currently working on two projects. One deals with children and the contested meanings of work in contemporary Australia, the other with feminist and non-feminist theories of patriarchy.

Ros Pesman is professor emerita at the University of Sydney, where she was formerly Challis Professor of History and pro-vice-chancellor for the humanities and social sciences. She began her academic life studying fifteenth-century Florentine politics and since then has also worked on migration and women's travel. Her publications include *Duty Free: Australian Women Abroad* (Oxford University Press, 1996); *Pier Soderini and the Ruling Class in Renaissance Florence* (2002); with Loretta Baldassar, *From Paesani to Global Italians: Veneto Migrants in Australia* (University of Western Australia Press, 2005); and the co-edited volume *Australians in Italy: Contemporary Lives and Impressions* (Monash University ePress, 2008). She is currently working on British women in Risorgimento and liberal Italy.

Wendy Pojmann is an assistant professor of modern European history at Siena College in Loudonville, New York. She is the author of *Immigrant Women and Feminism in Italy* (Ashgate, 2006; Aracne Editrice, 2008) and editor of *Migration and Activism in Europe since 1945* (Palgrave Macmillan, 2008). Her articles about women's movements, immigration, and oral history have appeared in journals such as the *Historian*, the *Journal of Women's History*, the *Journal of International Women's Studies*, and *Migration Letters*. Pojmann is presently working on a book that examines Italian and international women's associations in relation to the cold war and European integration.

Yvonne Rieker teaches on the topics of postwar immigration to Western Europe, including labor and postcolonial migration, and German-Jewish history. After finishing her studies in 1990, she started a project on childhood patterns in Jewish families in Germany, published in 1997 as *Kindheiten: Identitätsmuster im deutsch-jüdischen Bürgertum und unter ostjüdischen Einwanderern* (*Patterns of Childhood: Processes of Identification in German-Jewish Bourgeoisie and among Eastern European Immigrants 1871–1933*, Olms, 1997). From 1998 to 2002 she was engaged in a research project on Italian immigration to the Federal Republic of Germany. The results of this project were published in 2003 as *"Ein Stück Heimat findet man ja immer": Die italienische Einwanderung in die Bundesrepublik* (*"My Own Foreign Country": Italian Immigration to the Federal Republic of Germany*, Klartext Verlag, 2003). She also published, together with the late Michael Zimmermann, *Betrachtungen zur Ästhetik des Ruhrgebiets* (Klartext-Verlag, 2007). Her current work focuses on the migration of nurses to Germany.

Carol A. Stabile earned a PhD in English from Brown University, where she did research on gender, technology, and feminist theory. Her interdisciplinary research interests focus on gender, race, class, and sexual orientation in media and popular culture. She is the author of *Feminism and the Technological Fix* (Manchester University Press, 1994) and *White Victims, Black Villains: Gender, Race, and Crime News in U.S. Culture* (Routledge, 2006), editor of *Turning the Century: Essays in Media and Cultural Studies* (Westview Press, 2000), and co-editor of *Prime Time Animation: Television Animation and American Culture* (Routledge, 2003). She is currently finishing a book on women writers and the broadcast blacklist in the 1950s titled *Black and White and Red All Over: Women Writers and the Television Blacklist.*

Susanne Wessendorf is a postdoctoral research fellow at the Max Planck Institute for the Study of Religious and Cultural Diversity (Germany) currently working on patterns of "super-diversity" in a London neighborhood. Her PhD dissertation, which she completed in social anthropology at Oxford University, focused on the interrelationship of integration and transnationalism among second-generation Italians in Switzerland. She has a master's of philosophy from the University of Basel, Switzerland, in social anthropology, European anthropology, and linguistics and has been a lecturer at the Institute of Social Anthropology, University of Berne, Switzerland. Her recent publications include "Roots-Migrants: Transnationalism and 'Return' among Second-Generation Italians in Switzerland," *Journal of Ethnic and Migration Studies* (2007); "Culturalist Discourses on Inclusion and Exclusion: The Swiss Citizenship Debate," *Social Anthropology* (2008); and *The Multiculturalism Backlash: European Discourses, Policies and Practices* (Routledge, 2010), co-edited with Steven Vertove.

Index